INTERNALIZATION IN PSYCHOANALYSIS

INTERNALIZATION
IN
PSYCHOANALYSIS

W. W. MEISSNER

Psychological Issues

Monograph 50

INTERNATIONAL UNIVERSITIES PRESS, INC.

New York

Library of Congress Cataloging in Publication Data

Meissner, William W
  Internalization in psychoanalysis.
  (Psychological issues; v. 13, no. 2,
monograph 50)
  Includes bibliographical references and index.
  1. Internalization. 2. Psychoanalysis.
I. Title. II. Series. [DNLM: 1. Psycho-
analytic therapy. 3. Identification. W1 PS572
v. 13 no. 2 / WM460 M515i]
RC506.M35   616.89'17   80-13867
ISBN 0-8236-2726-8

CONTENTS

ACKNOWLEDGMENTS

Grateful acknowledgment is made to the publishers for permission to use material from:

Z. A. Aarons, "The Analyst's Relocation: Its Effect on the Transference—Parameter or Catalyst." Published in *International Journal of Psycho-Analysis*, 56:303–319, 1975.

M. D. Berg, "The Externalizing Transference." Published in *International Journal of Psycho-Analysis*, 58:235–244, 1977.

T. L. Dorpat, "Internalization of the Patient-Analyst Relationship in Patients with Narcissistic Disorders." Published in *International Journal of Psycho-Analysis,* 55:183–188, 1974.

R. R. Greenson and M. Wexler, "The Non-transference Relationship in the Psychoanalytic Situation." Published in *International Journal of Psycho-Analysis*, 50:27–39, 1969.

M. M. R. Khan, "The Finding and Becoming of Self." Published in *International Journal of Psychoanalytic Psychotherapy*, 1(1):97–111, 1972.

H. Loewald, "Psychoanalysis as an Art and the Fantasy Character of the Psychoanalytic Situation." Published in *Journal of the American Psychoanalytic Association*, 23:277–299, 1975.

A. Malin and J. S. Grotstein, "Projective Identification in the Therapeutic Process." Published in *International Journal of Psycho-Analysis*, 47:26–31, 1966.

S. J. Olinick, "On Empathic Perception and the Problems of Reporting Psychoanalytic Processes." Published in *International Journal of Psycho-Analysis*, 56:147–154, 1975.

R. Schafer, "Generative Empathy in the Treatment Situation." Published in *Psychoanalytic Quarterly*, 28:342–373, 1959.

Thanks are also extended to R. D. Mehlman for permission to use material from his paper on "Transference Mobilization, Transference Resolution, and the Narcissistic Alliance," presented to the Boston Psychoanalytic Society and Institute on February 25, 1976.

PREFACE

The pages that follow are a distillation of over a decade of work on the problem of internalization in psychoanalysis. My exploration of internalization processes originally stemmed from an interest in the problem itself and an awareness of the looseness and dissatisfactory state of psychoanalytic formulations on the subject. More recently, however, I have become convinced that the issue of internalization lies at the very heart of contemporary psychoanalytic concerns.

On one side is the emergence of a more articulated theory of object relations, which emphasizes the importance of relationships with significant objects both in development and in current adaptive functioning. A second, and even more pressing, aspect of contemporary psychoanalytic thinking has been the appearance of a psychology of the self. It does not take much argument to show that internalization is central to the dialectic between object and self, and that it provides the conceptual bridge between an object relations theory and a concept of self. In this sense, it is out of the warp and woof of object relations that the rudiments of the self are woven, by way of a variety of forms and sequences of internalization. Similarly, the continuing process of internalization gives rise to capacities within the emerging self for engaging in, maintaining, and gaining meaningful gratification from object relations.

The current controversy over the psychology of the self deserves special comment. In the first place, the contribution of internalization to the original formation and development of the self has received little more than lip service in self psychology (e.g., Kohut's "transmuting internalizations"). On a more far-reaching level, it is perhaps unfortunate that the psychology of the self has been cast more or less exclusively in narcissistic terms. This somewhat narrow and constraining investment with narcissism has left us with a conceptual struggle that places self psychology over against the more familiar conflict-defense and structural models.

The concept of internalization set forth in this book strikes out along what seems to me to be relatively new ground. It recognizes that internalization and structuralization are inextricably linked, even though as processes and in terms of effects they can be discriminated. A basic assumption of my argument is that both internalization and structuralization take place by way of commerce with significant objects. These two processes provide the stuff out of which the intrapsychic self is organized. Or, to put it more accurately, internalization and structure formation give shape and substance to the emergent sense of self, in terms of which the subject's internal world becomes organized. The basis of these processes is *not* exclusively narcissistic. The narcissistic contribution to the organization and functioning of the self is only part of the overall picture, which embraces a variety of libidinal and instinctual vicissitudes and derivatives, as well as ego and superego formations and functions.

This volume can thus be read in relation to the ongoing debate between Kernberg and Kohut. On a simple level, Kernberg's approach can be envisioned as a psychology of object relations, in which the origins of the self are cast in terms of internalized object relations. In contrast, Kohut's theory casts the origins of the self in terms of the internal vicissitudes of narcissism, along a developmental line almost separate from involvement with objects. He views the transformation and development of narcissistic configurations in the light of the relationship to selfobjects as opposed to objects invested with libido. At only one point does the reality of external objects appear to impinge on the inherent vicissitudes of narcissism and that is when maternal empathy is lacking. At subsequent levels of development, the involvement with selfobjects seems more determined by internal vectors having to do with the differentiation of archaic narcissistic formations than with the quality of the relationship to the object as such. In a sense, the approach through internalization weaves itself between these more or less polarized positions. It suggests that a psychology of the self is meaningless if it does not take place within the matrix of real objects, not merely object representations (Kernberg) or narcissistically invested selfobjects (Kohut).

Finally, there are the clinical implications and connotations of these approaches. I have tried to steer a middle course which acknowledges the impact of object relations on the patient's experience, not only developmentally but also, even more significantly, with the analyst himself. I have also tried to articulate in terms of internalization which factors shape and elicit the original pathogenic sense of self and which factors, within the analysis, contribute to dismantling that pathogenic core and allow for something more adaptive, positive, and constructive to take its place. A deliberate attempt is made to link the technical aspects of psychoanalysis to specific forms of internalization and to indicate the role of these processes in the reworking of the patient's personality. It is in this frame of reference that the analyst's interventions, particularly interpretations, have their appropriate place. But it also brings into focus other critical aspects of the analytic situation, particularly the quality of the relationship to the analyst, over and above his technical interventions.

For the rest, the reader must judge for himself. It is my humble hope that these formulations will deepen our understanding of the analytic process and provide a framework within which practicing analysts may come to deal with the vicissitudes of internalization with greater effectiveness, empathy, and understanding.

INTRODUCTION

To focus this study, we can pose some of the critical questions connected with the problem of internalization in psychoanalysis. From the beginning, Freud's inquiry into hysterical phenomena was pervaded by questions of how patients got better, how they changed in the course of the analytic work, and what factors in the analytic situation were responsible for these changes. At first the focus was on symptomatic change, and the factors of change could be encompassed by notions of abreaction and insight in a relatively simple energic model. As analytic experience broadened and deepened, however, the emphasis shifted to more enduring and more resistant characterological problems. With this shift in emphasis came a growing complexity in our understanding of therapeutic effects and the models of the mental apparatus. We should note the plural — models — since the attempts to understand the analytic process and change within it rapidly outgrew the explanatory power of a single theoretical frame of reference. What has evolved is a series of increasingly complex and overlapping models of the mind which provide complementary accounts of mental functioning (Gedo and Goldberg, 1973).

As the analytic focus expanded, there was an increasing structural emphasis in the theory and an ego-superego psychology emerged. The concern with problems of internalization grew apace. The emphasis changed from a question regarding the existence of conflict between mental structures, to an examination of how such structures came into existence and into conflict. The perspective not only became increasingly developmental, but also increasingly concerned with how internal structures are formed. The role of internalizations in psychic

1

development and in the psychoanalytic process assumed a central position in offering some explanation to these questions. Internalizations have a critical function in the understanding of structure formation, particularly in relation to external influences derived from object relations. In this regard, the theory of internalization is intimately linked to and cannot be divorced from an object relations theory.

The perennial questions on the nature of structural change and therapeutic effectiveness have gradually been recast in terms of their relation to problems of internalization. The critical changes taking place in the psychoanalytic process have come to be seen as related to internalizing processes mobilized by the analytic situation and work. The theory, however, remains inchoate and has been plagued by a number of conceptual and terminological difficulties. Our effort here will be to sort out some of these ambiguities and to clarify certain relevant aspects of the psychoanalytic process in terms of various internalization processes.

The present study focuses specifically on the clinical aspects of the analytic process. It is based on clinical experience derived from naturalistic participatory observation, and thus does not provide the kinds of information or validation that might be expected within a more explictly experimental study. Its emphasis is on the formulation and the understanding of experience rather than on the delineation, testing, and validation of specific variables.

As a corollary, we can say that our intent is not to explicate theory. But it is clear that the effort to formulate internalization processes in clinical terms cannot ignore analytic theory. Thus, although the study is not explicitly theoretical, it deals with elements derived from and intimately related to theoretical concerns.

In pointing to the clinical bent of this study, it should be made clear that we are not concerned with analytic technique. While it cannot be denied that matters of technique are of singular importance and that our formulations will unavoidably have specific technical implications, our intention here is not to develop these aspects. They can perhaps more fruitfully be left for another time and another place.

Rather, our interest lies in the multiple and complex roles of internalizations in the analytic setting. This is the substance and the focus of our concern. We shall elaborate the role of internalizations in several specific areas, including the genesis and structuring of forms of psychopathology, as well as the structuring and organization of the analytic situation. We shall look at their part in the analytic process, with particular emphasis on both their dynamic and their therapeutic functions.

1

THEORETICAL ASPECTS
OF INTERNALIZATION

Although this study is concerned with the clinical aspects of internalization, our formulations will have little meaning without first setting the theoretical context for our discussion. What follows will be essentially an amplification and reworking of my previous assessment of the theory of internalization (Meissner, 1970a, 1971, 1972).

Freud's ideas about internalization, and particularly his notion of identification, underwent a gradual evolution, which roughly parallels the emergence and elaboration of his structural hypothesis. He postulated identification as one of the primary mechanisms of structuralization. In his last and unfinished work, "An Outline of Psycho-Analysis," he wrote:

> A portion of the external world has, at least partially, been abandoned as an object and has instead, by identification, been taken into the ego and thus become an integral part of the internal world. This new psychical agency continues to carry on the functions which have hitherto been performed by the people. . . in the external world: it observes the ego, gives it orders, judges it and threatens it with punishments, exactly like the parents whose place it has taken [1940, p. 205].

The reference was, of course, to the superego, which was the major aspect of Freud's structural theory. And it was in regard to the latter that the theory of internalization was developed.

Freud left numerous hints and suggestions that his thinking on the problem of internalization was broader than the frame of reference provided by the superego (Meissner, 1970a). But it was only with the further development of ego psychology that the concept of internalization came in for further elaboration. Hartmann (1939) specifically focused the concept of internalization and broadened its significance. He viewed the problem of internalization in terms of the biological, evolutionary, and adaptive functioning of the organism. As he saw it, evolution brings about an increased independence of the organism from environmental stimuli and pressures. Reactions which were originally the result of interaction with such external stimuli are increasingly displaced into the interior of the organism, so that the organism becomes less dependent and less reactive to environmental stimuli and gains a greater capacity for delay and mastery.

In his attempt to highlight internalization as a general biological principle, Hartmann depicted it as a major mechanism in the service of the organism's increasing capacity for adaptation, differentiation, mastery, and synthesis. He commented:

> In the course of evolution, described here as a process of progressive "internalization," there arises a central regulating factor, usually called the "inner world," which is interpolated between the receptors and the effectors. We are familiar with it in human adults as one of the ego's regulating factors. ... The inner world and its functions make possible an adaptation process which consists of two steps: withdrawal from the external world and return to it with improved mastery [1939, pp. 57–58].[1]

In Hartmann's view, internalization, both in a phylogenetic and an ontogenetic context, allows for an increasing capacity for delay and detour as well as an increasing independence from the pressure of immediate environmental stimuli. Internalization amplifies the organism's range of adaptive capacities and enlarges its resources for mastery of external stress.

---

[1] The point of view articulated here is that of internalization as a process. This perspective has recently been challenged by Roy Schafer (1972). Schafer attacks Hartmann's spatial metaphors, which locate mental processes in a framework involving specifications of interiority versus exteriority. Schafer argues that "internalization" is nothing more than a spatial metaphor that does disservice to psychoanalytic thinking and theory. The only term that enjoys real reference in his view is "incorporation," which stands for archaic fantasies of taking objects into the body. Schafer adds emphatically, "Logically, internalization cannot mean anything more than that: it refers to a fantasy, not to a process" (p. 434). Schafer's argument is ingenious and raises some interesting and difficult questions for psychoanalytic theory formation. The present study will take issue with Schafer's views at appropriate points in the discussion. A more detailed confrontation with Schafer's argument can be found in Meissner (1976, 1979b).

As a more articulated psychology of the ego took shape, Hartmann's emphasis shifted to a concern with internal regulation. This is the ego's essential function in its struggle with the "vital forces" of the mind, and it serves as the guarantor of the ego's relative autonomy. Corresponding with the development of organized capacities for inner regulation, the ego's dependence on the environment decreases and the range of environmental conditions to which the organism can adjust increases. Internalization is defined specifically in regulatory terms: "We would speak of *internalization* when regulations that have taken place in interaction with the outside world are replaced by inner regulations" (Hartmann and Loewenstein, 1962, p. 48). Internalization thus comes to include the processes by which the inner psychic world is elaborated — including the specific forms of internalization manifested in incorporation, introjection, and identification.[2]

Schafer (1968a) modifies the Hartmann-Loewenstein definition of internalization as regulatory in the following terms: *"Internalization refers to all those processes by which the subject transforms real or imagined regulatory interactions with his environment, and real or imagined characteristics of his environment, into inner regulations and characteristics"* (p. 9). Schafer emphasizes the subject's role and activity in the work of transformation. He also points out that the internalized qualities are not always real, but may be, to one degree or another, imagined by the subject.

Another dimension is added by Loewald (1962), who stresses the relationship of internalization to object relations. He comments: "I use the term 'internalization' here as a general term for certain processes of transformation by which relationships and interactions between the individual psychic apparatus and its environment are changed into inner relationships and interactions within the psychic apparatus" (p. 489). The external relationships to loved and hated objects in the

[2] Internalization is used here as a general term, encompassing incorporation, introjection, and identification. Beres (1966), however, sees internalization as specifically the final step in a process by which attributes of an object become the subject's own. Superego identifications remain derivative of parental objects; they become authentically the subject's own only by a further step of internalization. The present usage would describe the same modification of superego introjects by way of subsequent identification.

subject's experience are transformed into internal relationships. It is these internal relationships that organize the subject's character structure and internal psychic structure. Loewald's formulation emphasizes that the critical problem in internalization is the transformation of object representations into internal objects and related internal structural modifications.[3]

Loewald (1962) also introduces the notion of degrees of internalization. This concept implies shifting distances of what is internalized with reference to the ego core, as well as shifting distances within the ego-superego system. It also implies that the character of the introjects undergoes some transformation as a result of different degrees of internalization. In these terms, the superego involves a structural pattern whose elements may either be further internalized as part of the ego core or may be reexternalized in the form of object representations.

Schafer (1968b) has reformulated this concept in terms of activity and passivity. Well-established identifications enjoy the highest degree of internalization and are therefore most closely integrated with the ego core. With a high degree of internalization, there is resistance to regressive pulls toward an introjective type of experience. Instead, the subjective experience is characterized by intentionality, will, or activity. Where a greater degree of externalization predominates, the subjective experience shows a higher degree of passivity. Schafer (1968a) comments:

> ...it must always be borne in mind that internalization is a matter of degree: the degree to which external regulations have been taken over by the subject and stamped with his self-representations; the degree of influence exerted by the internalizations; and the degree of stability of the internalizations, that is, their resistiveness to being regressively abandoned and restored to the

[3] Schafer would regard this essential transformation as merely metaphorical and as related to the fantasy of incorporation. The process view, however, maintains that whatever the nature of the transformation by which external object representations become modifications of the internal world, that modification has structural implications whose referents are in some sense real, even if psychological. The important question Schafer raises concerns the meaning of structure in psychoanalytic theory, whether merely metaphorical or not (Meissner, 1976, 1979b).

environment or lost altogether in the systemic dedifferentiations that involve primitive mergings of self and object representations [pp. 14–15].

The correlative term to internalization is externalization; externalization is the inverse of internalization. The term is commonly used as an equivalent of projection. Moore and Fine (1967) describe it as: "a term used to refer in general to the tendency to project into the external world one's instinctual wishes, conflicts, needs, and ways of thinking (cognitive styles)" (p. 39). In her discussion of externalization, Anna Freud (1965) uses the term to refer to "processes in which the person of the analyst is used to represent one of or another part of the patient's personality structure" (p. 41). Brodey (1965) modifies this usage slightly to indicate that externalization involves a projection which is combined with a manipulation of external reality so that only the reality that verifies the projection is perceived by the subject; reality that does not verify it is not perceived. In this sense, the mechanism of externalization becomes a crucial part of the structuring of the intrafamilial environment and of the interactions between parent and child.

Rather than making the notions of externalization and projection equivalent, we shall stipulate externalization as the more general term and as the correlative of internalization. Externalization refers to a process of transformation by which elements of the personality structure that function in more immediate relation to the ego core become less immediately related to the ego core and are modified in the direction of relatively independently functioning personality structures, or, with increasing degrees of externalization, in the direction of object representations. With this definition, projection becomes a special instance of externalization in which the externalized elements are derived specifically from introjects and are transformed into object representations and are so perceived. This reexternalization involves a distancing from the ego core in such a way that the inner aspects of the personality involved begin to take on the quality of an object representation.

To clarify these specifications of meaning, it may be useful to keep in mind the characteristic differences between phobic externalizations and paranoid projections. The phobic anxiety in an acrophobia or an agoraphobia arises as a nameless and depersonalized fear—an apprehension of danger connected with a specific stimulus context. The fear may take the form of a fear of falling or it may involve the acting out of exhibitionistic impulses, but the fear can readily be related to specific aggressive or libidinal impulses. The impulse derivatives and the related conflicts are externalized. A paranoid projection, however, takes a more specific form. The persecutory anxiety often appears as fear of aggression or libidinal interest (usually homosexual) from other objects or object equivalents, such as social institutions. The projection takes place within a specifically object-related context. If the patient is the victim of a communist plot or of machinations of the devil, these have an inherent object quality in that the derivation of the projection carries with it a specific object reference. There are also mixed cases where a phobic externalization may be transformed by projective elements, as in the primitive fear of thunder and lightning. Some admixture of phobic and projective elements may also be seen in the more organized phobias, as Melanie Klein (1932) has suggested with regard to Little Hans. Here the object-related and object-derived context of the phobia is clear in Freud's (1909) analysis.

The balance of internalization-externalization has its point of reference in the subjectively sensed and experienced identity with the inner self or ego core. At the subject pole of one's own inner experience of self-awareness, the sense of self is indistinguishable from the operation of the autonomous ego. The phenomenological view of the self as experiencing, willing, intending, as the source of autonomous activity, becomes synonymous with the notion of the ego as the ultimate structural term of self-conscious activity. The phenomenological and the structural analyses coalesce at this point (Meissner, 1977a). Internalization, then, is any process of transformation by which external relationships, object representations, and forms of regulation become part of the inner psychic structure and thus part of the "inner world." By the concept of internalization, we refer to the movement of structural elements, derived from sources in reality, in the direction of integration with that part of the psychic structure which is seen as central to inner identity — the ego.

By way of qualification, it is useful to distinguish between primary and secondary internalization or externalization. Secondary internalization refers to the internalization of something that was external, just as secondary externalization refers to the externalization of something antecedently internal. These secondary transformations require the establishment of self-object differentiation and the capacity to distinguish and recognize what is internal from what is external. In the absence of this capacity, internalization and externalization can only mean that the internal and external are being constituted by these fundamental, primitive processes. In other words, primary internalization or externalization merely refers to aspects of the process of differentiation that contributes to establishing a boundary between the inner world and the external world, or correlatively between self and object (Loewald, 1962). For the most part, we shall be dealing with secondary internalization and externalization. The primary forms of internalization and externalization occur in the earliest stages of psychic development and their basic nature remains obscure.

IMITATION

The first important step in clarifying the nature of internalization is to distinguish internalization from closely related processes which are not in themselves forms of internalization. One such process is imitation. Imitation clearly is not a kind of internalization, but it is closely related to and often involved in identificatory processes.

Imitation can be conceptualized as a form of learning (Meissner, 1974d). Imitative learning is described as "the initiation and practice of certain responses (gestures, attitudes, speech patterns, dress, etc.) which are not subject to prohibition by the social environment and which are assumed to be the result of an attempt to imitate a model" (Kagan, 1958, p. 296). Through imitation one person can learn from another by a process of behavioral modeling. The concept of imitation, however, states nothing about the requirements of the object

relation between the imitator and the model. The cathectic involvement may be minimal, and the model may simply act as
the bearer of a behavioral pattern which the copying subject can
imitate. Parsons and Shils (1962) distinguish imitation from
identification on the grounds that imitation involves acquisition
of specific behavioral patterns by copying from a social object
without any particular attachment to the object beyond the
mere process of acquisition. Identification, in contrast, involves
acquisition of generalized patterns of orientation, including
values, attitudes, and beliefs, based on a motivated attachment
to the object. Imitation thus serves as a mechanism for transfer
of specific cultural elements, such as specialized knowledge or
technical skills, while identification permits the transfer of more
general aspects of the culture.

Forms of imitation are often seen in the analytic situation. It
is not at all uncommon for patients to adopt the mannerisms,
personal habits of dress or behavior, and even verbal expressions of the analyst during an analysis. More important, however, is that patients begin to adopt attitudes and opinions of the
analyst. Patients begin to act like the analyst, or act as they
believe the analyst would act or think in certain real life situations. They may even consciously ask themselves what the
therapist might do or think or say in a given situation. These
forms of imitation are frequently a medium of effective learning
and consequent modification of behavior. A difficult question
for the analyst to assess is whether these imitations serve the
purposes of the analysis or whether they represent resistances.
When these imitative patterns are motivated by the need to
please, placate, or attach oneself to an idealized or feared object, they must be recognized as defensive. They may also serve
a narcissistic goal of becoming like the powerful object. Such
imitations may be seen as reflecting or even as inducing underlying introjective configurations. The patient who mimics analytic expressions in an attempt to placate and please a powerful,
idealized analyst is behaving in terms of an underlying introjective organization in which the self is seen as weak, dependent,
and easily threatened by the loss of external love or approval.

But imitations can also be a force in building positive identifications. Despite the distinction of imitation as a form of learning from internalizations as such, imitation does play an important role in the development of identifications. By imitating an adult model, the child acquires similar behavioral patterns. The child becomes more like the adult and thus prepares the ground for evolving identifications (de Saussure, 1939). Early patterns of imitative behavior initiate patterns of identification, which serve as the basis for the development of early partial ego functions (Hendrick, 1951). The patterns of behavioral action acquired through imitation are integrated by subsequent identifications, with the result that the emerging partial functions can be built into more elaborate executive capacities.

It is important to emphasize that imitation does not imply internalization. Imitation remains in the arena of interaction between psychic processes and the external world. The attempts to formulate more complex notions of internalization, such as identification, in terms of modeling or imitative behavior capture only a part of the process. We must remind ourselves that the interaction and complementarity of imitative learning and internalization processes are extremely complex (Meissner, 1974d). In a global sense, we can say that imitation, whether conscious, preconscious, or unconscious, has an inductive influence on identificatory processes, especially when it occurs in the context of a positive attachment to the object. This is particularly true in relation to development, as Hendrick (1951) has so aptly observed.

Imitation may derive from and reflect an internal psychic organization based on introjection or identification. Clinically, we often find underlying identifications reflected in imitative aspects of the patient's behavior. But the clinical evaluation of internalizations cannot rest simply on behavioral parallelisms. The acquisition of a skill, for example, does not involve any internalization or modification of internal psychic structure by reason of the imitative process itself. Imitative behaviors can only suggest underlying identifications; they do not demonstrate them. By implication, then, the distinction must be drawn between behavioral and structural change. Identification is not a category of behavior; rather, it is a mechanism of personality formation that produces perduring modifications in the subject (Sanford, 1955). Moreover, identification is essentially an unconscious process, while imitation tends to be more conscious and deliberate. Even if we speak of superficial and transient identifications in such imitative experiences (Hendrick, 1951), it is clear that they are not identifications in any real sense.

Imitation, however, often plays a significant role in the genesis of identification (Gaddini, 1969; Jacobson, 1954, 1964). The initiation of early identifications and the establishing of primitive executive functions are accomplished by a transition from imitation to the integration of such acquired behaviors as part of the self (de Saussure, 1939). The position of imitation is thus transitional between purely external perceptions and the forms of internalization (Beres, 1966; Ritvo and Solnit, 1960).

The modeling behavior of imitation is at first object-bound in that it requires the presence of the model. As an image of the model is articulated, the model's external presence becomes less necessary and imitation can take place by reason of the inner object representation (Axelrad and Maury, 1951). This certainly seems to be the case in patients who ask themselves what the analyst might say or think in a particular situation, or who recall some comment or interpretation of the analyst and then make use of it. Imitations, however, do not imply the enduring change in the self-representation or structuralization of the ego that is involved in identification. As we have suggested, imitative behaviors can express trial identifications and thus serve as an indicator of the matrix of identification (Kernberg, 1966). Behavioral patterns and identifications may overlap, but they are never coextensive.

In the developmental context, imitations function in a way that is distinct from, yet gradually integrated with, identifications (Gaddini, 1969; Meissner, 1974d). As development progresses, imitative activity serves the adaptive and integrative processes of the ego. Imitations retain, at a primitive level, a relation to incorporative fantasies. The underlying wish to possess and become like the object creates a dynamic pressure toward subsequent identification. Imitations, like the more positive introjections with which they are often closely involved, can converge toward and inductively support the ego's inherent tendency toward identification. The patient's imitative use of analytic attitudes, especially in the context of a positive therapeutic alliance, can have a powerful inductive impact on the development of meaningful, constructive identifications with the analyst.

Undoubtedly, the ego's developmental capacity can be inhibited or fixated at levels of imitative or introjective organization, but these processes nonetheless carry within themselves inductive potentialities for shaping identifications and for becoming constitutive elements of the identificatory process. Imitation may also serve a vital function in ego development by helping to establish and maintain object relations. In addition, imitation and introjection remain continuously active in the mature organism, as constitutive elements of identifications and as active processes by which the subject interacts with the object world, with continually evolving further identifications.

Finally, imitations may serve a defensive function, whether in conjunction with introjects or not. The imitative defense may serve both to ward off the anxiety of introjective conflicts and to prevent further identifications. This defensive function of imitative and introjective processes is at work in the "identification with the aggressor" (A. Freud, 1936). Similar processes may contribute to more serious ego defects and forms of character pathology such as Deutsch's (1942) "as-if" character (Meissner, 1974d).

INCORPORATION

One basic aspect of internalization involves how the characteristics of external objects are taken in and become part of the inner psychic organization. It is hardly surprising, in this light, that the physical act of oral ingestion became the primary model of internalization. In our discussion we shall interpret incorporation as referring to a specific psychic process that is conceived as somehow analogous to the physical process of ingestion.[4]

---

[4] It should be noted that Schafer's usage differs quite markedly from this. He uses

Freud linked incorporation to a developmental schema in which the sexual aim of the oral phase was incorporation of the object. This involved primitive wishes to be united with the object along with oral-sadistic wishes to destroy the object cannibalistically (1905, 1915a). Incorporation was thus regarded as the prototype of internalization, although in Freud's later discussions of internalization the role of incorporation was never specified (Meissner, 1970a). Rather than regarding incorporation as an unconscious component of all internalizations, we are suggesting that it is a specific psychic mechanism with phase-specific functions in the psychic economy.

The notion of incorporation has always been troublesome. One usage restricts it to the instinctual physical activity of actual ingestion (Greenson, 1954; Sandler, 1960). This particular usage seems effectively to set incorporation aside as a meaningful psychic mechanism and puts the process of introjection in its place. Closer to Freud's thinking in the matter is the formulation of Hartmann and Loewenstein (1962), in which incorporation is defined as "an instinctual activity, belonging primarily to the oral phase. It is considered a genetic precursor of identification; and the latter is formed after its model. Clinically, we often find incorporation fantasies connected with identification. And actual identification processes may through a kind of appeal to their genetic forerunners reactivate such fantasies" (p. 49). Loewald's (1962) view is close to that of Hartmann and Loewenstein in that he sees incorporation as referring to specifically oral aspects of internalization processes of all kinds.

For Fenichel (1953), on the other hand, the aim of incorporation is primary union with the object by way of primary identification. Insofar as primary identification refers to a symbiotic union before subject-object differentiation, his equation cannot be simply accepted as such. Incorporative fantasies, no matter

---

the term to refer to an idea that stands for a fantasy. He writes: "Incorporation refers to a particular content of primary-process ideation. In the primary process, owing to its concreteness and its wish-fulfilling character, the idea (thought) is not differentiated from the deed. In this light, incorporation may be said to refer to ideas that one has taken a part or all of another person (or creature or thing) into one's self corporeally, and, further, that this taking in is the basis of certain novel, disturbing, and/or gratifying sensations, impulses, feelings, and actions of one's own and of correlated changes in one's experience of the environment" (1968a, p. 20).

how primitive, seem to require at least enough differentiation to allow for a wish to reunite with an object that is sensed, however vaguely and diffusely, as separate. It makes more sense to say that incorporative fantasies express a wish to reestablish the symbiotic union implicit in primary identification. In this sense, the process of incorporation suggests a regression to such primary identification (Axelrad and Maury, 1951).

Other treatments of incorporation take their cue from Freud's (1917) formulations on melancholia and suggest that the term should be restricted to the mechanism of internalization involved in melancholia. In this sense, incorporation constitutes a regressive reaction to the loss of an object through which the object is taken into the ego. Freud's insights into these depressive mechanisms lean heavily on the analogy to oral incorporation. But his treatment of narcissistic identification is cast primarily in terms of introjection. It is not at all clear how the incorporative model relates to the mechanism of introjection here. Certainly unconscious incorporative fantasies are frequently, if not always, a feature of depressive syndromes. But the association of oral fantasies does not demonstrate that incorporation itself is the mechanism of psychic alteration.

Jacobson (1964) has pointed out that frustrating experiences have a positive influence on the emerging distinction between the self and the loved or need-satisfying object. Repetitions of separation and frustration induce fantasies of total incorporation whose purpose is to reestablish the lost unity. Early incorporative fantasies of merging with the mother provide the libidinal foundation for later object relations and identifications. In this light, the process of incorporation is the primary and most primitive form of internalization; it is related to primitive oral fantasies as an aspect of primary-process functioning. These fantasies are usually unconscious; when they become conscious, they are usually repudiated by nonpsychotic subjects. Such incorporative fantasies are undoubtedly associated with more evolved forms of internalization, but this association does not demonstrate that incorporation is the mechanism of internalization.[5] This observation has particular

[5] This conclusion is in radical opposition to Schafer's (1972) view that incorporation is no more than a fantasy and that this fantasy is the only point of reference for all forms of internalization.

pertinence for the more organized and elaborate forms of internalization involving introjection and identification. Analytic patients, for instance, may at times express fantasies of incorporation. One hysterical patient repeatedly expressed the wish to devour my penis — not to destroy it, but to take it in so that she could have it as her own. The wish reflected her unresolved castration complex and the underlying narcissistic concerns, but also, on another level, it expressed her wish to be like me as an admired and loved object. Later on, in the termination phase, she spoke of taking me in, of having something of me inside her as a source of strength and growth. While the content was incorporative, the processes were clearly introjective (at first defensively and later more productively) and even identificatory.

It is important to distinguish the motivation for incorporation, together with its related wishful fantasies, from the mechanism of the internalization. The mechanism cannot be identified with the primitive wish for union. In incorporation the totality and globalness of the internalization of the object is such that the object loses its function and character as object. The external object is completely taken into the inner world of the subject. As a result, boundaries between the inner world and the outer world are decathected and dedifferentiated. In this sense, incorporation plays a role in severely regressed states. The earliest primitive identifications with primary objects may be regarded as involving incorporation as a basic mechanism. Despite the presence of incorporation fantasies, other cases are not as clear. The internalization of the lost object in depressive conditions such as melancholia involves incorporative fantasies to an important degree, but, following Freud, incorporation is not the basic mechanism of the internalization.

Only in severely regressed psychotic states does the operation of incorporation become unequivocal. Incorporation is the most primitive, the least differentiated form of secondary internalization, in which the object loses its distinction as object and becomes totally taken into the inner subject world. Incorporation thus stands at one extreme in the continuum of internalization. In other terms, in the course of incorporation object representations completely lose their object character and are merged or fused with self-representations without distinction. This is quite different from the treatment of object representations in more evolved forms of internalization.

INTROJECTION AND PROJECTION

Introjection is the most critical form of internalization. Freud (1917) originally took the term from Ferenczi and applied it to his analysis of depressive states. This formulation was later extended to the problem of superego formation (1923). In Freud's mind, the processes in question were forms of narcissistic identification whose mechanism of internalization was introjection. Introjection came to imply the abandonment of an object relation and the correlated preservation of the object intrapsychically by way of introjection.

Since Freud, however, analytic notions of introjection have undergone a significant development. Early analytic thinkers, following Freud's lead, tended to treat introjection and identification as if they were more or less equivalent. Fenichel (1953), for example, regarded introjection as a form of oral incorporation which served as the "pathway of identification." In more recent years, however, there has been an increasing tendency to distinguish the terms as separate processes. The necessity for such a distinction was prompted largely by the emergence of a more articulated ego psychology.

Fuchs (1937) has proposed that introjection is a form of instinctual inclusion into the ego system, while identification is the fact or state of such inclusion. Here introjection is equivalent to a mental mechanism based on oral-narcissistic drives which operates within the ego-superego system. The abandonment of objects, particularly ambivalent objects, requires that they are unconsciously taken in and thus become the foci of structural organization within ego and superego formations. In this view, identification is an "ego-term" and introjection serves as an "id-term," referring to overlapping and interlocking aspects of the identificatory process.

According to Fuchs (1937), then, introjection is simply a kind of incorporation based on an oral impulse which in the course of development becomes a form of inclusion of object representations into the ego and superego respectively. As Knight (1940) has commented: "Introjection seems to be used regularly as equivalent to and synonymous with incorporation, and may be defined as an unconscious inclusion of an object or part of an object into the ego of the subject. It is a psychological process based on the tendency of the id to incorporate an object according to an oral pattern" (p. 334). Greenson's (1954) formulation is quite similar, but he adds that the purpose of introjection is to reexperience the gratification derived from the object. Introjection is thus primarily in the service of instinctual needs.

Such overlapping usages do little more than extend the ambiguity in Freud's thinking on the subject (Meissner, 1970a). Freud himself reserved introjection for situations involving object loss. This in itself presumes some degree of self-object differentiation. Attempts to place introjection at the earliest level of primary object involvement, before any awareness of objects as such, really only confuse the terminology and further obfuscate Freud's formulations.

Despite this confusion, there have been attempts to bring greater clarity to the distinction of introjection and identification. In superego formation there is a renunciation of sexual and aggressive impulses toward the parents in favor of introjection (Greenson, 1954). This introjection, by which the oedipal attachments are weakened, and the subsequent identifications help to preserve and develop the child's object relations. Early introjections, however, tend to be more severe than the actual parental objects. This suggests that the renunciation and introjection of these objects are somehow called into the service of developing mastery over instinctual forces. In this sense, then, introjects promote the binding of instinctual drives and, in the case of the superego particularly, the binding of aggression.

Such early introjections are generally more rudimentary and disorganized in form since they reflect and embody a more primitive level of oral libidinal and aggressive stress. The objects that frustrate primitive instinctual demands tend to mobilize an infantile rage, which is at once projected onto the objects and internalized as bad or destructive introjects. By the same token, good, pleasure-giving objects may be internalized as good introjects.

The reasons for the internalization of a bad or hostile object are often obscure, and the dynamic motivations underlying this phenomenon have been the subject of frequent consideration. Schafer (1968a) offers a catalogue of such motives, which include masochism, guilt, repetition of trauma in the interest of mastery, control of a threatening or unreliably gratifying object, preservation of infantile omnipotence, and preference of a bad object for no object at all. He comments:

> Some of these motives involve gaining libidinal satisfaction from relations with a hostile fantasy object; others involve defensive gains or aggressive satisfactions; and some are concerned with facilitating controlled and adaptive functioning in general or at least in extreme situations. Some are experienced passively (e.g., the vengeful incorporated object) and others actively (e.g., the anticipation of dangerous dealings with the object). These motives and modes of experience are not mutually exclusive. Each hostile fantasy object has to be studied from its instinctual (object-related and narcissistic), defensive, and controlled-adaptive sides; from its passive and active sides; and from the sides of internal wish and environmental press. Although simple one-to-one correlations may be tactically useful in clinical interpretations, they are not adequate for general theory [p. 115].

Certainly the adherence to such introjects is highly overdetermined and serves as the ground for considerable resistance in the psychoanalytic process. But I think it is worth pointing out that in every case of adherence to a hostile introject, in my own clinical experience, that adherence has been accompanied by positive yearning and unsatisfied longing for closeness and acceptance by the object. This more specifically libidinal aspect makes the strength of the adhesive bond to such introjects more readily understandable and more available to clinical intervention. It is also clear that the therapeutic task has to do with a process of mourning for the yearned-for and often unavailable object.

Similar cogent reasons underlie the internalization of good objects, whether the motivation is essentially defensive or adaptive. Good objects may be retained in order to avoid the pain of mourning or to preserve a constant sense of secure object relationship. In any case, the underlying anxiety created by the finite nature of human relationships (in that an object, no matter how good or stable or constant, is not a permanent possession but at some time must be surrendered, lost, and mourned) serves as an adequate ground for such internalizations.

At the early, primitive level, good and bad introjects remain separate and continue to be subject to the constant reworking of processes of introjection and projection. As development progresses, the alternation and interlocking of introjection and projection produce composite introjects in which the aspects of the ambivalence are mitigated. Melanie Klein (1948; Segal, 1964) has described this process dynamically in terms of a transition from the paranoid position to the depressive position. The child gradually achieves a more differentiated representation of the object as well as a more composite and differentiated self-representation.

In this connection, Greenson (1954) describes a hierarchy of self- and object representations. The earliest introjections tend to derive from primitive oral-sadistic instinctual drives. Later in the developmental progression, introjections tend to derive from less primitive instinctual levels. The early introjects undergo a process of gradual fusion into more organized, more composite, and more highly differentiated introjects. The introjection may involve parts of objects or whole objects to a greater or lesser degree. In regressive states, however, these composite introjects may become defused into more primitive component elements.

The progressive developmental reworking of introjects is underlined by Jacobson (1964):

. . . the terms introjection and projection refer to psychic processes as a result of which self images assume characteristics of object images and vice versa. The mechanisms of introjection and projection originate in early infantile incorporation and ejection fantasies and must be distinguished from them. . . . The small child's limited capacity to distinguish between the external and internal world, which is responsible for the weakness of the boundaries between self and object images and the drastic cathectic shifts between them, promotes the continuous operation of introjective and projective processes. Thus, it is quite true that during the first years of life the child's self and object images still have more or less introjective and projective qualities.

But the establishment of realistic object and self representations rests increasingly on the maturation of perceptive and self-perceptive functions, i.e., on reality testing, at the expense of projective and introjective mechanisms. However, while becoming more and more subtle and refined, the latter continue to play an essential part in the processes of identification and in the advance from primitive fusions to those selective identifications on which infantile ego and superego development rests [pp. 46–47].

Jacobson seems to regard introjection and projection as extreme psychotic phenomena found only where self-object boundaries are blurred or dissolving. These phenomena are psychotic to the extent that they involve the dissolution of boundaries of the self, the loss of self-object differentiation, and the fusion or confusion of self- and object representations. The critical element in her view is the merging of object images with self-images in such introjections. Jacobson's descriptions of introjection are thus more akin to what we have described as incorporation, in which the merging of self and object and the obliteration of object qualities obtain. It should be noted that Schafer (1968a) objects to Jacobson's formulation, insisting on the subjective sense of the introject as something apart in the patient's experience. It is not clear at this point in what sense or to what degree this apartness is essential to the notion of introjection.

All in all, the view that these authors propose is probably somewhat too narrow. Introjection has a broader range of application in the understanding of psychic phenomena, particularly in regard to superego formation. The assimilation of object representations into self-representations presumably does not occur when the object and self-images are clearly and realistically differentiated. Such merely representational formulas, however, may not be adequate to describe the introjective phenomena. More than the characteristics of the self-image, the notion of introject suggests a functional aspect of the inner organization of the self. Fictive and imaginative fantasies of the self, as in Walter Mitty-like idealizations, are clearly not structuralizing introjects, but they can be described as assimilations at the level of self- and object representations. These phenomena are familiar to us as modes of adolescent fantasy. But the organization and functioning of the superego and its relations to the self are of a completely different order. Here introjections are not merely fantasy productions, but internalizations that effectively alter the inner psychic structure in significant ways. This sort of inner structural modification cannot be adequately described in terms of restrictively cognitional or representational modifications (Meissner, 1974c).

Sandler (1960) approaches this problem from a somewhat different perspective. He views introjection and identification as relatively complex processes which require a degree of internal organization and the construction of a mental model of the object. These antecedent processes of internal organization he describes as "organizing activities" whose function is the construction of such mental models. Organizing activities are an expression of the ego's synthetic capacities and are quite distinct from identifications or introjections. They play a significant role in the building up of ego structures, whether primary or secondary. The basic schemata of objects and the self are organized in this way. Sandler's formulation tries to restrict introjection to the process of superego formation and thus separate it from identification, which he regards as relevant to ego formation. In his view, superego identifications are equivalent to combinations of introjection plus the correlative ego identification.

In the emergence of the superego, the child's organizing activity gives rise to certain preautonomous superego schemata or models. These models are derived from parental models which enjoy a limited objectivity and are colored to some degree by projective elements. Particularly liable to projection are the intolerable elements of sadism and aggression which are part of the child's ambivalent experience of the parental objects. Introjection, then, serves to subsume these schemata in forming the definitive superego construction. The introject acquires the capacity to substitute in whole or in part for the real object as a source of gratification or aggression. The schema derived from organizing activities becomes structuralized and acquires a quasi-autonomy of its own.

Sandler's formulation clearly goes beyond mere representational assimilation. The preautonomous schemata are in their own way representational, but the process of introjection adds the formal note of structuralization. In these terms, then, it cannot be maintained, as Hartmann and Loewenstein (1962) suggest, that the distinction between introjection and identification lies in the degree of integration of object representations taken in from the outside, nor can it be said that the degree of integration depends on the extent to which self-representations have been substituted for object representations. Introjection is not simply a matter of representational confusion, but involves a distinctive process of autonomous structuralization. This point touches on the metapsychology of structure and structuralization, which currently remains relatively obscure and demands clarification. It is also at this juncture that the present approach differs most radically from that taken by Schafer (1972). This question hinges on the meaning of structure and whether internalization can be regarded as a process leading to the production of internal structure, or whether it must be regarded as an imaginative byproduct of fantasy (Meissner, 1976).

Introjects are structural components of the psychic system which enjoy a certain autonomy that allows them to be distinguished from ego components. Loewald has described superego introjects as being "on the periphery of the ego system" (1962, p. 483). He provides us with the concept of degrees of internalization as a means of describing the more peripheral character of introjects as opposed to the more central character of components of the ego system. As we have seen, Schafer (1968b) has translated this into the language of activity and passivity. In his terms, introjects are imaginary, "felt" presences by which patients feel assailed or gratified and in relation to which they feel relatively passive.

Such passivity is not absolute but is in contrast to the activity and more purely self-originative quality of ego functions. Schafer thus contrasts introjects to "well-established identifications," which are linked more closely to self-representations and have a characteristic "feel" of intentionality, will, or activity. According to Schafer: "An introject is an inner presence with which one feels in a continuous or intermittent dynamic relationship. The subject conceives of this presence as a person, a physical or psychological part of a person (e.g., a breast, a voice, a look, an affect), or a personlike thing or creature. He experiences it as existing within the confines of his body or mind or both, but not as an aspect or expression of his subjective self" (1968a, p. 72). The introject is an inner presence of an external object, and as such it exercises a particular influence on the subject's inner state and behavior. The relations between subject and introject may be as varied as the relations between two separate persons.

Schafer insists on the independence of the introject's capacity to influence the subject as its most significant experiential quality. While his emphasis on the "felt presence" safeguards a confusion of introjects and cognitive processes dealing with objects, particularly in that it preserves the divorce between the sense of self-as-agent and the role of introjects, it does not satisfy clinical experience, which suggests that introjects are in fact taken into the subject's inner world and often lose their independent quality and somehow become merged with the subject's sense of self. Introjects may be internalized in differing degrees; the quality of felt, quasi-independent presence, which Schafer's approach underlines, indicates only one such degree or range of possible degrees that a given introject may enjoy. As we shall see later, one dimension of the analytic process bears on precisely this issue, in that it seeks to increase the degree of externalization so that the introject becomes such an objectively sensed presence in the subject's experience.[6]

On the other hand, the pathology of many patients can be aptly described in terms of the tendency for the introject to take over and dominate their experience of themselves so that it becomes mistaken for the self-as-agent. In addition to degrees of internalization, introjects are also subject to topographic modifications and may be to one degree or another unconscious, preconscious, or conscious. This is a matter of some clinical impor-

---

[6] I am not arguing here against Schafer's formulation, but only wish to emphasize that it excessively limits the notions of introject and introjection. Introjects can and often do function unconsciously. They may become phenomenologically confused with and mistaken for the sense of self in varying degrees, and they lie at the root of a wide variety of pathological expressions.

tance. Although introjects may not be recognizable as such, they may be active and effective as an unconscious influence. Within these parameters, the introject serves as a quasi-active presence which provides a structural means for the binding and the mastery of basic instinctual energies.

The question can be usefully posed here: What is the phenomenology of introjects? What are we talking about when we speak of introjects? What are the concrete referents, the descriptive elements, of the introjects?

Perhaps some clinical vignettes will help to focus the question. A young woman comes for a consultation in connection with the termination of a long course of intensive psychotherapy. She tells me of her persistent guilt, which she relates to her many misdeeds (mostly trivial and inconsequential), but which seems to center on a rather traumatic abortion in her teens. Along with the guilt, there is a pervasive feeling of her own inherent badness and worthlessness. She feels that any good she does is fraudulent, that she is unlovable and hateful, that if people knew what went on inside her, they would have nothing to do with her. When asked about her early life history, she recounts with intense emotion and tearfulness the early divorce of her parents, abandonment by her mother at the age of two, and frequent shifting around from one living situation to another.

If we relate this account to the organization of introjects, what can we say about them? The sense of self that this patient carries and expresses so vividly is organized around qualities of evil, worthlessness, and deep-seated insecurity about her own lovableness and acceptability as a human being. She is someone whom others would readily abandon because of these characteristics. One could argue that these attributions were the effects of early traumatic learning which had been variously reinforced in the course of her life. But the phenomenon seems more pervasive, powerful, and persistent than that account would support. On the basis of learning parameters, one might more readily expect modification through relearning. Yet what is striking is the disparity between the patient's actual life circumstances and the content of her account. She is currently successful in a number of areas in her life, has a stable and loving marriage, is advancing her education with great success, and has a real sense of growth and accomplishment which contributes significantly to the areas in which she can feel good about herself. Nevertheless, after years of productive therapeutic work, she retains a sense of her own evil, an evil that cannot seek and accept forgiveness—even, or perhaps especially, from God—and that ultimately merits only abandonment—even from God. The reenactment of the infantile trauma becomes obvious and has many determinants, both real and psychodynamic, but our concern here is with the way the patient builds an inner self with a depressive core that includes a stern, unforgiving, and condemning superego. This reflects the organization of the introjects.

Another vignette. A man in his thirties comes for analysis because of his long-standing depression and unhappiness with his life. He is dissatisfied with his work, and his marriage is filled with tension and uncertainty. He has no friends. He has no one besides his wife with whom he can socialize. If she decides not to go out with him, he goes alone or not at all. When he goes to the symphony, for example, he talks to no one; he remains aloof. At work he is known for his efficiency and effectiveness in a quite demanding research job. He stays in his office and talks with fellow workers only to conduct business. He even refuses to eat lunch in the company cafeteria or take coffee breaks. Those who are more relaxed and casual are scorned as "goof-offs" and "gold-brickers." Intensely competitive and distrustful, he is extremely touchy about getting full credit for his contributions and constantly checks and updates his résumé, with a feeling of almost gloating satisfaction at what it contains, combined with a sense of impotent envy that others in the company may have more impressive résumés. Yet he refuses all offers of increased pay or advancement because he is afraid that in accepting such rewards he will have to accept additional responsibilities or additional demands will be made on his time. Consequently, he is significantly underpaid for his position and seniority—a constant embarrassment to management.

At home this man endeavors to keep a rigid accounting of who pays for what. He demands that his wife keep an accurate record of how much money she spends and for what. They keep separate accounts, and there is constant friction about who is to pay for whatever they do. When they go out for dinner, for example, he makes her pay half the check. He stoutly maintains this attitude with rationalizations of justice and fairness. He does not want to have children on grounds that they will only take things away from him and he could not tolerate this. Sexual relations are understandably infrequent and unsatisfactory. His wife is usually unwilling to be giving or responsive. The quality of their interactions generally is tit-for-tat.

What are we to make of the introjective configuration in this highly obsessional and schizoid man? More information can be gleaned from his response in analysis. In truly obsessional style, his attendance was faithful, punctual, and unvarying. Only after about two years did he feel comfortable enough to be a few minutes late, or even to take time away from the analysis— although these occasions were rare and all quite legitimate. In the analysis his material remained superficial, mostly a trivial recounting of daily events, given with little or no feeling and no semblance of association—this despite sometimes strenuous efforts on my part to find a way through his defenses. Gradually the analysis entered a phase of silence, with long periods of silence that often lasted most of the hour. I could not decide whether we were caught up in an obsessional anal hold-out, or whether some more basic fear and conflict were at work.

We began to get some hints from material related to the patient's history. He had been an only child. His father, a teacher, was seen as a weak, bumbling, ineffectual man who never had the guts or balls to make it in life. The patient also described his father as a captive victim of the mother, who controlled and ran the father's life. He hated his father's inability to stand up for himself, particularly against the mother. He also hated his father's cheapness and poor-mouthed penny-pinching. The father always bought his clothes secondhand from the Goodwill; he stole matches and sugar from restaurants, pencils from school, etc. The patient's mother, on the other hand, was a fairly successful artist and sculptor, who frequently exhibited her work. In her younger days she had been active in the theater and had even had occasional bit parts in movies. The parents had put off having a child for nearly ten years, and after the patient's birth the mother was anxious to get back to her professional work. The patient saw her as egotistical, self-centered, eager for any scrap of attention, admiration, or adulation. He bitterly resented this and complained angrily about any requests she made for help from him in arranging her exhibits or doing her work. He felt that she had turned her back on him as a child, that her work was more important to her than he was, so why should he do anything for her now?

The picture he painted was of a shy, isolated, friendless, and somewhat morose child. He didn't play with other kids because his father warned him about wasting time, telling him that the kids in the neighborhood were low-brow and no good and that he should use his time well by reading and studying. In elementary and high school he was an excellent student, spending long hours at his books with few other outlets. He learned to play tennis in high school and played on the school team, but this was his only sport. He had no social life, no friends, no dates. His feelings of rejection by his parents were reinforced by their sending him to a boy's camp for the summer and later to a boarding school. This was proof that he was not wanted, particularly by his mother.

As might be expected, these elements played themselves out in the transference. As the transference neurosis developed, there was a strong sense of admiration for me as a somewhat idealized father-figure. He became powerfully aware of his wish to have a closer relation with me and to get from me the intimacy, approval, and help that he had wanted so desperately but never received from his father. He felt that if he could assimilate my wisdom and strength, that would enable him to be the strong man that his father was not and his problems would come to an end. Along with this was the expectation that by submitting himself to the analytic process I would work my powerful magic and he would be cured without any effort or responsibility for change on his part. His expectation that I would do it for him was the same expectation that his parents should have made his life different. His resentment that I did not meet his expectations and did not exercise my power and magic on his behalf paralleled his resentment of his parents for not having dealt with his difficulties differently.

As his disappointment and disillusionment mounted, the intense pull of his dependency wishes toward me increased and with it the conviction that I did not really care about him. All I wanted was his money; my real interests were elsewhere; I was more interested in other patients; I was more interested in writing and publishing papers (he had looked up my bibliography — my résumé — which he both admired and envied). The elements of the mother transference now took a dominant role in the evolving transference neurosis.

In terms of the introjective configuration, several important points should be noted. First, the identification with his father was highly conflicted, yet powerfully present. The patient made a point of buying expensive clothes and delighted in going out to expensive restaurants. His clothes were fashionable and impeccable — obsessively so. In all this he insisted on how different he was from his father. Yet he was withdrawn and isolated as his father had been. Like his father, he avoided responsibility in his work and was in his own way penny-pinching and ungenerous. He would spend hundreds on a new suit, but would quibble with his wife over the price of a drink in a restaurant. His refusal of any pay raise was almost a direct translation from the model provided by his father.

Second, the elements of his identification with his mother were also quite apparent. These were organized along narcissistic lines. His constant search for approval and admiration, his sense of insecurity and powerful need for narcissistic support from outside, his sensitivity to hurt and narcissistic vulnerability were all paralleled in his mother's personality. Without belaboring the point, the parents' personality configurations clearly had a powerful role in the organization of the patient's sense of himself and in the way he functioned in his everyday experience.

Third, these configurations played themselves out in the transference interaction. This was most clear in regard to the mother transference. I was seen as uncaring and indifferent, narcissistically absorbed in my own interests and concerns, and not wholly invested in or attentive to the patient's welfare. In narcissistic terms, we can see the patient's wish for a mirror transference to support the narcissistic need and vulnerability of his grandiose self (Kohut, 1971). Correspondingly, the patient's need to see me as a powerful, even magical, idealized parent—the opposite of his devalued and impotent father—derives from an underlying narcissistic need.

A fourth point. There is a certain reversibility or, I would prefer to say, polarity in the organization and display of these elements of self-and-other experience. In the present case, the elements played themselves out in the transference so that the analyst was seen as a powerful, wished-for father and as a narcissistically depriving (and therefore narcissistically needy) mother. There was an interplay of elements of power and impotence, capacity and need. In relation to both aspects of the transference, the patient was the needy and neglected child who sought desperately but frustratedly for love, acceptance, and approval from his parents. In the previous case of the young woman, there was a polarity of good versus evil, of judging versus judged, of condemning versus condemned. This woman saw her therapist, as well as me, and even more profoundly God, as good, lovable, and righteous, and as condemning. The polarity of condemning righteousness and power over against her own sense of being condemned and evil came from within herself. She was both condemner and condemned. Similarly, the young man was both the hurt and needy child and the powerful parent. What is displayed in the transference is an aspect of this polar organization of the introjects—usually that aspect is externalized which is the polar opposite of the aspect the patient attributes to himself. If the patient is weak and needy, the analyst is seen as powerful. This polarity may be reversed so that the patient's omnipotence is matched by the analyst's inadequacy and devaluation. Such reversals are unusual in neurotic patients, but they are not at all infrequent in borderline patients and may be regarded as characteristic of more primitive borderlines.

I have come to think of the organization of introjects, perhaps simplistically but at least descriptively, in terms of polarities organized along lines of aggression and narcissism (Meissner, 1978b). The aggressive polarity is between powerful destructiveness, on one end, and helpless impotence and vulnerability, on the other. I have characterized the former configuration as the *aggressor introject* and the latter as the *victim introject*. The aggressor introject is displayed in feelings of powerful destructiveness, evil, having a hateful power to hurt and destroy. The victim introject, on the other hand, is seen in feelings of helplessness, impotence, and inadequacy — the feeling that there is no recourse other than passive compliance and submission. The young woman, for instance, saw herself as both an evil force and a helpless victim. The interaction of aggressor introject and victim introject is also found in the dynamics of depression and suicide (Meissner, 1977b). The narcissistic polarity is between a sense of superiority, specialness, privilege, even grandiosity and omnipotence, on the one hand, and a sense of inferiority, worthlessness, and lack of value, on the other. I have characterized these configurations in terms of superiority and inferiority. The *superior introject* has all the qualities of the grandiose self, while the *inferior introject* carries with it feelings of inadequacy, low self-esteem, shame, embarrassment, and other hallmarks of narcissistic vulnerability.

An important clinical consideration is that these polarities are defensively organized and reciprocally related. The young woman's position as victim was sustained by defensive needs against her sense of rage and resentment (presumably directed toward her abandoning mother), which reflected aspects of her aggressive components. The brief consultation did not bring the relevant elements to light, but we can guess at the underlying narcissistic elements that continued to support her rage and guilt. Similarly, in my analytic patient, both sides of the narcissistic conflict played themselves out in mutually defensive interaction. His grandiosity and haughty sense of self-sufficiency were transparent defenses against his underlying sense of neediness and vulnerability. In turn, his need to see himself as weak and inadequate served to avoid those feelings of powerful contempt and grandiose isolation that cut him off from the narcissistic supplies he otherwise needed.

From a clinical perspective, then, these introjective elements are always found in combination. The polarities always operate in conjunction. If one sees evidence of a sense of vulnerability and victimization, one must look for signs of the opposite, for the sense of powerful destructiveness that bespeaks the aggressor introject. Similarly, signs of a sense of inferiority, worthlessness, and low self-esteem alert the analyst to keep a weather eye open for indications of specialness, privilege, entitlement, and narcissistic expectation. While they may not seem as clinically relevant, the reverse tendencies are equally important. When one polar aspect is worked through, the patient may have recourse to the other. The worthless, inadequate patient may come to adopt a position of superiority and overconfidence. In fact, my schizoid young man did retreat to a position of somewhat grandiose self-sufficiency. His attitude was that if I would not give him what he wanted on his terms, he would take nothing and show me that he could get along very well without me—the very message that he had given to his mother for years. Obviously an exchange of one polar position for another, of one introjective configuration for another, does not signal a release from the pathogenic influence of the introjects. It is only when both polar introjective configurations have been surrendered that the patient becomes free of their impact. This applies to both narcissistic and aggressive configurations and to their interaction.

This discussion of the phenomenology of the introjects raises a point which is central to our understanding of the role of internalization in the psychoanalytic process. The point is that the distortion of the therapeutic relation derives from specific introjective configurations within the patient. We shall have occasion to reconsider this question in our discussion of transference, but here we are focusing on a critical difference from seeing the patient's idiosyncratic experience of the analyst merely in terms of learned patterns of interpersonal expectations or as displacements from previous object relations. I am not arguing here that these phenomena do not occur or do not have a place in the analytic process; obviously they do. But when the evidence of internalization is also present, to ignore it may be to run the risk of glossing over an important aspect of the patient's pathology.

In reference to the transference, it is not simply that the patient displaces some elements or expectations from a previous context—a sort of generalization of object relations experience—but that he has internalized this particular set of characteristics and made them part of his functioning personality. Thus, my schizoid patient's seeing me as an idealized father reflected not only elements of object representations from his infantile past, elements of childhood wishes and narcissistic idealizations, but also his own inherent narcissism which predicated his position as the special, privileged son of the powerful, idealized father. It was this internal narcissistic configuration that lay behind his contempt and devaluation of his real father. The core of the pathology was not touched until this introjective configuration was focused, brought to awareness, and analyzed. Similarly, his maternal transference — seeing me as the uncaring parent who was more narcissistically invested in my own concerns, interests, and self-importance than in him — could not be effectively modified until it became clear to him that these characteristics were part of his own makeup. These aspects of the maternal introject were clearly reflected in his constant preoccupation with his résumé and in his continual disregard of the needs of others with whom he came in contact — with his fellow workers, most particularly with his wife, and even with me. When these elements are focused and their relation to the introjective configuration established, crucial questions are raised about the function of such introjects, their defensive utility, the reasons for their persistence, the motivations for the patient's adherence to them, and so on. If these internalized dimensions are overlooked or minimized, there is a risk that the displacement of object representations will be taken as explaining the patient's difficulties and that the genetic motivations will be taken reductively as the basis for therapeutic insight. While these aspects are important and do carry therapeutic impact, they are not the whole story. I would insist that additional important analytic work must be done in the examination of the introjective configuration itself. We shall return to this question in the discussion of therapeutic effects.

In the continuum of internalization processes, introjection stands between the more primitive mechanism of incorporation and the more highly integrated and organized process of identification. There is a tendency in psychoanalytic thinking to limit introjection to superego formation, following Freud's lead, but superego formation is only one, if the most important, of the expressions of introjection. There is also a tendency in classical discussions to focus on only one aspect of the introjective economy in terms of superego dynamics—usually the aggressive, victimizing aspect. The superego becomes the harsh, punitive, judging, condemning agency. But, as our discussion emphasizes, where there is a victimizer in the psychic economy, there is also a victim. Both aspects are essential to an understanding of the pathology and its dynamics.

In trying to clarify the notion of introjection, the status of object representations is extremely important. Introjection involves the replacement of a relation to an external object by a relation to an internal object. The internalization involved in incorporation was envisioned as a global process in which the object becomes totally part of the subject's inner world and loses its function as object. By way of contrast, introjection preserves some aspect of the object's objectivity and relation to the external world.

The critical notion here is that of the transitional object and the transitional object relationship. Modell's work (1968) has made it clear that the transitional object stands midway between what is created by the inner world and what exists in the external world. The transitional object is somehow in the environment, but its separateness from the self is only partially acknowledged. It is created by the subject in the sense that properties attributed to the object are a reflection of inner dynamics and aspects of the subject's inner life. The transitional object takes its shape through the interplay of mechanisms of introjection and projection. There is frequently a fluid oscillation between what is attributed to the object and what is taken into the self. As Modell notes: "The transitional object is not a part of the self—it is 'something' in the environment. However, it is endowed with qualities that are created by the subject by the oscillation of introjection and projection. Therefore, the mode of transitional object relationships is one where the differences between the self and the object are minimized. The object is not acknowledged as separate from the self" (p. 37). Through the correlative mechanisms of introjection and projection, the subject's inner world is organized in such a way that the structure of that inner world reflects the quality of object relations.

Modell's formulations derive from Winnicott's (1953) views

on the nature of transitional phenomena. Winnicott regards such phenomena as a mode of experience and object relatedness, in which the internal reality of the subject's wishes, desires, or convictions blends with the external reality in the contemplation of the object. Parental objects are transitional insofar as they are colored by the child's projections. Introjection involves the internalization of such transitional object relations. In the process of introjection, a transitional internal object is created that somehow replaces the external libidinal relationship to the parent. The internalized object retains its transitional character, even as it becomes a part of the subject's inner world.

This creation of a transitional internal object by way of introjection is familiar in the resolution of oedipal attachments. As I have suggested elsewhere (Meissner, 1978b), viewing the emergence of the oedipal involvement as an effect of introjective and projective elaborations, rather than as a biologically determined outcome, has certain implications. I do not mean to dismiss the biological determinants, but to see the oedipal involvement as simply an expression of age-related, physiologically preprogrammed events does not do justice to the complexity of the process. Seeing it as the effect of evolving projections and introjections brings into focus the fact that the oedipal engagement is a motivated process. The point is similar to that made in relation to understanding the transference: an important part of the process is that the intrinsic motivations related to specific introjective configurations be exposed, analyzed, and resolved. The pattern that the oedipal situation takes derives in part from the projection onto the parental figures of elements derived from the child's preoedipal introjective organization. But the process is more complex in that it also involves an ongoing interaction with the parents in which the parents react in terms of their own projections onto the child, which in turn derive from and reflect the parents' own introjective organizations. Given the complexities of these interactions, however, the shaping of the child's oedipal experience answers primarily to ongoing motivational needs which influence the quality of his projective molding of parental imagoes. Although the process is influenced by the preexisting introjects, its imminent shaping reflects the motivational currents of the actual context. The introjections and identifications that emerge through the engagement, processing, and resolution of the oedipal involvement are the complex product of earlier introjections as they are modified and reprocessed by ongoing interactions and motivational pressures. The factors influencing the oedipal introjections have to do not merely with previous object-related experience and correlative internalizations, but with current pressures for the definition, separation, and integration of the emerging and progressively clarifying sense of self.

In Freud's original formulation, introjection specifically involved the loss of an object. In terms of our present formulation, however, the loss is of the object as transitional object. Introjection preserves the subject's transitional mode of relating to the object, but the object as transitional is abandoned. The subject's attachment to the object is sustained under a new set of conditions imposed by the internalization of the object.

A further question is whether or not the introjection *requires* loss of the object. If we adhere to the transitional object formulation, it is apparent that the loss of the object as transitional does not imply the loss of the object as such. In fact, the loss of the transitional object may lead to important modifications of the object relationship which serve the purposes of development. This is probably what happens in the dissolution of oedipal involvements. The child's oedipal relation to the parents is a form of transitional object relationship. But the parents function less as transitional objects or as different transitional objects by reason of the child's introjecting them. The creative or illusory aspect which derives from the child's own inner world is, however, preserved in the introject. The oedipal introjects, as they become integrated, for example, into the structure of the superego, are not simply internalized aspects of parental objects, but are modified by and integrated with elements from the child's inner world — elements of preexisting introjective configurations. They thus retain the illusory or intermediary quality of the transitional realm. It can be seen from this account that introjection serves extremely significant functions in the psychic economy. It provides an important mechanism for the mastery of instinctual forces and serves as an organizing point for further instinctual vicissitudes. This is particularly true in regard to aggressive instincts, but applies as well to libidinal instincts.

There are certain implications of the relationship between introjection and transitional object relations. Like the transitional object, the introject carries with it the residue of object derivation and thus participates in both worlds. It can never become fully internalized into the ego core (Loewald, 1962). When it comes to conscious awareness, it is experienced as a felt presence, as something objectified within the reality of the self. The introject may be experienced as having varying degrees of integration with the subjectively grasped sense of self—Schafer's (1968a) reflective self-representation. In many pathological states, the pathogenic introject may be experienced as indistinguishable from the sense of self. Only through therapeutic clarification and focusing does the introject become differentiated and distanced from the subjective self (Meissner, 1977a). Introjective processes involve a range of internalizing mechanisms which vary with the transitional character of the object. Those which have a more primitive character and are more intensely endowed with derivatives of the inner world can be more clearly discerned as introjective. But as the derivatives of the inner world become less apparent, introjective processes function in a manner much closer to more autonomous identificatory processes. They maintain their distinction, however, in their potential distance from the ego core when conscious, in their embodiment of instinctual energies, both libidinal and aggressive, and in their propensity for projection.

The implicit measure of development and differentiation in internalization processes is the degree to which the separateness of the object is preserved in the process of internalization. In incorporation there is no room for the separateness of the object. The object is subsumed into the subject's inner world and loses its object function completely. Introjection, however, allows for an intermediate degree of separateness of the object. Consequently, a higher degree of internal structure and self-organization is required for introjection than for incorporation. In both processes the internalized objects may be partial or total; the distinction rests on the quality of object relatedness. The object quality is eliminated in incorporation (in terms of oral engulfment), but it is partially preserved in introjection—as an internalization of a transitional object relation.

To fill out the object relations schema in reference to patterns of internalization, the most highly organized and differentiated forms of internalization, which we are designating here as identifications, carry the process of separation from the object a further step. In identification the object quality of the model is fully preserved and is, in fact, one of the conditions of the internalization. The object is acknowledged, accepted, and preserved as autonomously existing in its own right and as separate and independent from the internalizing subject. The tolerance for the separateness of the object is a mark of the autonomy of the participating ego (Modell, 1968). For identifications of the patient with the analyst to be mobilized in the analysis, the patient must be able to experience the analyst as a separately existing, autonomous human being, who is both different from the patient and independent in his functioning. We shall return to a consideration of the conditions for such identifications later, particularly in our discussion of termination.

The progressive elaboration of introjects in the course of development brings about an evolution of inner structure. At each stage of the elaboration, psychic structure becomes more developed, more organized, more integrated. Each new level of structuralization is accompanied by a further evolution in the process of forming structure and internalization. Each progressive step diminishes the degree to which the inner world contributes to the constitution of object relations. Thus, at a pregenital level of psychic organization, the quality of object relations is much more highly dependent on introjective components, so that their projective derivatives carry more of the quality of such infantile components and directly color the person's object experience. Object relations come to have an all-or-nothing quality. They are based more on need satisfaction than on true libidinal object constancy, tend to be highly ambivalent, and are subject to a variety of preoedipal (oral and anal) instinctual vicissitudes. The oedipal and postoedipal reworking of introjective configurations again changes the quality of their organization and correspondingly modifies the character of projective derivatives and the related experience of objects. Introjection therefore comes to serve important defensive and developmental functions, particularly in regard to the mastery of instinct and the forming and sustaining of inner systems of regulation. Such patterns of internalization achieve a relative binding of significant amounts of instinctual energy in forms of internal organization and structure.

As we have noted, the structuralizing aspect of introjection is of central importance and is not adequately accounted for by representational formulations. The structural perspective brings into focus the concept that the introject becomes a source of intrapsychic influence and relative activity, which under specific circumstances substitutes for the object as a source of narcissistic gratification or aggressive impulse. In this way, the self is modified so that it acquires the specific characteristics of the internalized object, now functioning intrapsychically as a quasi-autonomous agency. The introject thus becomes a center of functional organization with its own relative autonomy in the intrapsychic economy. However, because the introject also involves a tendency to regression and is susceptible to a broad range of internal and external influences, its inherent stability as a structuralizing component of the inner psychic world is somewhat mitigated. Its organization and functioning tend to be predominantly along lines of primary-process influence and reflect more directly the vicissitudes of drive influences than does the less instinctually derived, secondary-process organization of identifications.

An important aspect in understanding introjective processes is their inherent relationship to projection. Projection refers to a process in which attributes derived from the subject's inner world are attached to a real object so that the object as perceived and experienced is constituted by qualities derived from both the environment and the subject's self. We need to remind ourselves that in referring to objects we are referring technically to object representations; the direct effects of projective mechanisms play on the qualities of object representations as such rather than specifically on external objects. In other words, projection brings about a modification of the object as transitional object, in the sense described above.

There is lack of parity in this usage since through introjection it is the self that is structurally modified, whereas through projection it is the transitional object representation, rather than the object itself, that is somehow modified or constituted. "Projection" can be seen as the correlative externalization to "introjection," in the sense that projection is derived from the intro-jects and directly reflects their content and level of organization. The correlative externalization to incorporation would be the loss, engulfment, or absorption of the sense of self into the ob-ject. We have no useful technical term to describe this phenomenon—the metaphoric term "engulfment" is as close as we can come. It tells us little about the nature of the proc-ess—but neither does the term "incorporation" for that matter. As for identification, there is no correlative externalizing proc-ess. Since nothing is "taken in" from the object, nothing is given back to the object. The relative autonomy and separateness of both subject and object do not give rise to conditions allowing for the externalization of elements of the self and their attribu-tion to another.[7] Identification may follow on the interplay of introjection and projection, as it typically does in superego for-mation and development (Sandler, 1960), but the projection is in no sense correlated to the identification.

The reciprocal relationship of introjection and projection serves to emphasize the inherently defensive function of intro-jection. In these terms, processes serving specific defensive ends can be more usefully denominated as introjective than as iden-tificatory. The concept of "identification with the aggressor" seems to be a case in point. In introducing this term, Anna Freud (1936) describes a clinical situation in which a child took on and mimicked the threatening or fearful aspects of an anxiety-provoking object. In her description, the child's iden-tification with the object's powerful and terrifying qualities was a means of mastering intolerable anxiety. Mowrer (1950) calls this process "defensive identification." Such an "identification" seems more accurately described as a combination of introjec-tion and subsequent imitative behavior. In terms of our usage

---

[7] This consideration focuses one of my difficulties with the term "projective iden-tification." It implies that identification takes place with an object that has been sub-jected to prior projective modification. This usage completely obfuscates the mean-ing of introjection and identification. However, it should be noted that most of the authors using the term "projective identification" make no attempt to distinguish identification from introjection. In my judgment such an approach ignores impor-tant metapsychological differences which have important theoretical and therapeutic implications.

here, identification with the aggressor is not an identification at all, since it is largely defensively motivated, results from significant projections that are influenced by the child's own aggressive vicissitudes, and is itself characteristically subject to subsequent reprojection and externalization. These are all hallmarks of introjective organization. The child introjects some characteristics of the anxiety-provoking object, specifically the aggression of powerful adult figures. The introjection here is closely related to projective mechanisms. The interlocking of introjection and projection permits the mastery of instinctual pressures and the tolerance of anxiety.

In addition to this specifically defensive function, identification with the aggressor serves as a preliminary step in superego formation. The contribution to the superego is more in the nature of an introjection than an identification (Sandler, 1960). In this connection, we can also note that Anna Freud's notion of "altruistic surrender" has been clarified by Knight (1940) as a combination of introjection and projection.

The confusion involved in linking the concepts of identification and defense is discussed by Rapaport (1967). He points out that the concept of identification often has two connotations: it is regarded both as a defense mechanism and as a mechanism of structure formation. How do these connotations of identification relate to the notion of introjection? Or, alternatively, what is the difference between identification as defense and introjection as defense? This raises the question whether the notion of defensive identification is at all meaningful or useful. Defenses are directed against instinctual derivatives, particularly aggression. In identification with the aggressor or in depressive states or even grief reactions, it is the sadistic and hostile impulse that must be defended against. My contention here is that the defensive mechanisms in these cases are specifically combinations of introjection and projection. Although identification may be involved to one or another degree, it is *not* directly involved in the defensive function per se. Identification can serve, as we shall see, to stabilize defensive structures derived through introjection, but its defensive function is derivative or secondary to such defense mechanisms.

In the case of identification with the aggressor, the defensive aspect is clear. The introject may remain caught up in relatively intense defensive pressures so that it is only minimally modified and its aggressive components remain effectively unneutralized. The result is a pathogenic introject which gains little in the way of effective integration with the rest of the psychic organization. However, identification with the aggressor takes place in a developmental context in which there is an ongoing and progressive interplay of projection and introjection in relation to significant objects. If the objects, particularly the parents, respond in ways that affectively mitigate and modulate the child's aggression, the opportunity arises for the introjective organization to be progressively reprocessed, the defensive pressures modulated, and the aggressive components relatively neutralized. Such a context provides the conditions for nondefensive, positive identifications which allow for more harmonious, constructive, and purposeful integration of elements of the aggressive introject. In cases of pathological development, however, we find a more or less severe superego distortion, with severely self-punitive and destructive dynamics and poor integration of superego structure. The former course, however, is the preferable one and achieves a higher level of superego integration, in which aggressive elements are constructively modified and integrated in the form of capacities for courage, fortitude, perseverance, self-assertion, and determination. The identifications that follow on the aggressor introject can be envisioned as secondary to the previous defensively motivated introjections and as effectively modifying and stabilizing the earlier defensive structures. This progression, of course, is accompanied by increasing distance from and decreasing susceptibility to instinctual derivatives.

Thus, in contrast to identification, introjection seems to be much more intimately involved in instinctual vicissitudes and more closely related to defensive ego functions. It is particularly affected by the economy of aggressive and libidinal instinctual drives. Introjects express and reflect instinctual dynamics and are involved in the binding and loosening of instinctual energies. They serve as the vehicles of intrapsychic expression of instinctual forces and are particularly susceptible to the regressive pull of id derivatives. The organization of introjects is therefore more along primary-process lines than is that of identifications. Identifications are subject to these influences only in secondary and derivative ways. Since identifications are less influenced by and less dependent on instinctual drives and function preferentially in terms of neutralized or independent energies, they are considerably less subject to regressive dynamics and are capable of functioning on a secondary-process level. Correlatively, they enjoy a considerably higher degree of inner cohesiveness and autonomy.

Rapaport (1967) was one of the first to point to the complex problem of the integration of defense formation and identifications. Anything in the organization of the psychic economy that serves to increase countercathectic resistance to drive discharges may be regarded as defensive in that it serves to heighten the threshold of discharge. The counterbalancing of structure and discharge means that any formation of structure is at least derivatively defensive in function. Hartmann (1939) has repeatedly emphasized that defensive operations may undergo a change of function and achieve a level of secondary functional autonomy. Such a change of function involves the integration of defensively derived modalities into the ego so as to increase the level of structuralization within the ego.

This process is extremely important, as we shall see, in the working and reworking of internalizations in analysis. Through the analytic regression, introjective configurations loosen and become available for analytic processing. In the analytic work new introjections derived from the analytic relationship come into play and progressively modify the patient's introjective configuration. These revised introjects are still defensively motivated, but become increasingly less so as the analytic relationship evolves. As more positive identifications with the analyst emerge, this process of reworking the introjects is extended and elaborated. The introjects are increasingly modified and undergo a change of function. They lose their defensive relevance and become integrated as character structures, increasingly effectively integrated with the rest of the adaptively functioning ego-superego system.

To return to Rapaport (1967), he assumes that the formation

of defenses is linked to introjections in that ego and superego become differentiated as structural integrates of what he calls "defense-identifications." These early defense-identifications may be assimilated by both ego and superego, but remain relatively passive in relation to drive derivatives. As far as I can see, Rapaport's defense-identifications are the equivalent of introjective configurations. As long as they remain at that level of organization, they retain the characteristic defensiveness and drive susceptibility of introjects. With the developmental progression through levels of increasing integration, the passive and drive-dependent regulation of such defense-identifications gives way to an increasingly active form of ego regulation. Our assumption here is that the change in function from levels of specifically defensive to adaptive functioning always involves the modification of preexisting defensive structures by identificatory processes, leading to the more autonomous stabilization, modification, and integration of defensive introjections by structuralizing identifications.

Freud (1923) first approached these problems in his analysis of the formation of the superego. As we have previously noted, Freud derived his model of narcissistic identification from his analysis of mourning. Such an identification involved an object loss with a subsequent internalization of the lost object. Object loss in superego formation meant the loss of oedipal attachment to the parents. Superego formation modified the oedipal attachment to the parents and was essentially a process of introjection of parental imagoes (Freud, 1923; Meissner, 1971). Freud's formulation points to the issues of oedipal renunciation, but it tends to gloss over their significant problems. The oedipal renunciation, rather than involving object loss in the strict sense, requires a surrender of incestuous ties and a substitution of more mature affectionate attachments.[8] The respective roles of introjection and identification and their interrelation in this context require clarification.

Sandler's (1960) contribution to the understanding of

---

[8] I am not referring here to regressive resolutions of oedipal conflicts, which may result in greater dependence and more infantile attachment. Such a regressive resolution results in a reactivation of earlier, more infantile introjective configurations with superego primitivization and pathogenic effects.

superego formation can help to clarify these ideas. In his formulation, a variety of preoedipal elements derived from early identifications, "organizing activities," and other functions become integrated into preautonomous superego schemata. These schemata provide a preliminary framework which represents and is derived from parental authority, but is also influenced by instinctual derivatives. In the phallic phase, the intensification of conflict between instinctual wishes and narcissistic needs, the increasing ambivalence toward parental figures, the intensity of oedipal involvement, the fears of punishment and castration, all serve to influence and modify the superego schema. The schema represents the admired and feared qualities of the parents and provides the basis for discriminating parental love and admiration from parental rejection and narcissistic depletion.

The complex conflict of the oedipal involvement is resolved by the more or less definitive introjection of parental imagoes (Freud, 1924). The oedipal resolution with its correlative internalization is accompanied by reduction of interest in and dependence on the parents. The internalized schema takes on a capacity to serve as a source of narcissistic gratification and thus supplants the influence of the parents as the major providers of self-esteem. Parental imagoes are internalized as transitional objects so that the transitional mode of relatedness to the parents is preserved. The relationship to the real objects is consequently altered in significant ways. While the transitional object relation was once part of the outer world, it now becomes a part of the inner world. The true superego schema becomes an autonomous source of psychic activity and internalized capacity. The superego thus assumes the functions of parental approval and/or disapproval.

The basic mechanism of this internalization is introjection, but it may be and often is followed by subsequent identification. Sandler and his co-workers comment: "After the formation of the superego through the introjection of parental authority, there can occur identifications with features of the introjects as well as with aspects of non-introjected objects. The capacity to identify with objects (via object representations) continues through life, irrespective of whether these objects are persons in the subject's environment or introjects" (Sandler, Holder, and Meers, 1963, p. 152). The process of identifying with parental introjects is described as "identification with the introject" (Sandler, 1960; Sandler and Rosenblatt, 1962).

In his discussion of internalization, Loewald (1962) makes the point that superego introjects enjoy a certain mobility which permits them to be integrated into the ego proper so that their distinctive superego quality is lost. Elements of superego structure may thus become integrated into the ego, but, under conditions of pathological regression, they may revert to the level of superego organization. Here we are speaking of degrees of internalization or, conversely, externalization. Loewald writes:

> This implies shifting distances of internalized 'material' from the ego core and shifting distances within the ego-superego system, as well as transformations in the character of the introjects according to the respective degrees of internalization. The superego is conceived as an enduring structure pattern whose elements may change and move either in the direction of the ego core or in the outer direction toward object representation. Thus elements of the superego may lose their superego character and become ego elements, or take on the character of object representations (externalization) [p. 503].

The position proposed here suggests that the mechanism of the crucial internalization by which superego elements are transformed is specifically identification. Identification serves to organize these superego elements as structural elements within the ego, thus lending increased stability, autonomy, and resistance to regressive pulls to these transformed elements. Rapaport (1967) describes this progressive shift toward the differentiation and integration of ego elements: "In the course of development, the more active the integrates the less, or the less directly, are they tied into that regulating network of integration to which we refer as the superego, and the more are they integrated and regulated by that network of integration to which we refer as the ego" (p. 705). Moreover, as Greenson (1954) has suggested, this identification which follows on parental introjection in the process of superego formation serves to further delibidinize and deaggressify the relationship to the parents, so that the child is able to preserve the relationship to the parents and to re-form it on a more developed level of object relations. As Jacobson (1954) describes this process:

The fact must be understood that, quite contrary to psychotic identifications which arise with the breakdown of realistic object and self-representations, of object relations and of ego functions, the object relations of the child profit greatly from the building up of ego and superego identifications. The latter do not either destroy or replace, they only transform and change the nature of object relations. By reinforcing the processes of drive neutralization, by reducing the sexual and aggressive object cathexes in favor of affectionate love relations and of ego interests, they contribute indeed very much to the development of firmly cathected, realistic, and enduring object and self-representations and of stable object relations and ego functions [pp. 244–245].

The process of identification with the introject, whether in superego formation or in other forms of introjection, is a process of internal structural modification within the ego.

The metapsychological impact of this formulation needs explication. As we are envisioning these processes, introjective configurations hold an intermediate position in the psychic scheme of things — intermediate between the objectified realm of object representations and the ultimate subjectively experienced ego core. Some of the introjective configuration may be indistinguishable from the person's experienced subjectivity, but introjective components are all at least potentially externalizable and are variously experienced as differentiated from the core of personal subjectivity. Thus we may experience such organizations as another force or focus of influence in our experience of ourselves, which may stand as separate and even in opposition to our own experience of personal intention or will. This phenomenon lies behind the tendency of analytic thinkers to conceptualize psychic events in terms of separate structures, or psychic agencies, and even to anthropomorphize them (the minds within the mind that Schafer [1976] has criticized so vigorously). To maintain this dimension of potential and sometimes actual differentiation, I have regarded introjective configurations as modifications of the self-system (Meissner, 1977a, 1977c). Identifications, however, do not possess the quality of potential differentiation or separation from core subjectivity. Rather, they are modifications of the ego system, or of the ego-superego system to the extent that superego derivatives are integrated with ego functions. They are thus metapsychologically quite distinct from introjective configurations and pertain to different realms of intrapsychic organization (Meissner, 1971, 1972). The end-products of identifications are specific structural modifications within the ego system.

The introject, as a configuration within the self-system, in this setting serves as the model for structuralization, which is achieved through identification taking place in the ego. Identification brings about a form of "depersonalization" of the internalized object relation (Jacobson, 1964; Kernberg, 1966). By this means, the degree to which the influence of specific internalizations depends on or derives from the relation with a given object is minimized and the respective internalizations become integrated into higher-order and increasingly more stable patterns of structural integration. These identifications Schafer (1968a) refers to as "system-building identifications." At higher levels of ego integration, these internalized elements are consolidated and reinforced, and they acquire a higher degree of autonomy. They are thus increasingly resistant to regressive pulls and become organized and function more in terms of secondary-process than primary-process modalities.

In addition, the internalized elements become integrated into the ego core of the personality. As such they are experienced less in terms of their object relatedness as an internal object within the organization of the self, and more as a subjectively experienced part of the functioning ego. It is important to distinguish such ego-integrated systemic identifications, which connote integration within the subjective sense of self, from introjects, which function specifically as primary-process presences but which may have lost the quality of distance from the sensed subjective self. The problem is complicated by the clinical fact that well-established ego identifications may under conditions of stress regress to the level of such introjective formations. Nonetheless, Rapaport's (1967) attempt to relate levels of activity and passivity to levels of integration in the hierarchy of control systems involved in ego-superego functioning seems to be quite valid. He conjectures that "the lower the level of the hierarchy of integration we are dealing with, the more it must be assumed to be passive and regulated by the id impulses, and the higher the integration level in the hierarchy the more active its self-regulative role" (p. 705). The mechanism of such integration, which brings about a higher level of active self-regulation through ego structuralization, is specifically identification.

IDENTIFICATION

We can now turn our attention to the third major mode of internalization, that of identification and identificatory processes. To keep the problem of identification in proper perspective, we can contrast it to the other modes of internalization we have been discussing. Using the object representation as a point of reference, we can discriminate the modes of internalization in terms of their object-related status. As we have noted, incorporation involves a relatively primitive taking in of the object in such a manner that the total object quality of what is taken in is obliterated and becomes totally merged into the organization of the self. Through incorporation the object representation becomes wholly and indistinguishably merged into the subject's self-representation.

This rather global and undifferentiated taking in and merging with the object can take place on a secondary level, particularly in certain regressed conditions, but it may also play a role in the course of early infant development, before any realized differentiation between self and object. At this level, we can speak appropriately of primary identification as the most primitive form of emotional attachment, before the development of any object relationship or of self-object differentiation. Sandler (1960) describes primary identification as a fusion or confusion of the rudimentary self-schema with that of the object so that the distinction of self from nonself does not exist. In these terms, primary identification can be taken to refer to a regressive reactivation of a primary fusion and merger with the object — a form of regressive symbiosis which reconstitutes the conditions of primary union (primary identification in its basic sense) before differentiation between self and object and before any separation within the symbiotic orbit. The mechanism of such identification must be incorporation (Meissner, 1971).

Primary identification plays a significant part in mental life, particularly in the developmental experience of the preoedipal child, and even in certain phases of mature psychic organization such as the regressive experience of merging with a loved object (Jacobson, 1964). It may also be an aspect of severely regressed psychotic conditions, such as certain schizophrenic states, in which the differentiation of self and object becomes fragmented and self- and object representations become fused (Sandler, 1960). Incorporation must thus be regarded as the most primitive and rudimentary form of internalization and is to be distinguished from more autonomous identificatory processes.

By way of contrast, the introjective mode of internalization derives from a less primitive relationship to the object. Elements or aspects from the object are taken in in such a way as to preserve the relationship between the derivative aspects of the internalized object and the external object. What is internalized by introjection is a transitional object relationship. The introjection makes the transitional object internal, but it does not destroy its transitional quality. Thus the internal object maintains an inherent tie to the object. That specific object tie is the basis of the experienced quality of the introject, even when it is closely integrated with the core of the personality. The introject retains its partial quality of objectivity, as well as an inherent tendency to return to its object-derived status by way of regressive reexternalization. It is through the underlying mechanism of projection that the internalized introjective object carries this capacity and propensity for reconstitution as an object representation. As we shall see, this characteristic of the introject has important implications for the analytic process and specifically for the theory of transference, insofar as it is the introjective elements that are externalized in the analytic relationship and form the basis of the transference neurosis.

To move to identification as such, here we reach an entirely different level of relatedness to objects and an entirely different mode of internalization. In both incorporation and introjection we can speak meaningfully of something else being "taken in" from the object, although it is taken in in different ways. In identification, however, there is essentially nothing "taken in." The sense of "internalization" thus shifts from an implicit reference to "taking in" from objects or incorporative fantasies to a connotation of enhancement of internal differentiation and organization. The implication of "taking in" is reduced or refined to the dimensions of modeling.

Identification is a process of internal organization and synthesis within the ego which is carried on essentially as a modeling and self-organizing process in which the object representation is left intact and no translation of object elements into the self-organization takes place. Thus, while incorporation and introjection can be understood as defensive measures and ways of dealing with the intolerable threat of separation from or loss of the object, in identification the object is left totally intact and distinct and its inherent separateness is not only tolerated but preserved.

An example may help to focus this difference. A depressed, primarily hysterical, and somewhat narcissistic young woman entered analysis, and over the course of time developed an intense clinging, dependent, and idealizing transference. The transference elements derived from her close, somewhat infantilizing and ambivalently dependent relation to a depressed, rather narcissistic, but critically controlling mother. The relationship to the mother was based largely on the mother's preoccupation with making her daughter a perfect, pretty little doll. In many ways the patient lived up to these expectations, but at the obvious cost of constant self-scrutiny for any little imperfection or fault, a diminished self-esteem, considerable feelings of inadequacy, and a lack of a sense of her own inherent worth as an intelligent and talented woman.

The transference was cast in this maternal mold. But in terms of the internalizations it reflected, the maternal introject played a major role. The patient herself felt devalued as a woman, as did her mother. This was reflected in a variety of castration concerns and in intense but suppressed rivalrous feelings toward a two-year-younger brother. She constantly saw her brother as having advantages and opportunities, as well as forms of recognition from both parents, simply because he was a boy—opportunities and recognition that were denied her because she was a girl. The identification with the chronically worn-out, self-sacrificing, neurotically complaining, "dished" mother was a powerful motif in her pathology. As the analytic work progressed, the issue of separation from the close and self-undermining entanglement with the mother and separation from the maternal introject, which had so dominated and determined her sense of self and self-worth, became a major focus.

I would like to emphasize here the important transition not only from the pathogenic introject to the analytic introject, but even more pertinently, from the analytic introject to identification. The transference was based in part on the pathogenic maternal introject. As the analytic process took hold, particularly through the work of clarification and interpretation, the elements of the maternal transference were delineated and their origins traced in detail to the maternal relationship. As this work progressed, the elements of self-doubt and feelings of inadequacy that had so characterized the patient's mode of relating to the world began to diminish and disappear. She became more confident, began to feel better about herself in a variety of difficult life contexts, and began to shift from a chronically worn, fatigued, stay-in-bed-and-mope, "dished" version of her mother, to an increasingly ambitious, energetic, and effective woman capable of pursuing a variety of interests and career objectives.

There seemed little question that this patient had acquired a new model, her analyst. Comparisons between how she saw me (frequently in idealized terms) and how she saw her parents were continual. She observed time and again how she wished that she had had a parent like me and—in terms of her somewhat ambiguous relations with both parents—how she wished her own parents had dealt with her insecurities and doubts about herself with the firmness and discipline she found in me. Her behavior increasingly reflected a process of making herself more and more like me—or at least like the image she had created of me. My own interpretive phrases and comments would come back to me, sometimes weeks or even months later. She thought about how I would deal with certain problems, how I would act in certain situations, or she would think of comments I had made—and she used all these to her adaptive advantage. The process was imitative and assimilative.

In retrospect, one could conclude that important learning was taking place and that processes of internalization were at work. But processes of what kind? In this phase of the analytic process, the behavioral modifications were tightly linked to her conviction that she was only capable of such performance as long as she was attached to me. She had found a new object of libidinal and dependent attachment — an object to replace her mother, and one which would give her more than her mother had given her. She replaced one dependency for another, one introject for another. An exchange of the pathogenic introject for a more benign introject, however, leaves the process of internalization incomplete and runs the risk of settling for a form of analytic compliance and a kind of false-self organization whose integrity remains dependent on the analytic situation (Meissner, 1978b).

Consequently, these issues had to be addressed and worked through. The patient's dependency on me was reviewed and analyzed. In the course of this work, some radical revisions took place in this woman's relation to her mother — in the direction of considerable independence and a staunch resistance to an onslaught from the mother, who wanted to bring her daughter back into the close-binding, dependent alliance of depressed and disadvantaged women. The most powerful stimulus to further internalization, however, was the termination. It was the first time in her life experience that the patient had been forced to give up and renounce someone whom she loved and admired.

The mourning process was intense. But as the mourning progressed and as she struggled with the sense of deep loss, there came increasing evidence of her courage and strength, her willingness to undertake and withstand pain in the interest of gaining the advantage to herself. More and more she began to realize and accept that she was an independent, autonomous human being with strengths, capacities, and resources that would enable her to withstand the buffeting of the harsh, cruel world. She did not have to run to her mother for protection and support, nor did she have to cling to me like a frightened child. Instead, she was a mature and capable adult, able to take care of herself and ready to deal with whatever life had to offer her. An important element in this realization was that even though she wanted me and valued her relationship with me more than anything in her life, she did not *need* me; she was ready to walk on her own feet, accept responsibility for herself and the direction of her life, and make of it what she could.

The theoretical problem is how to conceptualize this change in internalization. The change is from a pattern of behavioral and attitudinal qualities that were tied to and dependent on a specific object relation and on continuing attachment to that object, to a modification in which these same qualities became an autonomous possession of the subject and were divorced from dependence on the object. These qualities were internalized not only in the face of loss of the object (this would not distinguish introjection from identification), but also in the context of acknowledgment and acceptance of the separateness of the object.

There is an additional point of reference here. Acknowledgment of the separateness of the object carries with it certain other important realizations. Of particular importance are the realizations that the analyst is not merely separate but different, that this difference is to be accepted and valued, and that the qualities inherent in the other do not deprive the self and in no way diminish the self (this implies important modifications in the underlying narcissistic components of the adherence to the pathogenic, and even later to the analytic, introject). Finally, there is the realization that the qualities of the patient's own psychic makeup are to be valued and respected in their own right.

My emphasis here falls on the shift from modifications in the self-image, or even in the organization and functioning of the self, to a level of change that has to do with the development of autonomous ego capacities, which reflects a process of internal structural change within the ego itself. It is this level of structural development and modification that is effected by the process of identification. Later in our discussion we shall be more explicitly concerned with the conditions within the analysis that give rise to such identificatory processes.

A number of important discriminations need to be clarified in order to focus the idea of identification. The primary clarification is that identification involves both a process and a product of the process (Hartmann and Loewenstein, 1962; Sandler, 1960). The product is an internal modification of the ego structure. This change may be reflected in modifications of patterns of ego functioning, expressed in the individual variations in behaviors, motives, attitudes, and values acquired by reason of the identificatory process (Kagan, 1958). Process and product cannot be separated since each complements and completes the other.

Formulations of the identificatory process that consider identification only as a product and introjection as the process by which the product is formed can be misleading (Fuchs, 1937; Knight, 1940; Schafer, 1968a). As Schafer (1968a) makes clear, this approach does not account for the failure of certain introjects to be modified into identifications; it implies that introjection must always precede identification; and finally, it confuses levels of abstraction, since the analysis of component subprocesses does not violate the process status of the original concept. In other words, if one demonstrates that the process of identification involves or is related to other processes such as introjection or projection, that does not force the conclusion that identification itself is not a process. Moreover, the dynamic nature of identification and our capacity for reorganization and revision require that they be conceptualized in process terms.

The emphasis on process brings to mind an important consideration, which has been implicit in much of this account but here deserves special comment. Much of the preceding discussion has used the language of structure to describe internalizations. The language of structure often tends to carry with it implications of form, static organization, shape and dimension, and qualities related to capacities to maintain such form and organization against externally applied forces and influences. These terms might, for example, be applied to the structural properties of a building or a bridge. More important, however, for our understanding of internalization in analysis is the realization that internalizations are complex forms of human action. As action they are dynamic processes; they are motivated and impelled; they are carried out with reasons, purposes, and intentions which are only occasionally conscious. We must remind ourselves, both in our consideration of the role of such processes in the analytic setting and in our actual work with analytic patients, that internalizations (including identifications) are actions performed by subjects with motivations and for reasons. Part of the analytic work is to discover and specify such motives and reasons. Introjections and identifications are not something that happens to the patient; they are something the patient does. To emphasize this dynamic, action-oriented aspect of internalization and identification, so well articulated by Schafer (1976), does not in any way override or minimize the structural emphasis contained in the description of internalization as product.

A second clarification has to do with the extent to which identificatory processes are conscious or unconscious. It is generally conceded that identification is carried on at an unconscious level, but it may involve other processes that are relatively accessible to consciousness. It may involve conscious imitation (Gaddini, 1969; Sanford, 1955) or awareness of certain common qualities shared by self and object. While the process may be unconscious, there may be significant variations in the degree of awareness that identification has taken place (Greenson, 1954). Nearly half a century ago, Fenichel (1926) suggested that identifications are genetically unconscious but may become conscious as resultant modifications of the ego.

The identificatory product has both an internal and an external aspect. Internally identification effects change or modification in psychic structure, while externally it produces modification in the subject's relation to the object. Structural changes wrought by identification are located primarily and specifically in the subject's ego. This does not rule out modification in many other aspects of the personality and behavior besides the ego, but it proposes that peripheral modifications derive from and depend on the primary changes effected in the ego. Many of the secondary changes, however, particularly on the behavioral level, can take place without identification and can be understood in isolation, without an appeal to underlying identificatory processes. The modifications that uniquely specify and identify identificatory effects are intrasystemic. Secondary intersystemic changes are derivative from the intrasystemic ones and must be understood in relation to structural ego modifications in order to be established as partial products of identification.

As a process that takes place essentially within the ego, identification involves a number of ego functions in its various phases, and would seem to involve relations with objects in important ways. Identification takes place within a subject-object matrix (Miller et al., 1968), which has multiple internal and external determinants. The ego functions contributing to this process may include perception, memory, abstraction, selection, symbolization, organization, integration, and synthesis in a variety of specific patterns. Unique to the process of identification as such, however, are the internalization, synthesis, and structuralization taking place within the ego.

It is worth emphasizing again that the processes of internalization and structuralization that are intrinsic and essential to the notion of identification are not simply reducible to cognitive or representational parameters. Identification is a process of structure formation in the internal world of the psychic apparatus and not merely one of cognitive modification of the inner representational world (Sandler and Rosenblatt, 1962). It is in this sense, then, that the definitive changes brought about in the psychoanalytic process are conceptualized as autonomous structural ego modifications rather than as merely representational phenomena, in the sense of changes either in the object representation of the analyst or in the patient's own self-representation. These representational changes are indeed part of the process and can readily be identified, but they do not address or express the inherent changes in the patient's own psychic organization. In the case of the hysterical young woman cited above, these representational modifications, both in her perception of me as the analyst and of herself as a functioning human being, had been achieved without the crucial internalization effected by identification. It is this further step from the representational to the structural that is specifically brought about by identification as an internalizing process.

The process of identification provides one of the major mechanisms of ego development. Early in the course of development, the organization of the inner world is dominated by introjective processes, but identifications nonetheless take place in more or less partial and global ways. As the structure of the ego gradually becomes increasingly defined and differentiated through progressive identifications and other developmental influences, the identificatory processes become correspondingly more selective and better organized. The identification with crucial introjects, such as those which emerge with the resolution of the oedipal involvement, continue for a significant period after the introjection has taken place. In this process, identification serves to assimilate elements of the parental introjects in a gradual and dynamic process of structuring and restructuring within the ego.[9] As the ego undergoes this structural evolution, the quality of the subject's object relations undergoes a progressive and correlative change. Earlier identifications with parental objects are amalgamated with later and more developed identifications with the parental objects, as well as other significant objects with whom the child may become involved. But part of the process remains a deeper internalization and depersonification of the oedipal introjects. As Schafer (1968a) has noted, these early preoedipal and oedipal identifications have a pervasive and highly significant influence, perhaps greater than that of other later identifications. They often set the direction and limits of later identifications and lend their own peculiar intensity and meaning to them. This is particularly true in the much later adolescent reconstitution and reworking of these patterns of introjection and identification (Blos, 1962, 1967).

The role of identification, then, can be seen not so much in defensive terms, but rather as part of an ongoing developmental process. Identification does serve the objectives of mastery and

[9] The modeling process by which the ego modifies and organizes itself through identification can take as its object either the object representation or the introject. We can surmise that the interaction and integration of introjection and identification take place from the earliest levels of internalization. Conceptualizing early developmental processes, however, is open to considerable subjective distortion, particularly when we are dealing with internal processes that are difficult at best to discern in highly verbal and expressive adults. Infants do not provide the essential data. If the notion of introjection implies a defensively motivated "taking in" from the object, as we might easily imagine taking place in the context of separation and individuation, I would want to leave room in our understanding of development for nondefensive, constructive forms of internal ego building based on significant nonambivalent assimilations from the loved and caring (caretaking) objects. These would represent early and more diffusely organized forms of identification. Such crucial positive internalizations would related to Winnicott's (1965) notions of the "holding environment" and "good-enough mothering" and to Erikson's (1959) formulations regarding the development of "basic trust."

control of instinctual forces in a variety of complex ways, particularly through the stabilization and structuralization of the ego. It serves to consolidate autonomous ego functions and contributes to the more adaptive integration and utilization of id derivatives. Thus, the progressive modification of the ego through identification means that the structures and functions of primary autonomy and those of relative secondary autonomy (gained through previous introjections and identifications) are reworked, remodeled, and reintegrated into an emerging pattern of more harmonious and adaptive ego functioning. The respective functions become more stable, relatively autonomous, and more constructively integrated with drive derivatives. But the primary focus of identification is on the progressive synthesis and integration within the ego as a manifestation of the ego's inherent capacity for internal structural development and modification on the basis of non-ego models. Identification is an expression of the ego's synthetic capacity, in which aspects of a model are assimilated, whether they are derived from introjects or real objects, and subsequently integrated into the structure of the ego (Nunberg, 1948).

An important aim of the present study is to clarify the interplay and integration, as well as the points of separation and differentiation, between introjective and identificatory processes. In the progression from external object representation to internal object (introject) and from introject to ego structure, metapsychologically distinct and different processes are involved. Introjection and identification have different structural effects, involve different mechanisms of internalization, have different relationships to the libidinal and instinctual economy, and have different effects on the development of the internal life of the organism.

As we have noted, introjection is a kind of "taking in" from an external object in the interests of preserving union or of defense. By the taking in, the transitional object relation is sacrificed and a new relationship must be constructed out of the interplay of further projection and introjection. The conditions allowing this formation of an internal object and the correlative reorganization of libidinal and aggressive drives (introjection) are not the same as the conditions for the building of structure within the ego (identification). If ego projection and introjection result from the pressures created by instinctual energies, ego identification arises from its own internal tendency toward structural integration and its own inherent developmental capacities. Introjection and projection come into play specifically in response to instinctual vicissitudes and in the interests of defense (Meissner, 1971). In contrast, the inner modeling of the ego through identification is not directly motivated by instinctual vicissitudes.

The functioning of identificatory processes enjoys a relatively greater degree of autonomy in the sense that identifications tend to express the inner dynamic tendencies of the ego toward increasing differentiation and integration. The inner dynamism toward ego integration is paralleled by the developmental tendencies toward establishing meaningful and mature object relations. Identification can be seen, therefore, as operating in relative autonomy from instinctual pressures and derivatives as motivating sources of the process. Instead, it arises from specifically noninstinctual and relatively conflict-free tendencies of the ego toward self-integration and meaningful object relatedness. This inner integration of the ego and the correlative capacity for relatedness are intrinsically intertwined and cannot be divorced.

Identification can also play an important part in superego development. The usual psychoanalytic account of superego development is cast in terms of the pathological organization of the superego. Superego pathology reflects the predominance of unintegrated introjective configurations in the superego organization and their influence on its functioning — whether in terms of the predominance of the aggressor and victim introjects or the more narcissistically impregnated superior and inferior introjects. Another important dimension of the superego, however, is its adaptive integration with the ego in a nonpathological manner. The functioning of the superego tends to be recognized only in pathological states of conflict between ego and superego. When ego and superego are harmoniously functioning in mutual integration and reinforcement, we tend to lose sight of superego functioning per se.

An important mechanism in the integration of superego introjects with the autonomously functioning ego is identification with the introject. Identification with the introject is a process of constructive self-organization according to a pattern established or determined by the introject. However, since it derives from a relatively autonomous base, it is governed by more autonomous ego interests and secondary-process patterns of organization. The resulting identification tends to be relatively selectively adaptive, integrated with the preexisting patterns of ego structure and defensive organization. In terms of superego modification, it serves to reconstruct superego elements in terms of the organization of extant ego structure, thereby freeing them from direct instinctual involvement and placing them increasingly at the disposal of more neutralized and differentiated energies.[10]

The reintegration and superposition of a set of ego functions supersede superego functions, neutralize instinctual energies attached to more primitive forms of introjective superego organization, increase the autonomy of psychic structures from their involvement with both original objects and instinctual forces, and effectively diminish the susceptibility of psychic structure to regressive pulls and pressures from id derivatives. The identification brings about a "change of function" (Hartmann, 1939) so that these superego elements are effectively distanced from their more primitive involvement in issues of conflict and defense and are transferred to the relatively conflict-free sphere of ego functioning. Although the introject serves as the template for what is made available to identificatory integration, the actual integration is carried out, both selectively and adaptively, in terms of relatively autonomous ego tendencies and objectives.

An important area of clarification, to which considerable effort has been directed in recent years, is the relationship between the products of internalization and the emerging concepts of the self. A starting point for this effort was Hartmann's (1964) distinction between the ego as an organized system of structures and functions at the core of the personality and the self as an in-

---

[10] These formulations merely specify the implications of the previous description of identification in its relation to the introjects insofar as they apply to the development of the superego in its healthier and more adaptive integrations.

tersystemic unit, which serves as the reservoir of narcissism and becomes the object of libidinal cathexis in the development of secondary narcissism. Identification and introjection, in their respective ways, serve as the mechanisms by which modification of the self takes place. In introjection, for instance, object libido is redirected to the self so that self-modification is directly effected.

The attempt to make the concept of self identical with self-representation and a tendency to interpret identificatory processes in terms of the blending of self- and object representations have dominated thinking in this area (Beres, 1966; Brody and Mahoney, 1964; Jacobson, 1954; Sandler, 1960; Schafer, 1968a). Schafer (1968a), for example, is at pains to segregate the concept of self-representation from any systemic implications. He points out quite correctly that self-representations should not be confused with the ego system, since one involves an experiential frame of reference and the other a metapsychological frame of reference. Moreover, he scores Kohut (1966, 1971) for his concept of a narcissistic self that involves systemic properties having to do with energy, aims, and interaction with other psychic systems. Here our theoretical reflection carries us into the realm of questions that demand and still await clarification. What is the relation between the organizational subsystems of the psychic apparatus (ego, superego, id) and the organization of the self-system? What is the relationship between self-system as objectively conceived and self-representations? And where are we to locate the products of internalization processes, specifically introjection and identification (Meissner, 1979a)?

An important contribution to the conceptualization of these problems has been made by Sandler and Rosenblatt (1962). In terms of their analysis of the representational world, objects must be perceived and object representations formed before introjection or identification is possible. They draw a distinction between the ego as a psychic structure and the representational world. The ego forms representations of objects out of a matrix of images based on perceptual inputs from the object. The building up of object representations is essential for the implementation of ego development and progressive adaptation. Along with object representations, the ego also forms a self-representation or self-representations. The self-representation is a perceptual and conceptual organization specifically within the representational world. The progressive differentiation between self- and object representations and the increasingly realistic clarification of both of these are essential aspects of the ego's growth to mature functioning.

Within this theoretical framework, identification is defined in terms of the modification of the self-representation with the object representation as model. Thus Sandler writes: "We can define identification by saying that it represents a process of modifying the self-schema on the basis of a present or past perception of an object, and that such modification may be temporary or permanent, whole or partial, ego enriching or ego restrictive, depending on what is identified with and whether the need for such an identification is of short or long duration" (1960, p. 150). We should note that this formulation makes no mention of the structuralizing aspects of identification and can as easily be applied to imitation or other similar processes, which effect changes in the self-representation but do not imply significant ego modification. Identification in these terms is distinguished from introjection, in which the self-representation is not modified to become like an object, but rather the object representation is thought to have the inherent power and authority of the real object itself (Sandler, Holder, and Meers, 1963; Sandler and Rosenblatt, 1962).

The Sandler-Rosenblatt formulation thus differs significantly from the one advanced in this study. The present approach regards introjects as internal modifications of the self-system, not merely as qualifications of object representations. Moreover, identifications are regarded not just as representational modifications of the self-schema, but as intrinsic modifications of the ego itself. Identification brings about an internal structural change, which may be secondarily reflected in representational terms, but is not limited to such representational changes.

The Sandler-Rosenblatt approach to the representational world must be put in the context of the important distinction originally made by Hartmann (1964) and emphasized by Rapaport (1967). Both Hartmann and Rapaport draw a distinction between the "inner world" and the "internal world."

The *inner* world constitutes a kind of intrapsychic cognitive map of the external world, which is interpolated between receptors and effectors and serves as a means by which the ego regulates its interaction with the external world. The *internal* world, on the other hand, comprises the organization and integration of intrapsychic structures. Thus the inner world is representational, while the internal world is specifically structural.

We can reformulate the problem of internalization in the following terms: How is it that a representational aspect of the inner world can become a structural part of the internal world? It is clear that neither perceptions nor object representations nor memories are forms of internalization in the structural sense, but how this transformation takes place is still a difficult problem. To say that identification involves a modification of self-representation touches only part of the problem, since it ignores the structuralizing effects of identification. Moreover, it is by no means clear that self-representational changes correlate with structural modifications of the ego. It seems clear that structural ego modifications are inconceivable without corresponding reflections in the self-representation, but the question remains open whether modifications of self-representation can take place in a variety of forms, including pathological ones, without explicit changes in ego structure. The position taken here tends to oppose any easy equivalence of representation and structure.

It seems, moreover, inadequate to accept a secondary effect of a process and to make it the basis of definition at the cost of ignoring the primary effects. Self-representation depends on and reflects changes that have taken place in the organization of the self, whereas identification refers to the process by which the actual changes are brought about in the self. To be more precise, identification brings about changes in structure of the ego which is a participating subsystem of the self. Definition in terms of self-representation not only misses the mark in relation to the products of identification, but it leaves no room for the process of identification itself since the definition is cast in terms of an aspect that derives from the product.

There is a further problem in describing the relationship between the ego and the self. While the ego is clearly articulated in the theory as a structural subsystem within the personality organization, the same cannot be said of the self. A great deal of conceptual unclarity surrounds the concept of self. In the view taken here, the self serves as an intersystemic referent that embraces the total personality, including id, ego, and superego. The self is a structural system or suprasystemic organization which is conceptualized at a different level of abstraction and experiential reference than are the more established psychic agencies. In other words, the concept of the self, as it is employed in this study, embraces the notions of id, ego and superego as component subsystems, but implies a larger frame of reference within which intersystemic interactions take place (i.e., interactions between the respective subsystems of id, ego, and superego). It also implies a realm of psychic operation and structural organization that is not simply accountable in systemic terms. The organization of the introjects, which function as foci of psychic activity and influence, cannot simply be attributed to any one of the psychic systemic entities, but it nonetheless reflects the influence of the combined activity of all or some of them. The superego, in its pathological forms of expression, i.e., as divided from and in conflict with the other psychic agencies, approximates an introjective organization. However, superego configurations do not exhaust the range of introjective expressions and must be regarded as accounting for only a portion of them—admittedly, a significant portion. In this regard, the introjects are conceptualized as modifications of the organization of the self-system rather than as modifications of any one of the individual psychic agencies.

Hartmann's (1950) early clarification of the distinction between ego and self emphasizes that the self is the repository of secondary narcissism. The mechanism for the elaboration of secondary narcissism is specifically introjection (or in Freud's terminology, narcissistic identification). Introjection effects a modification of the self by the institution of an internal object; it takes in a libidinally cathected object and redirects the flow of libido toward the self.[11] Thus introjection brings about a self-

---

[11] Schafer (1968a) attempts to distinguish in this context between the self-as-agent and the self-as-place, locating the introject experientially in the self-as-place, but denying its involvement with the self-as-agent, which he apparently believes belongs

modification; identification is involved only secondarily in consolidating the developmental gains achieved through introjection. Structural changes in the ego necessarily affect the
organization of the self, since the ego is a component of the self-
system. Consequently, ego modifications modify self-representations and thereby affect the economy of narcissistic libido.
In this light, it would seem that formulations having to do with
changes in self-representation are much more closely related to
the effects of introjective processes than to those associated with
identificatory processes.

The problem of the organization of introjects and identifications can be usefully related to certain forms of pathological
self-formation. Winnicott (1965) has described the "false self"
and its role in the psychopathology of relatively severe
(schizoid) character disorders. I would propose that his formulation has much broader and more useful application in
considering the role of internalizations in psychoanalysis. In
Winnicott's terms, the false self is inherently defensive and is
based on the child's need to conform and comply with the
demands of significant objects in the caretaking environment.
In our present formulation, the false self is that more or less
experienced, but inherently experienceable, self that is
organized around specific introjects. In the course of development, the false self organizes itself around the child's emerging
introjective configuration, which is defensively motivated to
respond to parental demands and pressures and is mutually
responsive to the narcissistic needs and implicit narcissistic
pressures stemming from both parent and child in their complex interaction (Meissner, 1978b).

In exploring the introjective economy, the analytic process
elucidates and delineates the false-self configuration inherent
in the patient's neurosis. We shall refer to this process in detail

---

more properly to the functions of the ego. It should be noted that the distinction is
primarily experiential and not rooted in metapsychological grounds. While the ego is
the appropriate originative source for the sense of subjective intentionality and activity, it is not clear that other elements of the psychic organization cannot be involved in
such a subjective experiential sense as well.

later. Here we need only note that the analytic process applies itself to the regressive dissolution and undoing of this pathogenic false self and works toward the setting in motion of those forces which lead to a new internalization, which replaces the defensive and dependency-motivated compliance and conformity characteristic of the false self.

The reworking of the false-self configuration mobilizes potentialities for the emergence and growth of the true self. Winnicott's conception of the true self places it at the inner core of the personality, beyond meaningful communication with the environment and significant objects. Rather than envisioning this form of defensive and relatively schizoid isolation, the present approach sees the reworking of the false-self configuration and its determinants as opening up the inherent potential of the true self to emerge and grow. The patterning of this development is based on identifications, which are fostered and facilitated within the interaction between the analyst and the analysand. As we shall see, this progression is set in motion by the emergence and organization of the "analytic introject," which sets the conditions for and mobilizes growth potentialities.

The risks in the analytic process are similar to those inherent in the developmental process. The mobilization of defensively tinged forces within the analysis may lead the reworking of the patient's introjective configuration in the direction of an analytic introject based on conformity to analytic expectations and compliance with implicit demands of the analytic process. The technical problem centers on being able to mobilize identificatory processes without contaminating them with such introjective components as will shift the patient's self-organization in the direction of another—if more adaptive and less conflicted—false-self configuration. Such an analytic false self may represent a reasonable limit or goal with some patients, but it does not define the limits of the analytic process itself. In other words, the analyst and the patient may settle for a less conflicted and more adaptive, if limited, resolution, but this does not mean that we cannot hope for and in large measure achieve a more mature and autonomous reconstruction in a significant percentage of cases.

Our concern here has largely been with the interface between identification and introjection, particularly as exemplified in depressive states and superego formation. But we can turn now to the interface betwen identificatory processes and object involvements as such. Identification may take place without the intervention of introjective mechanisms in the direct context of an object relationship. Obviously the ego's capacity for such identifications becomes amplified in the course of development. At the level of childhood experience, the context of object relations is dominated largely by objects that are transitional in character, that is, the quality of the child's object experience is determined to a large extent by the interplay of introjection and projection, which strongly influences the experience of objects. The gradual refinement of this projective-introjective interplay and the evolving patterning of identifications bring increasing differentiation both to the structure of the ego and to its capacity to relate to objects more in terms of the real qualities than in terms of those constituted through defensively determined introjective-projective mechanisms.

There is consequently an appreciable shift from the predominantly transitional object representations to increasingly more realistic object representations. The ego must develop the capacity to accept and tolerate the separateness of significant objects, to relinquish instinctual demands and dependencies on the object, and thus to tolerate the painful reality of loss, separation, and abandonment. This capacity ultimately derives from and depends on the development of structure within the ego. As Modell (1968) has emphasized, the acceptance of painful reality and the tolerance of separation from objects are a function of precisely the same psychic structures whose development is required for the capacity for mature love. These structures are specifically developed through identificatory processes. Where instinctual pressures continue to influence object relations and to contaminate them so that they retain a transitional component, introjection continues to play a significant role. Where the transitional components become increasingly mitigated and object relations are based more specifically on the realistic characteristics of the objects, introjective mechanisms fade into the background and identificatory processes play the predominant role.

Identification in this instance is not significantly different from the process of identification with the introject. In this case, however, the structuralizing process within the ego takes as its model the object representation itself rather than the internal object. The degree to which that representation may be internalized by introjection does not alter in any way the nature of the identificatory process. In these terms, then, identification with a loved object is not only a corollary of the manner of functioning of internalizations, but is also quite distinct from the libidinal narcissistic modifications of the self that are inherent in introjective mechanisms. Thus identification contributes to the building of mature loving relationships, since it produces the very structures that enable and support mature object relations. Mature object relations and identification interact with each other in reciprocal reinforcement. In this sense, identifications increase the inherent capacity for object relatedness and, conversely, relatively more mature and realistic object relations provide adaptive models for higher-level identifications and integrations (Meissner, 1979a).

2

THE NATURE OF THE
PSYCHOANALYTIC PROCESS

The psychoanalytic process has often been a source of puzzlement, an enigma, even to those who make it the arena of their professional interest and commitment. Particularly for those who live closest to it, the practicing psychoanalysts, the psychoanalytic process is a source of continual wonderment, of ever-deepening experience and seemingly endless understanding. It is hardly surprising that this should be so, since the psychoanalytic process carries within it the richness of human experience and affective life. The attempt to study, evaluate, and understand this process, however, leaves the scientist in the somewhat ambiguous and enigmatic position of having to reduce this process to manageable technical terms. The study is fraught with inner tension as the process continually defies resolution and escapes elucidation.

In a sense, then, we are attempting a study foredoomed to a certain disappointment. The extent to which the rich complexity and depth of experience inherent in the psychoanalytic process can be captured in any set of definitions or terms remains a moot question. But the effort to close the gap between the experience and the explanatory power of theoretical concepts provides constant challenge and stimulation for the inquiring mind. This is particularly pertinent for psychoanalysts, since the pervasive concern of their clinical work is that they gain an ever-deepening understanding not only of the individual patient but also of the broader context of human experience in all its often perplexing diversity.

Within the clinical framework, the objectives and concerns are unalterably therapeutic, but they cannot be carried out in isolation from the influence of theoretical directions and persuasions. Clinicians begin with the complex experience embedded in their relationship with their patients, but they must strive to make the benefits of their experience and theoretical knowledge bear on the course of treatment. While the analytic process is in this sense guided by theory, it is a working through of critical variables, specifically in regard to the individual patient and his unique psychodynamics and dispositions. Clinical effort is constantly caught up in a dialectic between the general and the particular and, conversely, between the particular and the general.

In order to focus the present study, we must try to clarify what we intend by the psychoanalytic process. Our effort is necessarily more descriptive than definitive; it is concerned more with locating the area of concern and with examining the nature of the process than with defining the variables. The first and most obvious dimension of the analytic process is that it occurs in the context of a dyadic interaction. This interaction takes place at multiple levels and reflects multiple influences and determinants. In this sense, it is said to be overdetermined.

Behavioral manifestations represent only one of the multiple levels of interaction. Phenomenology embraces not only patterns of behavior that are observable and describable, but also less extrinsic processes, those which have to do with intrapsychic activity and which are reflected in the introspective experience of both the analyst and the patient (Kohut, 1959). Both the analyst and the patient are present in the analytic situation and in the interaction as behaving and experiencing agents participating in the process. They are in a sense participant-observers of the process — engaged in and experiencing it with each other, but also constantly observing themselves and each other in the ongoing interaction.

The psychoanalytic process engages the whole person, such that his participation in the process cannot be delimited in terms of particular functions or groups of functions. Most particularly, the process and the activity involved in it cannot be envisioned in purely cognitive terms, but must be seen in the full spectrum of affective and emotional experience as well. Moreover, the experience embedded in the process embraces not only reflective or conscious realms, but reaches out to include the world of unconscious cognitive and affective processing which is a constant feature of human psychic experience.

It should be fairly obvious that the inherent immediacy and the humanistic relevance of the psychoanalytic situation do not permit the style of objectivizing and fragmenting exploration that characterizes the experimental approach. This is not to say that aspects of the analytic process cannot usefully yield to experimental procedures or that in some derivative sense experimental techniques should not be applied to analytic material. It is to say, however, that such approaches involve a necessary distortion of the analytic process, which must be taken into account in evaluating any results. The analytic process entails a kind of naturalistic participant observation, in which the observer is inexorably as much a part of the process as the observed. The situation is inherently dyadic and does not lend itself to the polarization of observer-observed without distortion.

But the analytic experience is not limited to mutual observation and interaction, or even to introspective enrichment (Grossman, 1967). It also includes a dimension of intersubjective experience. This latter aspect is difficult to describe, but I think it is nonetheless a real portion of the experience of both the patient and the analyst. This element of intersubjective experience is closely allied with what we intend by "empathy" and is often a vital guide for the analyst's intuitive interventions (Kohut, 1959; Schafer, 1959). I would venture to say that this dimension of analytic experience is largely unconscious and has to do with that subtle and often ineffable "tuning" of the analyst's psychic processes to those of the patient and vice versa. The intersubjective experience may also make important contributions to establishing and consolidating the therapeutic alliance and may account for the patient's sense of being understood and accepted, almost regardless of the therapist's verbalizations or specific interventions. Similarly, a defect in this dimension may play itself out in countertransference vicissitudes, most dramatically in those involving a negative countertransference.

THE THERAPEUTIC RELATIONSHIP

At the core of the analytic process there is the real relationship between the patient and the therapist. A major contributor to our understanding of this real relationship has been Greenson (1967). In discussing the real, nontransference relationship, Greenson and Wexler (1969) stated:

> To facilitate the full flowering and ultimate resolution of the patient's transference reactions, it is essential in all cases to recognize, acknowledge, clarify, differentiate, and even nurture the non-transference or relatively transference-free reactions between patient and analyst. The technique of 'only analyzing' or 'only interpreting' transference phenomena may stifle the development and clarification of the transference neurosis and act as an obstacle to the maturation of the transference-free or 'real' reactions of the patient. Central as the interpretation of transference is to psychoanalytic therapy, and about which there can be no question, it is also important to deal with the non-transference interactions between patient and analyst [pp. 27–28].

The authors cite some of Anna Freud's (1954) remarks from her discussion of the widening scope of indications for psychoanalysis. With reference to the distinction between the "real personal relationship" and "true transference reactions," she observes:

> We see the patient enter into analysis with a reality attitude to the analyst; then the transference gains momentum until it reaches its peak in the full-blown transference neurosis which has to be worked off analytically until the figure of the analyst emerges again, reduced to its true status. But — and this seems important to me — so far as the patient has a healthy part of his personality, his real relationship to the analyst is never fully submerged. With due respect for the necessary strictest handling and interpretation of the transference, I feel still that we should leave room for the realization that analyst and patient are also two real people, of equal status, in a real personal relationship to each other [p. 618].

In addition to Greenson's (1967) formulations regarding the working alliance, the dimensions of the real relationship have been discussed in terms of the therapeutic alliance. The major theoretical contribution here is that of Zetzel (1966, 1970), who has defined the therapeutic alliance in terms of a specifically developmental framework. As Zetzel (1966) has indicated, this basic therapeutic relationship not only expresses the specific qualities of a one-to-one relationship, but also reflects the patient's developmental achievements in the realm of such one-to-one relationships. The quality and the stability of the therapeutic relationship reveal the extent to which the patient is capable of achieving a given level of development. This relationship draws on the strengths and reveals the weaknesses of attributes acquired early in the patient's experience of relating to significant objects on a one-to-one basis. As Zetzel (1966) observes:

> The realistic factors of this relationship must therefore be distinguished as far as possible from distortions, fears and unrealistic expectations. Consideration of the latter involves differentiation between distortions attributable to a reversible decompensation in the patient, distortions attributable to defects in the psychiatrist's technique, and those distortions which reflect such serious or irreversible problems in the patient that a question should be raised as to what psychotherapeutic goals may justifiably be anticipated [p. 141].

We may not expect patients to be immune from the effects of regression, and in fact a limited regression is an integral feature of the emergence of the transference neurosis and thus an essential part of the analytic process. The patient brings to the therapeutic relationship certain developmental attributes and definitive psychic structures which were originally formed in the one-to-one parent-child relationship. But these attributes are subject to regressive pulls, particularly at times of increased stress and during developmental crises. A distinction must thus be drawn here between reversible regressive impairments and developmental failures. If the capacity for meaningful one-to-one relationships was not successfully achieved in the earliest years, it is questionable whether the analytic process can provide a context for acquiring the related developmental attributes. The most important developmental prerequisites are the capacity to tolerate delay; the capacity to tolerate affective pain, particularly anxiety and depression; and the capacity to internalize and identify with significant objects. Without these inherent capacities, it seems unlikely that reasonable expectations can be entertained for the patient's achieving real autonomous growth.

Severe developmental failure and a more or less irreversible susceptibility to regression are quite apparent in a variety of psychotic patients. Other patients may be susceptible to somewhat more reversible regressive episodes, which tend to occur during periods of maturational or situational stress. Such patients are usually described in terms of borderline or severe hysterical or narcissistic character pathologies, or other forms of relatively primitive character organization (Kernberg, 1970b, 1971, 1974). Typically they suffer from developmental failures in important areas of one-to-one relationships (Zetzel, 1971). Prolonged exposure to significant regression or to excessive stress may serve to impair otherwise available ego functions, particularly the capacity to distinguish between fantasy and reality. The regression, however, is often transient and reversible, unlike that of the psychotic. In the course of treatment, such patients often prove capable of establishing a meaningful relationship with the therapist, which allows them to remobilize previous levels of developmental achievement and, often, to attain relatively high levels of functional and adaptive integration. For such patients, a persistent and stable therapeutic relationship is often an essential requirement for the maintenance of this level of functioning.

In some cases, the therapeutic relationship may constitute the first real and meaningful relationship the patient has ever had. Together with the earlier developmental impairments, this may make it extremely difficult for the patient to achieve definitive termination. Even if the patient achieves a level of object involvement and improved psychic functioning, the capacity to internalize and to achieve any sense of inner autonomy may remain substantially limited. The therapist must often remain available and therapeutically involved with the patient on an extended and increasingly attenuated basis. Such a patient may not be able to work through the issues of a genuine separation and termination of the analytic process.

An effective evaluation of these parameters of the therapeutic relationship is by no means easy, and the incidence of misjudgment in the initial evaluation of such patients is often high (Knapp et al., 1960). Some patients seem to be much better than originally anticipated, while others seem to be considerably worse. Patients who seem to be better are often decompensated or depressed at the time of evaluation so that they appear and evaluate themselves at a level somewhat below that of their optimal developmental achievement. Many patients, however, are diagnosed, even by experienced and knowledgeable clinicians, as relatively analyzable neurotics, but during subsequent analysis they prove to be susceptible to significant levels of regression (Zetzel, 1968, 1970).

Accordingly, it can be seen that an important differentiation must be made between the real aspects of the doctor-patient relationship, the distortions of the relationship related to earlier developmental failures, and the emergence of specific transference manifestations during the course of the treatment. The critical question is whether developmental failures have so impaired the growth capacity of patients that they are unable to derive from the therapy what is required for their further psychic growth and the resolution of their present difficulties (Kernberg, 1970a). The critical area where this discrimination plays itself out is that of internalization. The position advanced here is that the capacity for internalization based on early developmental achievements is a specific requirement for successful and effective working through in the analytic process. In other words, the capacity for internalization remains, even if retrospectively, a major index of analyzability.

Several other dimensions of the therapeutic relationship are worthy of comment. The patient enters into a relationship with the physician as one who is seeking help from an authority figure. This serves to mobilize certain basic attitudes of the patient and sets certain characteristics of the interaction. Frequently patients bring to the therapeutic relationship magical expectations, in which they attribute special powers to the therapist which in fact the therapist does not have. This introduces an imbalance to the analytic relationship and gives it an authoritarian stamp which is often counterproductive.

Every good physician, whether consciously or unconsciously, tries to induce in the patient an attitude of trusting confidence in his professional capacities and skills. If the patient responds with an attitude of compliance and unquestioning obedience, the ground is laid for a therapeutic misalliance which ultimately works against the objectives of the analytic process. There is danger, of course, that the analyst's own insecurities or narcissistic needs may lead him to take an authoritarian stance which then contributes to the therapeutic imbalance. It is important to remind ourselves, with Zetzel (1966), that these distortions of the analytic relationship are not simply transference distortions, but rather reflect an underlying impairment in the capacity for one-to-one relationship and interaction.

In the face of his illness (physical or psychological) and his incapacity to control and master the source of his difficulty, the patient is placed in a position of relative helplessness which mobilizes his need for infantile dependence. Many, if not most, analytic patients approach the therapeutic relationship from this relatively regressed position. It is part of the analyst's work to redress the balance and enable the patient to participate in the analytic process in a more effective and therapeutically productive way. Instead of infantile dependence and magical expectations, the patient must achieve some sense of his responsibility as an active and productive agent within the analytic process. The patient is not merely the passive recipient of the analyst's therapeutic actions, but is rather an active participant, with the analyst, in a process in which both of them share and to which both of them contribute in different ways.

Similarly, the analytic situation and the quality of interaction between the analyst and the patient are meant to provide a context that maximizes the patient's capacity for spontaneity and relatively free self-expression. As we shall see, this is essential to what is known as "free association." The risk is that within the structure of the analytic situation, the patient, out of his needs and in response to acutely felt pressures of dependence, will adopt a position of conformity to whatever the analyst seems to expect or demand. Often a patient will assume this position even when it is not at all clear what the analyst expects and where no explicit prescriptions are made. Patients often create rules and regulations, which guide their behavior in the interaction with the therapist, and they identify these rules and regulations of their own making with the therapist's expectations.

The patient's conformity may be extremely subtle, and it often remains an abiding issue in the analytic process from beginning to end. Patients may conform to unexpressed, implicit, or even patient-derived expectations of the therapist or the therapeutic situation. They may be assiduous in coming on time, pay their bills punctually and dutifully, or be elaborately productive in terms of verbalized material in the analytic hours or even in terms of vivid and graphic dreams. The distinction of autonomous and spontaneous self-expression from therapeutic conformity can be a very subtle one both in clinical fact and in theory.

I am not referring here to a manifest resistance on the patient's part, but rather to an apparent lack of resistance. The pressures to be a good patient are often quite powerful in the analytic setting, with the result that what on one level may pass as the well-motivated engagement of the patient in the analytic process may at another level have to be seen in terms of conformity. What may contribute meaningfully and usefully to the working through on one level may at the same time undermine and frustrate efforts to achieve specific therapeutic goals at another level.

Just as we can reasonably point to dangers inherent in the patient's excessive or too-ready conformity, we can also indicate dangers in the other direction. Patients may deal with unconscious pressures toward dependency by adopting a precipitous and reactive autonomy which adheres to the ground of the alliance and prevents the patient from responding to the regressive pressures of the analytic situation. Such premature and defensive autonomy—a common phenomenon in obsessional patients—preserves the alliance at the cost of the analytic regression. It is thus a form of resistance. And it is a far cry from the gradual emergence of the more authentic and less defensive autonomy in later stages of the analysis—as an analytic achievement derived from the working through and resolution of basic dependencies.

Thus the issues of responsibility, activity, and autonomy within the analytic relationship can be played out in extremely complex ways, often with a subtlety that escapes the analyst's attention. The inference here is that a more autonomous structuring of the therapeutic relationship, involving the most meaningful aspect of the interaction between doctor and patient, is an essential ingredient of the working through of meaningful identifications within the analytic process. Where this more autonomous structuring is subverted, whether from the side of the patient or from the side of the analyst, there are important implications for the nature and quality of analytic internalizations and for the ultimate outcome of the analytic process.

Central determinants of the patterning of the analytic relationship stem from early one-to-one object relationships and experiences with the primary objects. In many good analytic patients, that is to say, patients with a high degree of analyzability and with healthy, although neurotic, character structures, the issues discussed above may play a moderate and rather minimal role. These patients are often capable of engaging in a productive and relatively autonomous relationship with the analyst, so that the significant area of therapeutic work lies elsewhere — specifically in the neurotic conflicts and fixations embedded at the oedipal level of development. But for many other patients — and the number seems to be gradually increasing — the capacity for a productive and relatively autonomous relationship is to one or another degree comprised. If such patients are capable of sustaining the analytic work, the nature of the therapeutic relationship, its determinants, and the working through of the issues involved become a significant part of the analytic process.

The Analytic Work

The analytic process can be described in terms of certain variables that play a role in its operation. Each of these elements will be subjected to more detailed exploration later, but for the moment we can satisfy our needs with a rough catalogue. The analytic process necessarily involves a certain amount of therapeutic work on the part of the patient. First on the patient's work agenda is the requirement of free association. Free association is of central importance to the analytic process, and the efforts of the analyst in structuring the analytic situation and in working continually with the patient's resistances are directed primarily toward facilitating free association.

It has long been recognized that the term "free association" is something of a misnomer. It is neither totally free nor simply a matter of association. Rather, it is a process of free-floating introspective attention, as Freud (1900) so aptly described it, combined with a more difficult process of directed attention and evaluative reflection. The patient must first take a relatively free, uninhibited, open position toward the content of his own intrapsychic processes. This implies a certain regressive openness to otherwise repressed and unconscious needs, pressures, drives, and impulses. But the process requires more. The patient must also join the analyst in the therapeutic effort of evaluating, interpreting, searching out the meaning and implication of what is thought or felt, relating it to other significant experiences, integrating it with the ongoing process of the analysis and particularly with the present experience of his relationship and interaction with the analyst. This attitude is what has been referred to as the therapeutic split in the patient, in which one part of the ego undergoes the necessary therapeutic regression while another part actively and productively collaborates with the analyst in attempting to understand and integrate this experience. Free association provides the stuff on which the analytic process works. In addition, it is a contributing factor to the analytic regression, which forms such an important aspect of the analytic process.

A second level of the patient's work within the analytic process is that of gaining insight. Not only must the patient be able to regress in order to gain access to important repressed material, but he must mobilize his cognitive and affective resources to gain some meaningful insight into his conflicts and difficulties. Here the processing of meaning is of central importance. It is this part of the analytic work that most engages the patient's understanding with the analyst's attempts to explore and comprehend the patient's psychic contents and productions. The effectiveness of this aspect of the analytic work is best facilitated by a sound and persistent therapeutic alliance. The gaining of insight and the work involved in it are not simply matters of cognitive processing (Pressman, 1969). Rather, the interplay of analytic interpretation and the generation of insight takes place within the context of a meaningful object relationship which is embedded in the therapeutic alliance. The giving of an interpretation and its acceptance and integration by the patient represent more than a simple exchange of information. There is a giving and receiving, a sharing and an interchange between two human beings who are mutually and reciprocally involved in a meaningful and productive therapeutic relationship.

But the work of the analytic process does not end with the production of meaningful material through free association and the generation of insight. The insight must be made real and palpable; it must be realized not merely in cognitive terms but in affectively meaningful terms. Moreover, the infantile fixations and the rigidity of the patient's neurotic position, which lies behind and expresses itself through the patient's resistances, must be resolved. Only then can the insight be effectively integrated with the rest of the patient's psychic experience and become an operative force for therapeutic change. What is required is the working through of the analytic material and its related insights. This process often consumes the largest portion of time in the analysis. In the course of working through, the patient must often regenerate the basic insight over and over again in a variety of contexts and from a number of differing perspectives. It is in the process of working through that effective therapeutic change begins to take place.

The working through has to do immediately with the patient's resistances to the therapeutic process. Resistances can be described as anything that impedes the therapeutic progression. The diversity of resistance provides a large catalogue, but this catalogue can essentially be assessed in terms of the predominance of instinctual determinants of the resistance as opposed to ego determinants or superego determinants. Early in the course of his theorizing, Freud conceptualized such resistances in terms of fixations and libidinal attachments that yield to change only with the greatest reluctance and often manifest great rigidity. With the emergence of a more articulated ego psychology, resistances could be conceived in terms of defense mechanisms and the anticathectic or antilibidinal forces at the ego's command. To this was added the consideration of superego dynamics, particularly in terms of underlying guilt motivations, whereby the acceptance of therapeutic insights and the progression toward healthier and more satisfactory functioning are impeded. This view relates particularly to the response in treatment of masochistic and depressive patients and also, most particularly, to the negative therapeutic response. Most recently, however, therapeutic resistances have been understood in terms of underlying narcissistic expectations and entitlements.

Freud's original vision of resistances was cast in the language of force. He envisioned the unconscious, and often conscious, efforts of the patient to resist the inroads of therapeutic interventions in somewhat physicalistic terms. The frame of reference provided in current analytic theory, however, is considerably more motivational. It is concerned with the complex significance of meanings and the symbolic dimensions of the patient's experience, particularly in terms of unconscious significances, as well as with their integration into the patient's ultimate frame of reference.

If one asks more specifically about the function of resistance in psychoanalysis, one must bring into focus its role in the avoidance of regression. The inevitability of resistance and its importance in the analytic process are closely linked to the phenomenon of regression. One of the essential dynamics involved in the analytic process is that the clarification, working through, and ultimate diminution or loosening of defensive operations or resistances lead to a kind of destructuralization, which allows for the mobilization and emergence of more regressed psychic contents. Many of the technical aspects of the analytic process, particularly free association, are directly intended to facilitate this regressive movement within the analysis and thus make more available the more infantile, less differentiated, and less structured aspects of the patient's personality and functioning.

The direct result of this regressive movement is the emergence of the transference neurosis, which usually reflects the dynamics of oedipal levels of development and involvement. In the classical psychoanalytic view, the oedipal triangle serves as the major focal point and determining influence in the production of neurotic symptoms and other disorders of character and adjustment. These are specifically reactivated and focused in the relationship with the analyst. As Freud commented, the transference neurosis is perhaps the most powerful tool that the analyst has available to effect therapeutic change, but it is also the most difficult and frequently serves as the strongest source of the patient's resistance.

The rationale for the analytic regression is that it allows for a reopening of infantile conflicts, here specifically oedipal conflicts, which then offer the possibility for reworking and reorganizing along healthier and less neurotic lines. The regressive pulls, however, create an increased titer of anxiety for the patient, since in some ultimate sense it is the dangers and fears attached to those basic infantile conflicts that serve as the source of the patient's pathology and give rise to the anxiety signals that trigger the defensive operations (often keeping them mobilized in rigid resistance to the analytic process). Thus the mobilization of developmental potential through regression is both a source of therapeutic change and a source of increased anxiety and threat. Moreover, the opening up of infantile levels of conflict runs a certain risk of further regression as an alternative to more positive and constructive resolution.

It has often been observed that the analytic regression is a modulated and buffered regression. Precipitous or excessive regression may extend beyond the patient's capacity to tolerate the resulting anxiety and to integrate the new experiences and insights that it generates. The patient must be protected from such malignant regression within the analytic process, since it is frequently countertherapeutic. This is the primary reason why the assessment of ego strength is of critical importance in the evaluation of analyzability. Where the patient has sufficient ego strength to resist regressive pulls and to tolerate the necessary limits of therapeutic regression, the potential for a successful analysis is inherent. Where these capacities are not available, the analytic process may be more damaging than helpful. The essential element in the analytic process, which provides the necessary safeguard and the framework within which an effectively moderated regression can take place, is that of the therapeutic alliance. Where the patient is able to engage in, sustain, and progressively deepen the therapeutic alliance as the analytic process moves along, he is correspondingly more able, by reason of the supportive aspects of the alliance, to tolerate increasing degrees of regression and the correlated anxiety.

In the early years of psychoanalysis, an analytic regression to the level of the triangular oedipal situation was deemed adequate for therapeutic purposes. Increasing clinical experience, however, and particularly the experience gathered in the last score of years, has suggested that for a significant percentage of patients the resolution of conflicts at the oedipal level is no longer adequate; the therapeutic process must reach beyond the oedipal context to the levels of pregenital fixation and early object relations.

As we have already suggested, the problem with the analytic regression to this pregenital level is that patients with such basic traumata, with such early levels of fixation or developmental arrest, often have difficulties in establishing and maintaining meaningful one-to-one relationships. In consequence, their capacity to enter into and sustain a productive therapeutic alliance is compromised. Patients who are experiencing the effects of an episodic regression, whether from situational or developmental crises, may be better able to meet the demands of therapeutic involvement and alliance than those who are suffering from the effects of specific developmental arrests. The analyzability of these latter patients and the advisability of their entering into the psychoanalytic process remain open to serious question.

From another perspective, the analytic process can be envisioned as moving through more or less determinate phases. Like ancient Gaul or a good speech or even a good story, the analytic process can be divided into three parts—a beginning, a middle, and an end. The divisions are somewhat arbitrary and the lines between them cannot be clearly or unequivocally drawn. Yet, however crude, the division allows us to make some initial differentiations.

The first phase of the analytic process is concerned with the establishing of the analytic situation and particularly with the forming of the therapeutic alliance. A second phase is introduced by the beginnings of the analytic regression, which allows for the emergence and intensification of the transference neurosis. This phase usually involves dealing with the patient's resistances and working them through in order to allow for a therapeutic regression. The emergence of the transference neurosis and its increasing play in the analytic process open the way for the therapist to interpret and bring understanding to the patient's ego of what the patient is experiencing within the analytic context.

The final phase of the analytic process is taken up with the working through of transference elements and with the problems of separation and infantile dependence related to the termination of the analysis. The termination of a successful analysis brings into focus, in relatively specific and direct ways, the issues of autonomy and independence. As the end of the analysis approaches, the patient's passive-dependent wishes are intensified and increasingly become the focus of analytic work.

In this respect, the analyst's position in the final phase differs considerably from that in the initial phase of the analysis. In the beginning the analyst functions as a more or less parental figure, who responds to the relatively regressed and passive-dependent aspects of the infantile neurosis. But in the final phase the analyst functions more like the parent of a late adolescent in attempting to foster and sustain a growing autonomy and independence. As this process evolves, the passivity and dependence, as well as the conformity, which are essential parts of the analytic process in its early and middle stages, become increasingly ego-alien. They are seen as residual infantile wishes which must be resolved in the work of the terminal phase.

THERAPEUTIC FACTORS IN THE ANALYTIC PROCESS

In our attempt to understand the nature of the psychoanalytic process, it is important to specify those aspects of the process which result in specific therapeutic gain or which can be conceived as somehow responsible for the therapeutic progression and change experienced by the patient. The history of psychoanalysis reveals a significant shift and redirection of emphasis in the understanding of such therapeutic factors in analysis. In general, it can be said that the shift has been from an emphasis on affective factors to a more explicit emphasis on the cognitive factors involved in the integration of unconscious contents with more conscious levels of activity and organization, to a further focusing on the elements involved in the object relationship between the therapist and the patient and the dynamics of this therapeutic object relationship (Meissner, 1975).

In the very early stages of his thinking about the therapeutic process, particularly during the period of his collaboration with Josef Breuer, Freud laid particular emphasis on catharsis as the effective parameter of therapy. The model employed was the abreactive model, according to which a real traumatic experience caused a certain reflective response to be forced out of consciousness so that the affect became strangulated and was unable to achieve normal expression and thereby integration with the rest of the patient's conscious experience. The therapeutic approach aimed at the release of this repressive strangulation and the recovery of the traumatic affective experience. In their preliminary communication, Breuer and Freud (1893) wrote that "each individual hysterical symptom immediately and permanently disappeared when we had succeeded in bringing clearly to light the memory of the event by which it was provoked and in arousing its accompanying affect, and when the patient had described that event in the greatest possible detail and had put the affect into words" (p. 6).

The reasons for the strangulation and repression of affects were matters of some doubt at the time. Breuer seemed to favor the hypothesis of hypnoid states, which more or less postulated, without explaining, the patient's susceptibility to such dissociated, repressed affects. Freud, however, saw the process more in reactive terms, and this led him in the direction of thinking in terms of defensive processes operating against traumatic inputs. The latter view led to a theory of repression and ultimately of defense, as well as to the idea that dynamic mental forces struggling for expression and locked in conflict were somehow related to the psychopathological symptomatology. The model of abreaction, however, proved to have a limited validity, particularly as its therapeutic effectiveness extended little beyond relatively transient symptomatic improvement. Freud became increasingly sensitive to and aware of the resistive forces at play in the mental apparatus. With this growing awareness, the emphasis in his therapeutic approach shifted toward a concentration on the patient's resistances and became more concerned with the overcoming of amnestic barriers than with the simple abreaction of strangulated affect (Zetzel and Meissner, 1973).

As the nature of the analytic process gradually became better understood and as an ego psychology evolved, the emphasis on the role of interpretation and the genesis of insight as therapeutic factors in the analytic process became progressively more central. Within a more specifically functional, ego-psychological framework, interpretation and the gaining of insight were seen as bringing into operation specifically cognitive and preferentially secondary-process capacities of the ego as a corrective to the more unconscious and instinctually derived, often primary-process aspects of the patient's more regressed, neurotic functioning.

Early on, the work of interpretation and the gaining of insight followed as an extension of the emphasis on remembering and working through, that is, on the recovery of amnestic material, as opposed to the unconsciously determined repetition that was involved both in the patient's neurosis and in the transference neurosis which developed in the analytic setting. The analytic process was thus conceived as facilitating the recovery of significant memories and enabling the patient's ego cognitively to process and integrate the understandings derived from the analytic work and from the analyst's insight-fostering communications. In this regard, the patient's capacity to maintain the distinction between fantasy and reality and to sustain a meaningful and productive working alliance with the analyst became factors of major import.

However, as a result of increasing experience, and perhaps also as a byproduct of the diversity of patients seen in the analytic setting in recent years, the view of the role of interpretive interventions has been enlarged. Not only is the interpretive effort seen in terms of mobilizing ego functions within the context of the working relationship between the patient and the analyst, but it has become more and more clear that an interpretive dynamic takes place within the context of an ongoing object relationship, which is the core reality and essential dimension of the analytic process. The interpretive effort can no longer be envisioned simply in terms of undermining resistances and clarifying cognitive content and relationships; it has to be seen as possessing a dynamic all its own, a dynamic which has to do with the vicissitudes of the object relationship within the analytic process.

The focus has thus shifted to a concern with the object-related experiences and developmental vicissitudes that underlie the patient's capacity to respond to, accept, and integrate interpretive initiatives from the analyst. In an increasing proportion of analytic patients, it is clear that these dynamics pertain to the very early history of one-to-one object relations, to some of the very earliest aspects of mother-child relationship and interaction. Although in patients who more or less fit the classical analytic paradigm, in which triangular oedipal conflicts are conceived to be central to the neurotic pathology, these aspects of the transference and therapeutic relationship play a minimal role and thus the interpretive dynamics are not at the forefront of analytic concern, in the more narcissistic and schizoid forms of character pathology, which are seen with increasing frequency in the analytic setting, these dynamics have become increasingly central to the analytic work.

It should be noted that there has been a corresponding shift in our understanding of the therapeutic effectiveness of interpretation. The focus is no longer merely on the cognitive level where meanings are illuminated, understood, and integrated, but on a deeper level of patient-analyst involvement which has to do with important modifications that take place through processes of internalization. The interpretive effort can be seen in terms of providing a matrix within the analytic object relationship for significant internalizations which somehow underlie and accompany the giving of the interpretation and its acceptance and integration by the patient. In this regard, one can discern different levels of therapeutic modification. On a more superficial or functional level, one sees the attainment of understanding and the integration of meanings and relationships of meanings (the cognitive level). On a deeper level, one finds the more internal structural modifications taking place by way of internalization.

Viewing the interpretive dynamic from this perspective raises a related set of concerns to which analytic theorists have paid little attention, but which nonetheless seem to be of primary significance in understanding the analytic process. Taken at its more limited cognitive level, the acceptance, understanding, and integration of interpretations and the gaining of insight can be conceptualized in terms of a learning process. I do not mean to infer that these are the only elements of learning that play a role in the analytic process, but they are certainly central ones. In any case, the learning dimensions of interpretation and insight raise important questions about the relationship between learning phenomena in general and the genesis and induction of internalizations within the analytic process.

It seems strange that psychoanalytic theory has more or less shunted the whole problem of learning to the side. This lack in the analytic theoretical armamentarium was exquisitely sensed and felt by David Rapaport, who came to psychoanalysis from a rich background of psychological theory. Psychologists, particularly experimental psychologists and learning theorists, have occupied themselves with the problem of learning for the last century of more. Certainly Rapaport was deeply concerned with the problem, and the major emphasis of his theoretical contributions was in the direction of laying the groundwork for a more meaningful analytic formulation of learning factors.

There can be little doubt that learning plays a significant role in the analytic process, even beyond the indications we have already given (Birk and Brinkley-Birk, 1974; Greenspan, 1972, 1975). As the analytic process moves along, considerable learning takes place in the patient's mind. The process of making explicit the details of real situations and events carries with it an increasing awareness and concretization of aspects of reality of which the patient may not have been previously aware. The same can be said of aspects of the patient's own inner experience. The relatively new experience of verbally expressing and formulating currents of thought and affective life brings a certain definition and clarification to aspects of the patient's experience, both in the realm of external awareness and in the arena of introspective self-awareness, which had previously been unavailable to the patient. This clarification and increasing objectivization represent a form of learning and often carry important therapeutic benefits.

Similarly, in the analytic regression, the patient becomes more conscious of and more in touch with aspects of instinctually derived affective experience, aspects that may have been previously threatening and were impregnated with danger as long as they remained in the realm of unconscious fantasy. Experiencing these aspects of affective life in the context of a supportive therapeutic relationship can have an effect similar to desensitization, so that the patient is much better able to tolerate these affective experiences and to integrate them with the rest of his experiential life. In a parallel fashion, the patient undoubtedly becomes increasingly aware of aspects of his behavior and attitudes that are nonadaptive. The clarification of these aspects of behavior makes it increasingly possible, if not likely, that the patient will begin to take steps to modify his behavior in order to bring about more adaptive results.

The increasing clarification and delineation of the patient's reality, both in terms of the real physical environment and in the context of object relations, represent aspects of a learning process. Similarly, as the analytic work progresses, the patient becomes increasingly aware of and undertakes a detailed delineation of the realm of his own inner fantasy — another aspect of the learning experience within the analytic process. The interplay between the analysand's learning and clarifying experience and the interpretive efforts of the analyst constitute an important matrix within which learning variables play themselves out.

It is extremely important not only that analytic thought develop an understanding of these learning dimensions, but that they be integrated within the larger perspectives of analytic work. The most important area that theories of learning have neglected is the relationship between learning factors and other internal structuralized modifications that play a role in human development and experience. Since internalized modifications play a central role in the analytic process, they have been much more readily included in analytic theory. What is needed at this juncture, however, is an integration of the various dimensions of the analytic experience (Meissner, 1974c, 1974d).

As a last consideration, we should note the therapeutic influence of internalizations themselves. Since this issue is the central focus of our study, it will not be detailed here. Suffice it to say that the theory of both the developmental and therapeutic aspects of internalizations has been generally left on a rather vague and nonspecific footing. The subject was introduced by Freud initially in his conceptualizations of superego formation, and later on in his attempts to articulate aspects of ego development (Meissner, 1970a). Yet, despite the extreme importance of internalizations, little explicit attention has been paid to the theory of internalization. The most significant exception to this is Schafer's remarkable monograph (1968a). Our objective in this present study is to extend and deepen the theory of internalizations with specific reference to the analytic process.

3

CLINICAL ASPECTS
OF INTERNALIZATION
IN THE PSYCHOANALYTIC
SITUATION

In approaching the problem of internalization in psycho-analysis, we shall follow the usual distinction between the psychoanalytic situation and the psychoanalytic process (see Zetzel, 1970). In this chapter we shall focus on the analytic situation, by which we mean the setting within which the analytic process takes place, and primarily the positive real relationship between the patient and the analyst on which the therapeutic alliance is based.

The complexities of the conceptual structure of the psycho-analytic situation have been explored and discussed in Stone's (1961) excellent monograph. Our intent here is to focus more specifically the contribution that the patient's extant inner struc-ture, developed and achieved through the various forms of in-ternalization, brings to the organization of the psychoanalytic situation. We should keep in mind as well that the structuring of the psychoanalytic situation is not a static phenomenon, but rather provides a dynamic and often dramatically shifting con-text within the psychoanalytic process. In this regard, we can see the contribution of internalizations to the psychoanalytic situation as a matter of shifting configurations, which can be ex-pected to follow certain predictable patterns through the various phases of the analysis.

Our objective here is twofold. Our first goal is to identify the role of internalizations in various forms of psychopathology, particularly those that may find their way to the analytic couch. Our second concern is to clarify the role of internalizations, both on the part of the patient and on the part of the analyst, in structuring the analytic situation. We shall discuss these two considerations in terms of the three forms of internalization we have already delineated.

INCORPORATION

Insofar as incorporation is a primitive mechanism which reflects relatively undifferentiated forms of object involvement, it can only play a very limited role in the psychoanalytic situation. Patients whose capacities for internalization are more or less confined to incorporative modes must be seen as functioning on a psychotic level. For such patients analytic intervention is contraindicated. This is not to suggest that these patients are beyond the reach of therapy, but it does presume that the essential ingredients for undertaking the psychoanalytic process are missing. The loss or fragmentation of ego boundaries and the merging with objects reflect the operation of severely regressive psychotic processes. The ego remains undifferentiated and disorganized and there is a lack of differentiation between self and object, so that the capacity to discriminate between fantasy and reality (essential for analytic work) is not meaningfully operative.

A more troublesome question arises with regressive states that come about in the course of analysis. Here we are concerned with the emergence of the so-called psychotic transference. Both Balint (1968) and Searles (1961a, 1963) point out that the regression in the psychotic transference carries the patient to a level of symbiotic relatedness which is essentially beyond the reach of the usual interpretive techniques. Although Searles is discussing the psychotherapy of severely disturbed schizophrenics, he emphasizes the necessity for such a regression not only in these patients but in most patients, even neurotics. He insists on a therapeutic regression to the level of a symbiotic maternal transference, out of which the patient can begin to differentiate and experience therapeutic growth. In severely regressed schizophrenic patients, regression to such an incorporative mode is quite possible and clinically verifiable, but it is not clear that similar levels of regression are, or can be, reached by more integrated personalities.

Balint (1968) makes a point similar to that of Searles in his discussion of regression to "the basic fault." Here we must question the role of regression in the therapeutic process and the depth to which regression can be carried and remain a therapeutic force. If patients regress beyond a certain point, the regression may become malignant and may serve only to overwhelm the patient with excessive anxiety which is beyond his capacity to integrate constructively. The point can be usefully made, however, that in their discussion of severely regressive phenomena, both Searles and Balint are directing our attention to the working through of internalizations that take place at a more primitive level than can be made available to secondary-process interventions such as analytic interpretations.

Another difficult question concerns the extent to which the regressive episodes occasionally seen in analytic patients can be described in terms of the incorporative mode. I have never seen this degree of regression in the analytic context, but may well have witnessed it in psychotherapy with schizophrenic patients. If analytic patients do regress to a modality of symbiotic relatedness, this regression would seem to involve primitive levels of introjective experience in which the interplay of relatively undifferentiated introjective and projective elements distort the transference relationship. In this regard, Frosch (1967) has suggested that the Wolf Man was a psychotic character and that his treatment, both with Freud and later with Ruth Mack Brunswick, was marked by a series of regressive episodes in which he developed a transference psychosis.[1]

The extent to which such severe regression in the analytic setting is therapeutic, as Searles suggests, remains a matter of controversy. In discussing the treatment of schizophrenic patients, Searles (1961b) himself observes that "only with the resolution of the symbiotic mode of relatedness is the patient capable of genuine object-relatedness and able, therefore, to cope with the matters with which psycho-analysis of the neurotic individual

[1] In this connection, Blum (1974) has delineated the Wolf Man's borderline personality organization, which may explain these regressive psychotic episodes. See also the material in Gardiner (1971) and Meissner (1977c).

ordinarily deals" (p. 551). As Searles explains, "the patient [now] becomes involved in a better differentiated, more selective, process of de-repression of identifications from the past, with acceptance into his own ego of those identifications which are predominantly useful to him, and relinquishment of those which have proved unuseful or pathological" (p. 551). What Searles points to here is the reactivation of significant introjects and their working through in the therapeutic process. He is quite aware that the resolution of symbiotic issues and the capacity for greater differentiation and ego functioning are essential dimensions of the psychoanalytic process. Whether the symbiotic relatedness described so well by Searles is to be regarded as incorporative or as essentially introjective, that phase must be essentially resolved before any capacity for analysis becomes operative.

Although the symbiotic relatedness in schizophrenic and other patients with more primitive psychopathology may be incorporative, I would have reservations about describing the regressive symbiotic relatedness of most analytic patients in such terms. This may better be described in terms of primitive forms of introjection and projection, which give rise to relatively early forms of symbiotic maternal dependence within the transference. Whether these regressive reactivations of primitive introjective configurations can be described as transference psychoses depends on the maintenance of other relevant ego functions, such as reality testing and reality orientation.

INTROJECTION AND PROJECTION

When we come to the interacting and interrelated processes of introjection and projection, we come to the most significant internalization processes for the structuring of the analytic situation and ultimately the workings of the analytic process. We shall first delineate the role pathogenic introjects can play in a variety of forms of psychopathology, only some of which may be susceptible to psychoanalytic intervention. However, even in cases where suitability for analysis is questionable or absent, these pathogenic formations play an analogous role. We shall then turn to the analytic situation itself and trace the role of interlocking introjections and projections in the structuring of the analytic context. Our objective in this discussion is to specify the organization of introjects characteristic of particular forms of psychopathology.

Pathogenic Introjects

We shall begin at the most primitive levels at which introjective and projective mechanisms are elaborated and work our way toward more differentiated and more highly integrated forms. On the psychotic level, the introjects serve as the effective organizing force for almost the whole of the patient's internal personality organization. There is little — hardly any — room for the relatively autonomous functioning of ego capacities. It should be remembered, of course, that within any discriminable level of personality organization or diagnostic category there is a spectrum of degrees of impairment and pathogenicity.

SCHIZOPHRENIA

In most severely disturbed and chronically regressed cases of schizophrenia, the patient's inner world is fragmented and pervasively consumed by the introjects. These introjective configurations can be regarded as internalizations of part-objects that have achieved only a minimal degree of integration. The object fragments are subject to contamination by primitive, unneutralized cathexes involving unresolved aggressive and libidinal (usually oral) instinctual derivatives. Because these instinctual components prevent the further integration of the part-objects, internalization results in an inner world that is structurally weak, vulnerable to drive influences, easily subject to regression, and indicative of severe developmental defects and deficiencies. The fragility, fragmentation, and susceptibility to regressive drive influences of these introjects serve to undermine any islands of autonomy or more or less severely conflicted ego functioning that may be present.

These primitively organized introjects are very susceptible to projection, and the constellation of paranoid features so frequently found in more compensated schizophrenics reflects this underlying set of mechanisms. Schizophrenic projections tend to be all-encompassing and to reflect intensely the underlying drive determinants, particularly those related to aggression. These pathogenic introjects overwhelm the patient's inner world, so that the opportunity or capacity for emergence of a functional ego is generally minimal. It should also be noted that the schizophrenic introjects, as internalized object relations, are highly determined by projective influences stemming from external sources, particularly those found operating within family systems (Boszormenyi-Nagy and Framo, 1965; Lidz, Fleck, and Cornelison, 1965; Meissner, 1978a). In such projective contexts, the interplay of projection and introjection encompasses not only the inner world of the patient, but also the emotionally toned affect system that constitutes the inner world of the family matrix. Consequently, the transference in these patients is influenced not only by the ordinary mechanisms of projective distortion, but also by the patient's developmental experience as the unwitting victim of parental and other familial projections.

An important point can be made here with reference to certain clinical aspects of these pathogenic introjects. As we have seen, the descriptive content of introjective systems involves the polarities of helpless victim and destructive aggressor, superiority and inferiority, powerfulness and powerlessness. In schizophrenic patients we find the extremes of helpless victimization and pitiful powerlessness coexisting with infantile omnipotence and grandiosity. These polarities are part and parcel of the economy and the organization of the introjects. In the most regressed forms of schizophrenia, they are permanently entrenched. The sense of victimization and powerlessness in the schizophrenic is radical and very nearly ineradicable.

The schizophrenic introjective organization is marked by fragmentation, confusion, and, at the most primitive level, by incorporative modes of relating in which self-object differentiation is obliterated and ego boundaries are dissolved in the psychotic loss of identity and fusion with the object. Moreover, in the schizophrenic patient the introjective fragments remain relatively active and unrepressed so that the inner organization of the self-experience is characterized by a chaotic shifting from one introjective configuration to another—from helpless and defenseless victim to destructive and powerful aggressor, from worthless and totally inadequate nothingness to full-blown grandiosity. These configurations may even be seen operating simultaneously. The result is a state of inner instability and chaotic confusion in which any relatively permanent self-organization and self-image become impossible, or nearly so. It is the simultaneous, conflictual presence and activity of these contradictory introjective configurations that create the conditions for this internal disorganization. Moreover, the introjective configurations tend to assume extreme forms. The sense of victimization is of total helplessness, while the sense of aggressive destructiveness involves absolute annihilation without any redeeming or mitigating elements. Inferiority is characterized by abysmal nothingness and complete worthlessness, while grandiosity has little or no limit.

The impact of this introjective organization in the therapeutic situation is profound. Since the introjective fragments are highly susceptible to projection, the relationship to the therapist is constantly contaminated by projections, usually fragmentary and often rapidly shifting in nature. The therapist inevitably feels pulled and pressured into a variety of countertransference positions corresponding to the patient's projections. Typically, for example, the therapist may feel compelled to undertake extraordinary measures to help or rescue the patient from difficulties. The therapist moves into the position, unwittingly, of omnipotent protector, magical rescuer, powerful therapeutic manipulator—a perfect match for the patient's sense of vulnerability and powerlessness. It is a help at times to see these interactions as re-creations of patterns of interaction that are identifiable in the patient's family. Not infrequently, the patient will repeat these patterns with the therapist or, in the hospital setting, with ward personnel. The patient creates patterns of splitting, externalization of conflicts, and divisions within the staff similar to those experienced within the family. A further consequence of the schizophrenic introjective organization is that there is little room for enough autonomous functioning to provide a basis for the therapeutic alliance. In this regard, issues related to the alliance assume a much greater position in the therapeutic work with these patients than with others. The interplay of these elements in the therapy of schizophrenics has been explored by Searles (1965), among others.

MANIC-DEPRESSIVE PSYCHOSIS

When we turn to manic-depressive psychosis, we meet a somewhat different situation. In the depressive phase the patient is enmeshed in the most powerful grip of depressive introjects; his inner world is so dominated by the primitive forces built into the introject that all projective or other externalizing defenses are undermined. The patient becomes the helpless victim of an internalized persecuting and accusing superego introject. Although in this phase of the illness the aspects of the introjects underlying the patient's feelings of worthlessness, helplessness, and inadequacy dominate the internal economy, it should be remembered that the powerful, destructive, and aggressive components of the introjects are also operative. These aggressive components are usually described under the heading of superego dynamics, but it is clear that the superego aspects of the depressive phase are only a part of the operation of the introjects.

With the transition to the manic phase, the picture changes radically. The omnipotent, grandiosely superior, and aggressive aspects of the introjects now become predominant. Instead of being internally directed, against the powerful and helpless patient, these introjective components become externally directed in the form of grandiose schemes and activity.

This picture is quite different from the one envisioned for schizophrenia. In the schizophrenic patient the conflicting introjective components are present in a constant state of disorganizing interaction. In the manic-depressive patient, however, the polar aspects of the introjective organization seem to alternate. At one time the deflating aspects predominate; at another time the inflating aspects take over. The reasons for this alternation are not altogether clear. They may in part reflect the operation of defensive vicissitudes in that the grandiosity serves as a defense against the inadequacy and vice versa.

It should be remembered that the economy of the introjects is caught up in and intensely involved with the patient's defensive needs. In this sense, the polarities we have described must be understood as serving the purposes of reciprocal defense as well as mutual reinforcement. The patient's powerlessness, for instance, is defended against by assuming a position of relative omnipotence. At the same time, however, the patient's failure to sustain the inherent expectations of such an omnipotent position drives him back to the extreme of helplessness and powerlessness. Here we can see that these vicissitudes of the introjects not only reflect drive determinants, but are specifically and inherently caught up in the dynamics of pathogenic narcissism.

In another light, the manic defense may be seen as an alternate form of externalizing defense to the paranoid. In schizophrenic states, manic defenses and behavior are not infrequently observed, particularly in so-called schizo-affective states. Similarly, paranoid defenses and projections are by no means infrequent in manic-depressive processes, and in fact serve as a negative prognostic indicator (Meissner, 1978b).

Beyond the vicissitudes of defensive motivations in manic-depressive psychosis, the alternation between the polar aspects of the introjects seems to be strongly influenced by underlying biological determinants. Although the nature of these neurological factors is at this point poorly understood, it is gradually yielding to intensive investigation. Recent studies suggest that specific neurotransmitter catecholamines (dopamine and norepinephrine) are functionally increased in specific brain areas before the switch from a depressive to a manic phase. Thus while the defensive aspects of the pathogenic introjects can be delineated, the differentiation between schizophrenic and manic-depressive modalities may have to do with the interplay of other determinants than the merely psychological.

The point to be emphasized here is that the manic-depressive introjective organization is strikingly different from the schizophrenic one, even though both function at a psychotic level. The manic organization forms itself around the narcissistic, superior introjects and, to a certain extent, the aggressor introjects, while the polar opposites (inferiority and victimization) are repressed or even split off and projected. Similarly, the depressive organization forms itself around the introjects that convey a sense of victimization and inferiority. The disease expresses itself in the cyclic shift from one set of introjects to the other, together with the frequent dissociation and projection of the opposite forms. In this regard, manic-depressive psychosis can be seen as a more organized form of psychotic disturbance than schizophrenia. The introjective configurations in the schizophrenic patient are both fragmented and internally disorganized; they are set in continual conflict and contradiction with each other. In contrast, in the manic-depressive patient the introjects tend to be better organized and to form polar clusters that have a certain degree of inner consistency.

BORDERLINE PERSONALITY DISORDERS

When we turn from the psychotic organization to the borderline personality organization, we are confronted with what Kernberg (1970b) has described as the lowest level of character pathology. Kernberg organizes the character pathologies along a continuum, according to the degree to which repression or splitting mechanisms predominate in the patient's inner organization. Hysterical personalities, obsessive-compulsive personalities, depressive personalities, and the better-integrated masochistic personalities are placed at the upper level of the continuum, while many infantile personalities, most narcissistic personalities, Deutsch's "as-if" personalities, and other forms of antisocial personality structure fall on the lower level. Since the borderline personality organization tends to be impulsive and infantile, with the imperative need to gratify impulses breaking through periodically in acting-out episodes, it belongs at the lowest level.

Emphasizing this underlying character pathology, Kernberg (1967) offers a variety of descriptive characteristics that allow for a presumptive diagnosis of borderline personality organization. He points to a chronic, diffuse anxiety, which exceeds the binding capacity of other symptoms and character traits; to multiple neurotic symptoms including phobias, obsessive-compulsive symptoms, multiple elaborate or bizarre conversion symptoms, dissociative reactions, hypochondriasis, and a combination of paranoid and hypochondriacal trends; and to a primitive sexuality, which can be described as polymorphous-perverse. The personality structure tends to run along lines of the paranoid or the schizoid personality, or even the hypomanic personality, but depressive-masochistic character traits are explicitly excluded. Impulsive character traits and various forms of drug addiction merge with acting-out features. Narcissism is often a predominant element in the borderline personality. In fact, these patients can look clinically much like narcissistic personalities, but the difference is an important, if confusing, one. There is often a core of paranoid anxiety based on the projection of rather primitive oral rage.

More recently, Gunderson and Singer (1975) have identified features that characterize many descriptions of the borderline syndrome. According to their study, borderline patients show intense affect, which is usually hostile or depressive, and have a history of impulsive acts, either in the form of episodic self-mutilations and overdosings or in the more chronic pattern of drug dependency and promiscuity. Although borderline patients have a relatively good record of social adaptiveness characterized by good achievement in school or work, the appropriateness of their social behavior may reflect underlying identity disturbances, which are masked by mimicry and the capacity for superficial imitation. In addition, borderline patients have a history of occasional brief psychotic experiences, which tend to have a paranoid quality, and they characteristically give bizarre, illogical, and primitive or autistic responses on unstructured projective tests such as the Rorschach. Finally, there is a characteristic vacillation in their interpersonal relationships between transient, superficial involvements and intense, dependent relationships often marred by devaluations, manipulations, and intense demandingness.

Turning to the level of structural organization, which lies closer to our concerns with the introjective organization and its contribution to borderline pathology, Kernberg (1967) emphasizes the aspects of ego weakness in borderline patients, specifically the lack of anxiety tolerance and impulse control and the lack of developed capacities for sublimation. The shift toward primary-process thinking, which is detectable on projective testing or in response to unstructured or stressful situations, may reflect a variety of dysfunctions in the personality organization, but for our purposes it can be related to the susceptibility of the introjective organization to regressive pulls and the powerful influence of primitive drive derivatives. This in turn is related to the activation of more primitive defensive organizations including splitting mechanisms. These defensive configurations work against the integration of cognitive processes and promote the partial disorganization and fusion of primitive self-object images, as we have discussed in relation to the interplay of introjective and projective processes.

The essential deficit in the organization of the borderline personality involves the predominant role of the introjects and their continuing interplay with projective devices. Kernberg (1967) comments: *"Vicious circles involving projection of aggression and reintrojection of aggressively determined object and self images* are probably a major factor in the development of both psychosis and borderline personality organization. *In the psychoses their main effect is regressive refusion of self and object images; in the case of the borderline personality organization*, what predominates is not refusion between self and object images, but *an intensification and pathological fixation of splitting processes"* (pp. 665–666). Thus Kernberg lays special emphasis on splitting as the essential defensive operation in the borderline personality. The major developmental defect then lies in an incapacity to synthesize positive and negative introjections.

Specifically, Kernberg believes that the nonpathological internalization of object relations requires a differentiation of self- and object images, as well as an integration of self- and object images acquired under the influence of libidinal drive derivatives with corresponding self- and object images acquired under the influence of aggressive drive derivatives. The borderline patient's inability to integrate libidinal images with the extremely aggressive and self-punitive strivings connected to early self- and object images is a consistent feature of the pathology involved. The integration or synthesis of such opposing introjects may be the most important source of neutralization of aggression (i.e., through the fusion of libidinal and aggressive drive derivatives). Without this, the ego is deprived of an essential source of adaptive energies.

Some qualifying comments are in order. The description of the borderline personality given by Kernberg (1967) offers a global delineation of a group of character pathologies within which important diagnostic discriminations are possible. Kernberg's account establishes the borderline conditions as a separate realm of psychopathology intermediate between the neuroses and the psychoses. Within that realm of psychopathology, however, there is a spectrum of disorders, which can be differentiated in terms of the stability of ego organization, the quality of object relations, and the coherence of narcissistic structures. Some borderline patients, for example, show few of the signs of ego weakness, including splitting, which are so central to Kernberg's account. Ego weakness or primitive defensive organizations may not be at all operative in these patients, or they may find expression only in acute regressive crises (Meissner, 1980a). Yet these same patients may show clear borderline features in other aspects of their functioning. By the same token, some borderline patients show a significant degree of regressive potential with frequent episodes of acting out and even psychotic behavior, while others never show any signs of such regression.

These and other considerations have led me to suggest that within the spectrum of borderline disorders, the more primitive forms are characterized by ego deficits and a lack of self-cohesion, or at least a high degree of susceptibility of such structures to regressive pulls. The higher forms are characterized by the relative integrity of the ego and a relatively stable self-cohesion. In these higher forms, the pathology is more directly attributable to the organization of the introjects than to ego defects or ego weakness. In the more disorganized forms, the pathology may reflect additional ego deficits, or the ego deficits may be a result of the primitive organization or functioning of the introjects. Thus, some borderline conditions reflect the persistence of pathogenic introjects (and thus represent a pathology within the self-system), while other borderline conditions indicate a more severe pathology in the self in addition to pathology in the ego. The former patients often present as seemingly neurotic, even as candidates for analysis. They reveal the borderline organization of their personality only in certain regressive crises or in the analytic regression. As Zetzel (1971) has observed, these borderline patients are frequently only identifiable by careful attention to the quality of the patient's object relationship with the therapist. By way of contrast, the more dis-organized patients tend to present in acute regressive states, usually in a hospital or clinic setting. These patients are frequent-ly mistaken for psychotics, but again the response to treatment is diagnostic. With good therapeutic management, these patients are usually able to reverse the regressive decompensation and re-turn to more characteristic levels of functioning, even without the use of antipsychotic medications. The quality of the object rela-tion that emerges in therapy can be diagnostic for these patients as well. The borderline patient's world is characteristically struc-tured out of the continual interplay of introjection and projection. As we have already observed, the organization of these introjects is based on the transitional qualtity of object relations, and the polarities of these introjects tend to play themselves out in defen-sive ways. External objects may be idealized and seen as totally good, strong, and powerful. Such idealization of the therapist is a common experience in the therapy of borderline patients; it serves to provide the patient with an unrealistic powerful object to which he can attach himself as a protection against unneutralized and destructive aggressive threats. The opposite pole may find expression in the patient's sense of omnipotence and a devalua-tion of the object (Adler, 1970). In this regard, we frequently find a shift between an extremely demanding, dependent relation to an idealized, magical object and fantasies and behaviors that betray a feeling of the patient's own magical omnipotence. In the latter instance, the therapist is seen as weak and inadequate and is consequently devalued. This devaluation is partly a corollary of the patient's sense of omnipotence, but it may also serve as an ex-pression of the patient's disappointment at the therapist's frustra-tion of his powerful oral dependency needs, or it may even, especially in the terminal phase of treatment, serve as a denial of the patient's intense feelings of dependency and helplessness in the face of the loss of the object. A related, highly characteristic defense of the borderline patient is the tendency to use projection, usually in the development of dangerous retaliatory or persecutory objects against which the patient has to defend himself. The institution of such persecutory objects serves to rein-force and preserve the sense of victimization, which is bound into the elements of the introjective economy that escape projection.

Essentially the splitting mechanism reflects the patient's alternation between the polarized pathogenic introjects. The processes of introjection and projection revolve around these polarities. For example, patients may project their omnipotent and destructive impulses, creating persecutory and threatening objects which then tend to confirm and underline their sense of victimization. Correspondingly, patients may see important objects as potential victims and see themselves as powerfully destructive and possessing magical qualities, in this way preserving their sense of narcissistic omnipotence and specialness.

Thus the basic pathogenic structure of the borderline personality organization can be seen specifically in terms of the organization and interplay of pathogenic introjects, with the defensive mechanisms of projection and splitting preventing the further integration and synthesis of the introjective components. The essential note here is that the borderline patient's inner world is caught up in intense defensive needs and subject to intense drive pressures, corresponding to the organization of these introjects. The relative lack of secondary autonomy and consistency of the inner organization is reflected in the rapid alternation of affective states, object-related schemata, and susceptibility to transient regressive pulls of various kinds.

Kernberg (1976) has commented on the rapid mobilization of transference paradigms, the role of projections in borderline transferences and their relation to internalized object relations (introjections), the vulnerability of the therapeutic alliance, and the corresponding importance of countertransference dynamics in the treatment of such patients (1975b). These difficulties can be seen as a direct outcome of the introjective organization in these patients, and as a result of the importance of projective derivatives in shaping transference dynamics.

NARCISSISTIC PERSONALITY DISORDERS

The definition and formulation of the narcissistic personality disorders have become matters of some controversy, as well as the subject of intense psychoanalytic study. Kernberg (1970b) regards the narcissistic disorders as an intermediate area of character pathology distinct from the lower order of borderline disorders. Perhaps the most consistent attempt to delineate the psychopathology of the narcissistic personality disorders has been that of Heinz Kohut (1971). Kohut distinguishes the narcissistic disorders from the psychotic and borderline states, on the one hand, and from the more classical transference neuroses, on the other hand.

The differentiation of the narcissistic disorders from the lower levels of character pathology hinges on the tendency in the lower forms to a more or less chronic abandonment of cohesive narcissistic configurations and their replacement by delusional formations as a means of escaping inner fragmentation and the loss of archaic narcissistic objects. In contrast, the narcissistic disorders show only minor and transitory oscillations of the narcissistic configurations with occasional fragmentation and infrequent restitutive delusional formations. These patients are able to maintain a relatively stable grandiosity, which is quite distinct from the haughty and delusional grandeur of the psychotic. The healthy elaboration of narcissistically cathected objects, which are admired and idealized, tends to sustain these patients in the narcissistic transference, and the quality of projections differs considerably from the powerful destructiveness and persecutory quality of psychotic objects.

On the other side, in neurotic patients the pathology is not located primarily in either the self or its narcissistic objects, but rather concerns structural conflicts over libidinal and aggressive strivings. These conflicts take place in the context of a more or less cohesive self and have to do with objects that have become more or less adequately differentiated from the self. The essential psychopathology of the narcissistic personality, however, concerns the self and its archaic narcissistic objects. These narcissistic configurations may be insufficiently cathected and thus susceptible to temporary fragmentation and regression, or, if they are sufficiently cohesive, they remain unintegrated with the rest of the personality structure, so that other aspects of the emerging personality organization are deprived of reliable and more mature narcissistic investments. The difference in the pathological organization of the narcissistic disorders and the transference neuroses is a direct reflection of the cathexis of selfobjects with archaic narcissistic libido in one instance and the cathexis of separate objects with object libido in the other.

In the transference neuroses, the ego is threatened by the breakthrough of forbidden object-instinctual impulses. This danger is usually translated into terms of threats of physical punishment or emotional abandonment. In the narcissistic disorders, however, the anxiety relates primarily to the vulnerability of the self and the dangers it faces from either temporary disorganization or the intrusion of archaic forms of grandiosity or aggrandized selfobjects. The principal discomfort is related to the inability to regulate self-esteem and maintain it at minimal levels. Thus the narcissistic personality tends to experience embarrassment, self-consciousness, shame, hypochondria, and depression rather than the more neurotic aspects of guilt or anxiety. In this respect, the order of threat and anxiety in the therapy of narcissistic patients is somewhat the reverse of that in the transference neuroses. In the narcissistic disorders, the fear of the loss of the object or the loss of the object's love seems to predominate over issues of punishment and castration anxiety. The situation is more or less the reverse in the transference neuroses, where castration anxiety tends to be more prominent than the underlying fear of loss of love or fear of the loss of the object.

Kohut (1971) delineates the essential narcissistic configuration in the narcissistic personality disorders as the "grandiose self" and the "idealized parent imago." He writes: "The equilibrium of primary narcissism is disturbed by the unavoidable shortcomings of maternal care, but the child replaces the previous perfection (a) by establishing a grandiose and exhibitionistic image of the self: *the grandiose self*; and (b) by giving over the previous perfection to an admired, omnipotent (transitional) self-object: *the idealized parent imago*" (p. 25).

To link Kohut's formulations to our previous discussion of the organization of introjects, several comments are in order. First of all, Kohut speaks of the economy of selfobjects, that is, objects cathected with narcissistic libido and thus experienced as not altogether separate from the self. We have noted the transitional character of object relations involved in the organization of introjective configurations and how they depend on the interplay of introjective and projective operations for their integration. These object relations comprise both subjective and objective components, derived from the self and from the object, and hence would seem to be equivalent to Kohut's self-

objects. It must be remembered, however, that Kohut's formulations are focused expressly and almost exclusively on the
narcissistic dimensions of structural organization so that other
components take a secondary role.

Kohut's concept of the grandiose self expresses the narcissistic
dimension of the subject's inner world. The correlative cathexis
of the object with narcissistic libido constitutes the idealized
parent imago, which can be seen as expressing the narcissistic
dimensions of the projected aspects of the transitional object
relationship. Thus the relationship of grandiose self to idealized
parent imago is apparently another way of describing the interplay of introjective and projective elements with specific
regard to the economics of archaic narcissistic cathexes (Giovacchini, 1975).

The relevance of these formulations for the analytic situation
and the analytic process is stated with some precision in the
following terms:

> In the narcissistic personality disorders...the therapeutic activa-
> tion of the specific, psychologically elaborated, cohesive nar-
> cissistic configurations becomes the very center of the analytic
> process. The narcissistic "object" (the idealized parent imago) and
> the narcissistic "subject" (the grandiose self) are comparatively
> stable configurations, cathected with narcissistic libido (idealizing
> libido; grandiose-exhibitionistic libido), which enter into com-
> paratively stable amalgamations with the (narcissistically per-
> ceived) psychic representation of the analyst. A degree of cathectic
> constancy toward an object is thus attained...albeit that of a nar-
> cissistically cathected one. The relative stability of this narcissistic
> transference amalgamation, however, is the prerequisite for the
> performance of the analytic task (the systematic process of work-
> ing through) in the pathogenic narcissistic areas of the personality
> [Kohut, 1971, p. 32].

It should be noted that these stable narcissistic configurations,
around which the cohesiveness of the self is organized, can be
conceptualized as narcissistic introjective configurations.

The further implications of Kohut's formulations for the
analytic process are matters of considerable interest and current
controversy. Kohut seems to imply that the major contribution of the analyst lies in recognizing these archaic nar-

cissistic formations and in being able to tolerate, without reacting to or interpreting, the patient's narcissism. He envisions the
quasi-independent metamorphosis of the patient's pathogenic
narcissism in the direction of a more modulated and better integrated narcissism.

The establishing of the narcissistic transference achieves an
activation of the grandiose self and facilitates the arrested
growth process, leading to the internalization of the ideal self-
object and the move from a more primitive narcissistic fixation
toward a more mature integration of narcissistic libido. The
danger, in Kohut's view, is that the analyst's own unresolved
narcissistic conflicts may get in the way of the patient's idealizing of the analyst and thus inhibit the gradual process of
modulating the patient's pathogenic narcissism.

The issues here are indeed complex and do not readily yield
to resolution. Kohut's attempts to focus the narcissistic issues in
a more or less isolated and somewhat independent fashion have
met with strenuous objections. Kernberg (1974), for one, has
argued that the dynamics of narcissism, whether normal or
pathological, cannot be considered independently of either the
vicissitudes of libidinal and aggressive drive derivatives or the
organization of structural components, particularly those derived from internalized object relations. In terms of our discussion of the role of the introjects, it must be remembered that the
problem of pathogenic narcissism is not restricted to the narcissistic personality disorders, even if Kohut's delineation of
these disorders can be clinically substantiated and validated.
The introjects themselves are essentially the reservoir of narcissistic investment and reflect the vicissitudes of both
pathogenic and healthier narcissism.

It is difficult to escape the impression that the controversy
over the treatment of narcissistic disorders may be running
afoul of differences in the narcissistic organization at various
levels of psychopathology. On the basis of my own clinical experience, it seems clear that multiple issues involving the
dynamics and functioning of the introjective configurations, including their inherent narcissistic grandiosity and correlative
vulnerability, must be worked through to an adequate point
before the stance Kohut emphasizes can become an operative

part of the therapeutic process. It may be, however, as Ornstein (1974) has suggested, that Kernberg's clinical base consists of a generally lower order of pathological functioning, in which the issues of primitive aggression and other pathogenic aspects of structural integration and defensive alignment play a significant role. In contrast, Kohut's clinical base may encompass a somewhat higher level of psychopathology in which those concerns are of less moment and the emergence of the types of narcissistic transferences he describes is more readily validated. Another factor in the differing approaches to these disorders may stem from the analytic styles and orientations of the respective theorists.

The point to be emphasized here is that the organization of narcissistic personality disorders can be conceptualized adequately in terms of the organization of introjects and their correlative projections and that these play a significant role in the structuring of the analytic situation. In these terms, Kohut's emphasis on the activation of the grandiose self and the idealized parent imago as aspects of the introjective organization within the analytic situation is central.

PARANOID AND SCHIZOID PERSONALITY DISORDERS

Although the paranoid and schizoid characters also lie at the lower level spectrum of character psychopathology (Kernberg, 1970b), their distinction from each other and from more severe forms of narcissistic disorder or even borderline personality organization is often clinically difficult. Both paranoid and schizoid manifestations are frequently found in these other forms of character pathology. Our intention here, however, is to focus on the specific contribution of introjective internalizations.

In the paranoid character, the habitual use of projection as a defensive channel dominates the pathological organization. If we keep in mind the correlative interaction between projective mechanisms and the underlying introjective organization, we can appreciate the central role of the introjects in the organization of the paranoid patient's inner world and their critical part in motivating the defensive projections. Although the projective aspects of the pathology are more readily observable, it is important not to lose sight of the underlying introjective alignments (Meissner, 1974a, 1978b).

The line between the schizoid and paranoid defensive positions is very fine. We should remind ourselves here of Melanie Klein's paranoid-schizoid position (Segal, 1964) and its connection with introjective and projective mechanisms. Guntrip (1969) attempts in part to separate the components of the paranoid-schizoid position. He regards the schizoid position as a deeper level of pathology than either the depressive or paranoid positions, representing a state in which the infantile ego has withdrawn more or less completely from object relations and seeks safety away from the anxieties of persecution or guilt. He comments:

> The paranoid individual faces physical persecution (as in dreams of being attacked by murderous figures) and the depressed individual faces moral persecution (as, for example, in feeling surrounded by accusing eyes and pointing fingers), so that Klein regards both positions as setting up a primary form of anxiety. In fact, most individuals prefer to face either depressive anxiety (guilt) or persecutory anxiety (amoral fear), or an oscillation between them, rather than face the extreme schizoid loss of everything, both objects and ego. *Both persecutory anxiety and depressive anxiety are object-relations experiences while the schizoid position cancels object-relations in the attempt to escape from anxiety of all kinds* [p. 57].

But if the schizoid withdrawal is a withdrawal from external object relations, it must also be said that it is not a withdrawal from internal object relations. The schizoid patient in fact retreats to a world of "internal objects," the equivalent of the introjects we have been discussing here. Object involvement involves risks on all sides: the lack of objects involves a fear of ego loss by depersonalization, bad objects entail the fear of ego loss from destructive persecution, and good objects involve the fear of ego loss by engulfment in smothering passivity. Guntrip observes:

> Once the fear-dictated retreat from outer reality has been set up, the schizoid individual had two opposed needs both of which must be met unless death is to supervene: *the need to withdraw from in-*

tolerable reality and the need to remain in touch with it, to save the ego in both cases. This is what enforces the final ego-split into an active suffering and a passive regressed libidinal ego. The flight into regression begets a counter-flight back into object-relations again. But this return to objects must still compromise with fear and the need to remain withdrawn. This leads to the creation of an object-world that enables the ego to be both withdrawn, yet not 'in the womb', the Kleinian world of 'internal objects', dream and fantasy, *a world of object-relationships which is also withdrawn 'inside' out of the external world* [p. 82].

It becomes clear that the schizoid personality disorder is not a pathology without objects, but rather a pathology centering on internal objects and their introjective and projective vicissitudes. In this sense, the exquisite vulnerability of the schizoid personality must be seen as an inherent dimension of the pathological configuration of the introjects.

NEUROTIC CHARACTER DISORDERS

As we move to the higher-order integration of the neurotic character disorders and transference neuroses, the overtly dramatic presentation of the introjects tends to become considerably modified. Here the introjects are much more differentiated, much more highly integrated, and considerably less susceptible to regressive pulls or the influence of drive derivatives. In these patients the character structure is not as pervasively dominated by the introjective vicissitudes, so that the capacities for conflict-free and relatively autonomous functioning are significantly increased. Moreover, in patients at this level of personality disorganization the capacity for adaptive and relatively autonomous identification is much more available. It is at this level of pathology that the analytic process is most decisively successful.

Even though the introjective components are neither as flagrant nor as dramatic as those we have discussed, they nonetheless play themselves out in significant ways. Certainly this is clear in depressive or masochistic personalities, where the patient's self-image is largely organized around the depressive introject, which sees the self as inferior, inadequate, worthless, or undeserving. Although this pattern of introjective economy is also seen in more primitive forms of personality organization, here the opposite pole of the introjective components is embedded in an internal organization, namely the superego, which is seen to be punitive, destructive, and undermining. It is important to note, however, that the introjective organization in these cases embraces not only the superego, but other aspects of the organization of the self as well. Nor is the tendency to internalize absolute by any means; in cases of depressive or masochistic pathology we may find externalizing distortions that reinforce the patient's position of victimization and degraded self-esteem. Unlike paranoid distortions, these usually take the form of mobilizing elements in reality to bring about a self-devaluing or self-defeating outcome for the patient. Thus the masochistic wife will find a sadistic and demeaning husband, with whom she can carry out her masochistic pattern of behavior. The issue is not so much projective distortion as the externalization of an inner masochistic conflict.

An important consideration in the evaluation and treatment of hysterical character disorders is the extent to which the hysterical configuration is serving as a defense against underlying depressive issues. The more the depressive issues dominate the clinical picture, the more such hysterical patients tend to reflect a primitive level of personality organization, verging on narcissistic or even borderline levels (Zetzel, 1968). In these lower-level cases, even where hysterical symptoms predominate in the clinical picture, the introjective vicissitudes constitute a key aspect of the patient's inner dynamics. These introjective dynamics have implications for the analyzability of hysterical patients, since if the introjective vicissitudes inhibit the freeing up of ego capacities for the work of analysis, the prognosis is not optimistic. But even in more specifically neurotic hysterical disorders, we are postulating here that the introjective organization is an aspect of the patient's inner integration. The neurotic hysteric has presumably reached a level of oedipal involvement and triangular conflict, so that the internalizations and specifically introjections operate at a more differentiated level having to do with superego formation and integration. In consequence, the patient's capacity to use more advanced forms of defense, such as repression, and the ability to maintain the distinction between fantasy components (derived from the inner world structured around the introjects) and reality components (which correspond to more autonomous and unconflicted levels of functioning) are important aspects of the personality organization.

In the hysteric the dysfunction related to the disorganization of drive components and drive derivatives is focused in and expressed through the introjective organization. Compared with the previously discussed character pathologies, hysterical patients have greater areas of differentiated ego structure and autonomous ego functioning, which allow them to use more effective defensive structures in dealing with drive derivatives and achieving higher levels of adaptation. The introjects are integrated in a way that promotes greater resistance to regressive pulls and greater autonomy from drive influences. In this frame of reference, then, drive derivatives are not seen as unorganized disruptions of instinctual impulses breaking through repressive barriers, but rather as specific forms of integrated functions built into and expressing themselves through the structure of the introjects. The ego's defensive maneuvers are directed toward and deal with the introjective configuration, which serves as the inner organizing source and reference point for the patient's pathology.

A similar statement can be made about forms of obsessional neurosis. Obsessional symptomatology also expresses itself at various levels of character organization, with the more severe cases tending in the direction of paranoid or schizoid levels of personality organization. But even at higher levels of obsessional personality organization, the obsessional defenses are linked to introjective components that usually involve an inner sense of magical power and destructiveness, which reflects the potency and pathogenicity of the introjects. The obsessional's rigidity and the hyperstructuralization of the defensive organization are directed against the disruptive and pathogenic expressions of introjective components. Frequently the superego restraints and prohibitions can be traced relatively directly to the significant objects in the patient's developmental history. At this level the introjective components are usually concentrated in a relatively well differentiated superego, but again we must remind ourselves that the introjective components are not limited to superego pathology. Not infrequently, such superego components will be externalized and projected onto external objects, and this is a frequent aspect of the therapeutic interchange in analysis. We shall have more to say about these processes in the ensuing discussion of the contribution of introjective components to the structure of the analytic situation.

The Role of Introjection and Projection in the Psychoanalytic Situation

There can be little question that introjection and projection play a significant role in the psychoanalytic situation. Here I should repeat that by the psychoanalytic situation, I mean the setting or the structural matrix within which the psychoanalytic process takes place. Stone's (1961) conception of the analytic situation "includes the common and constant features of the analytic setting, procedures, and personal relationship, in both conscious and unconscious meanings and functions. The view ranges from the integrated reality situation and its clinical purposes, to the essentially biologic elements, which give the situation its unique power. . . . principally, the complex dynamic relationship between analyst and patient" (p. 9).

As we noted earlier, Stone's emphasis on the personal relationship between the analyst and the patient is reinforced by Greenson's (1967) concept of the working alliance and by Zetzel's (1970) formulations regarding the therapeutic alliance. While later treatments have tended to focus exclusively on the doctor-patient or analyst-analysand relationship, and specifically on the therapeutic alliance, there is a great deal more to be said about the analytic situation. Still, the analytic relationship remains in the center of focus as the primary and essential structuralizing element of the analytic situation.

In general terms, the analytic situation implies the shifting configuration of factors that provides the ongoing context within which the analytic process works itself out. In this sense, the analytic situation obtains from the very beginning of the contact between the analyst and the analysand and can be envisioned to last as long as there is any meaningful contact between them — even if that contact extends beyond the designated termination of the analysis. But the analytic situation can also be defined in a more paradigmatic and specific way to articulate those characteristics which are typical of the analytic setting and which characterize the analytic process in all of its phases, but which may be operative to greater or lesser degrees as the analytic process moves along.

In its paradigmatic and descriptive sense, the analytic situation involves the following factors, which contribute to the structuring of the therapeutic matrix in varying degrees. These contributing factors can be arranged in an order of increasing significance and centrality. To begin with, the analytic encounter takes place in a quiet and undisturbed setting at regularly scheduled hours of predetermined and unvarying duration and with sufficient regularity to ensure the intensification of the emotional responsiveness between the patient and the analyst. The organization of these details of meeting and the structuring of the physical setting of the analytic context, including the establishing of a fee and its payment, place the analysand in a position of dependence and set the stage for the emergence of emotional attachments and transference phenomena.

Moreover, the patient reclines on a couch in a position of relaxed concentration. The analyst sits outside the patient's line of vision and remains relatively silent and unobtrusive. This allows for the free play of the patient's mental processes and prevents the continual input of stimulus patterns and metacommunications from the therapist that inheres in the face-to-face sitting-up situation, where the patient is constantly presented with the therapist and his reactive behavior to the patient's productions. These situational elements contribute meaningfully to the induction of the analytic regression. Further, the patient is asked to free-associate. The attempt to free-associate, that is, to abstain from the inhibiting and focusing devices so characteristic of secondary-process thinking, serves to increase the tendency to regression and the production of primary-process material from earlier developmental strata in the patient's experience.

As we have already stated, the most important and determining aspects of the analytic situation involve the interpersonal relationship between the analyst and the analysand. From one side, the analytic relationship is affected by transference phenomena which derive from early, usually infantile levels of the patient's experience. The displacement of these patterns of affective responsiveness and reaction, which were originally experienced in relation to significant childhood figures, has a significant role in the shaping of the analysand's relationship to the analyst. It should be noted that such transference elements begin to play themselves out from the very start of the relationship to the analyst, but that their significance and intensity can be expected to increase *pari passu* as the analytic process develops and in relation to the degree of analytic regression (by which earlier strata of the patient's experience become more available).

The degree and intensity of the transference displacements can vary across an extremely broad continuum. At relatively minimal levels, transference elements may function only as generalized aspects of the patient's prior experience. At more intense levels of involvement, however, transference phenomena can be understood in terms of directly specifiable aspects of the analysand's relationship with significant objects — usually the parental objects, but not exclusively so. Often enough, transference determinants are available from siblings and from other significant family figures. To some extent, these determinants may operate independently of displacements from parental objects, but frequently enough they are amalgamated with the determinants deriving from parental figures.

The evolution of such transference influences is generally accepted as the basic mechanism for the development of the transference neurosis. This mechanism, however, is usually restricted to the displacement of elements of the object representation of the transference figures, primarily parental objects, to the object representation of the analyst. I would like to suggest something different. I would like to suggest that the full flowering of the transference neurosis depends not simply on displacements from parental object representations, but involves projections derived from the patient's own introjects.

The distinction I am suggesting has a history. In his review of the notions of transference and countertransference, Orr (1954) differentiates the view of transference held by what he calls the Vienna school from that held by the English school.

> The nature of transference phenomena will be differently described by those who hold that superego formation is a product of the resolution of the oedipal conflicts, on the one hand, or, on the other, by those who date the origins of the superego back to the projective and introjective struggles with oral-sadistic tendencies. Thus, the projection of the archaic superego or, for example, of imagos of the "good" or the "bad" mother will characterize the transference for one group, while the displacement of affects related to the loved or dreaded parents in the oedipal phase will govern the transference as viewed by the other [p. 629].

Here the distinction between transference by displacement of object-libidinal or aggressive drives and transference by projection is clearly drawn—but it is drawn in the context of the contest with the Kleinian view of early development, particularly with regard to the superego (Zetzel, 1956). This argument flourished in a theoretical climate in which there was little room for anything other than superego projection and in which little cognizance was taken of superego precursors or of preoedipal structural developments. It should be obvious that on both counts the theoretical posture of analysis has moved well beyond these historical restraints.

However, if we look at the implications of Orr's distinction for our current understanding of transference, there is an implicit link between displacement transference and oedipal dynamics on the one hand, and between projective transference and preoedipal dynamics on the other. That this implied division has persisted in analytic thinking is borne out by a recent explanation of the "externalizing transference":

> In classical transference (Moore and Fine, 1967) in terms of what is transferred, the emphasis is upon the displacement to the analyst of infantile aims towards infantile objects. The conflict reissued in the transference is between wishes towards and fears of the analyst. In the externalizing transference the emphasis is upon allocation of internal structures and their antecedent archaic self and object representations to the analyst. The conflict reissued in

the transference is between and within psychic structures and antecedent self-object representations. These elements are at bottom ambivalently held as contradictory opposites. This is not to say that in classical transference there is not an externalization of object imagos (Nunberg, 1951; Zetzel, 1956) nor that in the externalizing transference there is not a displacement of infantile object libido on to the analyst but, rather, that the emphasis is decisive for the development of the two contrasting types of transference. It would appear that as transference becomes rather more an occasion for the revival of narcissistic pre-oedipal, pregenital and prestructural elements and rather less an object-libidinal oedipal, genital and structural matter, the 'externalizing' rather than so-to-speak a 'displacing' transference takes place. Furthermore, in the classical transference, displacement is the complement to repression whilst in the externalizing transference, allocation of aspects of the self to the outside world is the complement to splitting of the ego and the process of defence [Berg, 1977, p. 235].

Although we can accept these descriptions as valid types of transference, the implication that each form is tied to a given school of analysis or to a specific level of pathology is strongly to be repudiated. As we have previously observed, more primitive forms of character pathology, particularly the borderline conditions, are often found to mobilize introjective residues in the form of transference paradigms — a point clearly made by Kernberg (1976). This process is undoubtedly related to a tendency toward splitting in the borderline personality organization, but this does not mean that borderline patients do not manifest displacement forms of transference. Nor does it mean that splitting does not occur to some degree in neurotic patients — I would in fact suggest that it occurs regularly in most, if not all, neurotic patients. In any case, whether projection is related to splitting or not — and it is obviously my view that it is often not related to any identifiable splitting — neurotic transferences in most instances in my experience come to express projective elements.

We thus have at least two transference models to work with — two models that may be mixed in varying degrees in all of our patients, with the degree and the manner of mixing being distinctly characteristic for each patient. The point that I would like to urge is that in trying to understand the transference dynamics, we choose whichever model best fits the available evidence. Many transference manifestations work on a displacement model. An attempt to describe or understand these in projective terms does not serve the analytic effort well, and only confuses matters—both theoretically and in the work of the analysis. However, where the evidence clearly points in the direction of the projective model, it does not serve the analytic process or its understanding to try to force the data into a displacement paradigm. To do so is to omit and ignore important aspects of the patient's inner life and psychodynamics. The analyst should make no presumptions about the structure of the transference phenomenon being dealt with. He should wait for the clear evidence that transference elements are connected with aspects of the patient's own inner structure—in terms of the present account, with aspects of the introjective configuration which provides the basis for the patient's sense of self.

Nonetheless it is my persuasion that in the full expression and emergence of the transference neurosis, the projective elements come to dominate the transference experience. Moreover, it is important and useful that they do so. In this connection, a recent discussion of the dynamics of a homosexual patient by Aarons (1975) is of note:

> It was not enough for me to know and interpret to the patient that I was the object of his homosexual strivings; he had to know and feel this himself for the transference to become effective. This is a case in which there was a transference of the feelings and general reactions of the patient without a projection of the image of the original object of those feelings on to the analyst (which I would call 'projective object specification' in the transference). In other words, it is not sufficient to show the patient that he behaves and feels towards the analyst as he did toward his parent. It is necessary for the patient to 'see' the analyst as a parent. In addition to a displacement there must be a projection [pp. 314–315].

In our discussion of the theory of introjection and projection, we noted that projections serve as derivatives and correlative expressions of the underlying organization of the introjects. In this sense, the transference neurosis involves not only displacements from object representations of the parents, but more specifically a projection of specific elements from the patient's own self-representation to the object representation of the analyst. There is little doubt that in the complex phenomenon of transference not only generalizations from previous object-related experience and displacements from previous object relations, but also specific projections from introjective configurations play themselves out in intricate interaction. The relative role of these various object-derived influences may vary from patient to patient and from one phase to another in the evolution of the transference.

In the view taken here, generalizations from previous object experience are the common stuff of familiar, everyday transference reactions — the sort that take place in many contexts of human intercourse in addition to the analytic situation. Object displacements may figure to a considerable extent in the ongoing experience of objects, but their role tends to be more restricted than that of more specifically cognitive generalizations, as they usually require a prolonged and emotionally involving interaction with the object of displacement. In the analytic setting, such displacements are easily and frequently observed, even in early stages of the analysis. The emergence of specific projections, however, requires the regressive reactivation of developmentally derived introjective configurations. This comes about only as the result of relatively significant regression, which may be operative in certain restricted regression-inducing contexts of the patient's everyday life, but is presumably exceptional and infrequent. The susceptibility to regression, however, does play an important role in this regard, since pathogenic introjective configurations can be quite easily reactivated in primitively organized borderline personalities as well as in psychotics. In relatively well organized forms of character pathology and neuroses, however, this reactivation is relatively less frequent and is generally induced only after considerable analytic regression.

It is impossible to state categorically that the transference neurosis always depends on projective elements, since the evidence for the derivation of such projections from the underlying introjects is not always clear. I am suggesting, however, that projective elements are characteristic of the full-blown transference neurosis, and that a fully emerged transference neurosis has not developed until such projective elements can be identified. Such a demonstration is complicated by the fact that the analysand's introjective organization derives developmentally from the internalization of object relations and most powerfully and most convincingly, of course, from the parental objects.

I am belaboring this point because I am convinced that it has important implications for our understanding of the role of internalizations and how they are modified in the analytic process. The objection might be raised, in fact has been raised, that the argument becomes circular insofar as the introjects are derived from specific object relations and these same object imagoes are reexternalized in the transference through projection. In other words, we are talking about the same thing as a displacement from the object imago, and there is no need for the complication of the introjective intermediary.

But this objection misses a vital point in our preceding discussion. Introjection is not simply an internal copying of some qualities of an object. To think of it in these terms makes the process reductively mechanical and deprives it of all the complex motivational components that underlie development and personality formation. Internalizations are complex human actions embedded in motivational fields that derive from and reflect the quality of object relations and their complex interactions. What is internalized reflects the quality of the interaction; in other words, it is not merely dependent on the object, in isolation from the interaction. It also reflects internal motivational influences (including but not exclusively reduced to drive determinants). These influences not only give rise to the internalization and sustain it, but also qualify the content and character of the introjective configuration itself. Consequently, what is reexternalized by projection is not only derived from the object imago, but also reflects the outcome of the interplay of these various factors — as well as the qualifying effects stemming from the immediate motivations tied up in the reactivation of these introjective configurations in the context of the analytic situation and in relation to the particular analyst. All of this is a highly motivated, dynamic process which cannot be reduced to merely mechanical terms.

The point of my argument here is that the unique quality of psychoanalysis as a therapeutic modality is its capacity to activate and revitalize the pathogenic introjects and to bring them to life once again through the mechanism of projection, by which the transference neurosis is constituted and vitalized. Bychowski (1956) has referred to the "release of introjects." He comments: "It is to be expected that the psycho-analytic process leading to profound changes in the psychic structure, and consequently to interdependent shifting of cathexis and countercathexis, will provide the best field of observation for the release of introjects" (p. 336). I would suggest further that the therapeutic impact of the transference neurosis, the major tool of psychoanalytic treatment, lies precisely in its regressively reactivating the patient's object involvement in the developmental context, the internalization of which is embedded in the structure of the patient's introjects and which must be creatively reworked in order for these pathogenic introjects to be productively modified. From this perspective, then, the working through of the transference neurosis is accomplishing something quite distinct from a mere reworking or modification of object representations; it is in effect undertaking a more meaningful and searching reorganization and re-creation of the patient's own self.

We should remind ourselves at this juncture that the fabrication of the transference neurosis re-creates in a sense a developmental situation that was itself structured by the complex interweaving and interplay of introjections and projections. In this sense, the oedipal situation is not merely a given matrix, out of which significant internalizations occur as the vehicle of dissolution, but is itself the product of the constructive and creative capacities exercised on the growing child's part through the interplay of such mechanisms (Meissner, 1978b). It should also be noted that that developmental context is not merely elaborated out of the infant's own introjective and projective contents, but is played into and responded to by the interweaving of projections and introjections from the parental figures, as well as by the emotional matrix of their interaction both with each other and with the child. The interweaving of these introjective and projective processes also occurs at earlier, pregenital levels of the child's developmental experience. The reactivating of these processes in the analytic regression essentially serves as a substitute model of a prior developmental matrix, within which these processes played themselves out and in terms of which they made their contributions to the patient's personality integration. In these terms, the interplay of introjection and projection expresses inner dynamic mechanisms similar to what Mahler (1968) has otherwise articulated in terms of the separation-individuation process.

This introjective aspect of the transference neurosis has been addressed by Schafer (1968a):

> One cannot categorically assert that all of the object representations involved in transference are introjects or other presences. Yet, in many instances of significant transference reactions, the analyst can hardly avoid recognizing that considerable feeling had remained bound up with the differentiated image of a presence, and that this image is being experienced by the patient as exercising influence on him. A usual step in the analysis of these transference reactions is to recognize that something in the patient seems to act on him in the way he first maintained the analyst was acting on him, or that he is attempting to act on something internal and is doing so by projecting that something onto the analyst. In this attempt by the patient, the presence is serving as a net to catch suitable current objects — in this case, the analyst — to be used for externalization or actualization [p. 133].

If we remind ourselves of Schafer's view of introjects as "primary-process presences," the relevance of the introjective dynamics to the structuring of the transference neurosis is all the more apparent.

The introjects can be activated by way of externalization, or more specifically projection, as Schafer suggests, but activation can also take place by way of a more subjective and internalized revivification of the introjects themselves. However one envisions the transference distortion, whether in terms of specific projections or of displacements of object representations, the introject as an inner possession of the self becomes revitalized in the transference neurosis, so that the patient becomes subjectively more aware of his own self-image in terms of the regressive dictates of the transference neurosis. Here we are suggesting that the reactivation of these introjects is not only contributed to by the projection, which effectively distorts the relation to the analyst-object, but itself feeds the intensity and vitality of this projection. Thus the full-blown transference neurosis reflects the reactivation in the present of interlocking introjections and projections and translates the vicissitudes of an earlier developmental matrix.[2]

Another important consideration is that the revitalized developmental matrix is contributed to on both sides by the respective participants. In the oedipal situation, it is not only the child who projects and introjects, thus contributing to the structuring of the triadic involvement with the two parental figures, but both parents are also actively engaged in contributing significant projections not only onto each other but onto the child as well. In the neurotic resolution of such interactions, and more dramatically and poignantly in even more primitive developmental resolutions, the child's introjections are powerfully and pathogenically influenced by the parental projections.

Within the analytic setting, similar mechanisms can be brought into play. The regressive induction and activation of the pathogenic introjects in the patient may be paralleled by the elicitation of more or less correlative projections from the analyst. Thus the patterning of introjections and projections between the analyst and the patient can provide the unconscious emotional matrix out of which the transference neurosis is articulated. In this sense, the interweaving of transference and countertransference elements takes place to a greater or less extent in the evolution of every transference neurosis. It is part of the analyst's therapeutic endeavor to tune in on and modulate his own projective responses in such a way that they do not play into and reinforce the patient's introjective constellation. In this way, the analyst not only undermines the patient's introjective organization by depriving it of essential projective supports, but also provides the patient with a correlative developmental matrix within which the working through of the pathogenic introjects can begin to take place.

[2] It should be emphasized that the purpose of these formulations is to relate frequently observed and common analytic experiences to the organization and functioning of internalizations. Thus, although regression and the revival of the infantile neurosis have been formulated quite successfully in a variety of theoretical terms, they require specific explications here in terms of internalization. The perspective provided by internalization as a theoretical frame of reference is like an additional lens or filter to be added to other more familiar ones, each of which enables us to clarify different aspects and contributing elements of the analytic process.

It is specifically within this context that countertransference issues and deviations in analytic techniques have their most telling impact. The introduction of certain parameters (Eissler, 1953, 1958) may be indicated in order to maintain the analytic situation, overcome disruptive resistances, or establish or reinforce the therapeutic alliance. However, behind such deviations in technique stalks the shadow of countertransference distortions — whether the deviant intervention is appropriate and therapeutically indicated or not. Although this intervention may promote gains at one level, it may also elicit and reinforce the pathogenic projective-introjective interchange at other, less conscious levels. This possibility may only reveal itself in aspects of the analysis at considerable remove from the immediate context of intervention, but it must be anticipated nonetheless. Correctness of technique serves as a safeguard for preserving the area of therapeutic interaction. In any case, the need for the analyst to be reflectively aware of these currents of introjection and projection as they affect him and play into the analytic interaction cannot be underestimated (Langs, 1975b).

We can see that the relationship of the analytic situation to the activation of pathogenic introjects is extremely close. Not only does the psychoanalytic situation induce the activation and revitalization of pathogenic introjects, but their intrusion into the analytic context provides the important structuring influence out of which the transference neurosis evolves. But the effects of the introjects do not exhaust the significance of internalization processes in the structuring of the analytic situation.

IDENTIFICATION

Since identifications are less caught up in defensive vicissitudes than introjections and function on a more or less autonomous level of integrated ego functioning, they do not serve so much to structure the analytic situation directly as to underlie and qualify the ego's capacity to involve itself productively and constructively in the analytic process. What is at issue is the implementation and facilitation of the patient's capacity for identification.

Identifications give rise to the secondary autonomous structures of the ego and superego that enable the patient to relate to the analyst as a real and separate object (Meissner, 1979a). Identification is the developmental process by which a sufficiently differentiated and integrated ego structure has been established, allowing the patient to relate to the analyst in a meaningful and productive way, to tolerate the anxiety provoked by the analytic regression, and to engage in a meaningful alliance with the analyst in undertaking the analytic work.

These capacities are particularly focused in the therapeutic alliance (Zetzel, 1970). It is specifically the strength inherent in the therapeutic alliance that enables the patient to tolerate the regressive reactivation of the pathogenic introjects along with the painful conflicts and drive derivatives associated with these pathogenic introjects. And identifications provide the base on which the therapeutic alliance is erected.

One of the objectives of the analytic process is the gradual enlargement of the patient's capacity for identification, specifically with the analyst, but not necessarily exclusively so. This elaboration of the therapeutic alliance stands outside the matrix of introjective and projective interplay that underlies the transference neurosis. In fact, in some sense, the therapeutic alliance and the transference neurosis stand in opposition. As the transference neurosis begins to intensify and flourish, the therapeutic alliance is placed under considerable stress. An important aspect of the analysis is the continual reinforcement and preservation of a meaningful alliance in the face of regressive vicissitudes.

In thinking about the interweaving roles of the therapeutic alliance and the transference neurosis, we need to remind ourselves that introjective and identificatory processes play themselves out at all levels of the child's developmental experience. The nature and quality of these processes vary at different levels of developmental organization, but the two processes continue to interact in complex ways. In general, as the child develops, the defensive need to resolve intolerable ambivalences drives the patterns of internalization in the direction of introjection rather than identification (Meissner, 1974b). But this does not mean that these processes occur in an either-or fashion or that defensively motivated introjections are not concurrently shadowed by meaningful identifications. Identifications may arise not only through a reprocessing of introjective contents — identification with the introject — but may also operate more directly in relation to evolving object representations. In some sense, the ego's capacity for internalizing significant early developmental experiences, such as those related to basic trust, must involve certain global and rudimentary patterns of identification which are difficult to specify.

If this is the case, we can infer that the identificatory elements that provide the substructure for the therapeutic alliance derive from all levels of the patient's developmental experience. The therapeutic alliance is consequently neither a simple nor a univocal aspect of the psychoanalytic situation. Rather, its quality and its basis differ for every patient and must be regarded as varying, depending on the phase of the analysis and on the level of regressive reactivation experienced by the patient. The patient's experience of a trusting relationship and the quality of the identifications associated with it are considerably different at early developmental strata, when the first rudiments of trust are being elaborated, than at much later developmental strata, when more complex, derivative issues of trust are being elaborated and worked through. Here I do not mean to suggest that trust alone is the dimension on which the therapeutic alliance rests. Certainly there are other significant dimensions, such as issues of autonomy and initiative.

It is interesting in this regard that the Eriksonian epigenetic schema provides a reasonably ready vocabulary with which to address the issues embedded in the therapeutic alliance, but again this does not mean that these are the only issues involved. For instance, issues of narcissism and the capacity for non-pathogenic narcissistic investment in the self (self-esteem) play a major role and bring up as yet unresolved questions. What can be said here, however, is that the analytic effort moves in the direction of reopening developmental crises in such a way that the introjective resolution is reactivated and made available for a reworking in which the therapeutic resolution will shift from an introjective mode toward a more specifically identificatory one. As this process takes place, the nature of the therapeutic alliance is modified and undergoes highly specific vicissitudes of its own. These modifications occur independently, but not separately from the working through of the vicissitudes of the transference neurosis. Thus, the structuring of the analytic situation is a composite of the interlocking components of both the therapeutic alliance and the transference neurosis.

In her attempt to analyze the therapeutic alliance, Zetzel (1970) focused on the one-to-one relationship in the child's early environment, particularly the mother-child relationship, as the essential place where the capacity for alliance was rooted. To see the therapeutic alliance simply in these terms, however, makes it a unitary capacity, which is more or less limited to the patient's capacity to trust the analyst. But the therapeutic alliance is considerably more complex. While it is certainly accurate enough to point to the one-to-one context within which the alliance operates, that should not limit one's perspective in understanding the therapeutic alliance. A variety of developmental attainments may play into the therapeutic alliance and qualify the patient's capacity to relate to the real person of the therapist. These factors stem not only from the early one-to-one maternal involvement, but may also derive from the more complex involvements in the later triadic situation, as well as from other later involvements with significant figures. The point I am trying to make is a relatively simple one — that the characteristics and dimensions of the therapeutic alliance do not derive reductively from a single stage of developmental experience, but rather span the full range of the child's developmental vicissitudes and reflect at various stages of the analytic process the different qualities of this developmental experience. The therapeutic alliance and the capacity for it reflect certain developmental processes which must be distinguished from the regressive introjective components that contribute to the elaboration of transference distortions and the transference neurosis. These separate, though not unrelated, developmental experiences underlying the therapeutic alliance involve the process of identification.

The focus of our discussion at this juncture is on the more or less static quality of the idenficatory contribution to the structuring of the analytic situation. We are in a sense anticipating the more dynamic role of identifications in regard to the evolution of the therapeutic alliance in the analytic process. However, it will serve our purposes here to provide some sense of the progressive shifts in the alliance during the course of an analysis and the role of identifications in promoting and supporting them. We are only attempting a rough schematization at this point and shall return to this important consideration later in our discussion of the analytic process.

The beginning of an analysis poses the expectable problems of starting a relationship and putting in motion a process that may be as important in the patient's life as any experience. The patient feels highly vulnerable in the supine position and in the unusual conditions of the analytic situation. Moreover, the patient soon begins to feel the pull of regressive pressures, which only add to the sense of vulnerability. These pressures increase the titer of anxiety, stimulate defensive reactions, and present the problem of finding some basis in the relation with the analyst for a sense of security and confidence. A considerable degree of stress, then, is put on the patient's inherent capacities for trust.

This initial phase of establishing the alliance may vary considerably from patient to patient in its form of expression or in the length of time it takes. It is unusual in my experience for patients to enter the analytic situation in such a way that the alliance is easily or readily established. More often than not, it takes specific work to accomplish this first step. Some patients may negotiate this phase in a very few sessions; others may take years to work through it. In one exceptional case, a young woman, with rather severe obsessional tendencies and considerable narcissistic vulnerability, spent the first several years of her analysis coming late, often missing all but a few minutes of her session. Sometimes she missed appointments altogether. This woman spent long hours on the couch in silence. She addressed significant material only in the most guarded terms, and then only when she felt that she herself already understood the material so that I would not be able to surprise her with anything she hadn't already thought of.

The defect in such patients is in the capacity to trust. The analytic situation puts patients in a situation of vulnerability and dependence which begins to stir infantile needs. They seek some ground on which they can engage the analyst in non-threatening terms. Insofar as patients can fall back on iden-tificatory systems that allow a basic sense of trust to enter the relationship, they can begin to tolerate that degree of lowering of narcissistic defenses which will permit them to entrust themselves to the risks and uncertainties of a precarious rela-tionship such as the analytic one. To the extent that such capacities are imperiled or constrained by pathogenic introjec-tive influences, entering into the analytic relationship becomes all the more difficult and problematic. Thus, it can be seen that almost from the opening moment of the analysis, important in-ternalization systems are brought into play and influence the course and direction of the analytic work.

As we have pointed out, the opening phase of the analysis puts the patient in a position of problematic dependence. That dependence normally increases as the analytic work proceeds and as the analytic regression takes effect. The analysis moves toward the increasing mobilization of the infantile residues in the patient's personality, toward the activation of the infantile neurosis, and with it the reemergence of infantile introjects. This development puts increasing pressure on the therapeutic alliance as the transference neurosis comes into the analytic relation. Yet, although the pathogenic introjects come to play a prominent part in the analytic relation, the identificatory elements persist and provide the basis for the continuing alliance. If the regressive ac-tivation of the introjects comes to overwhelm identificatory systems or if a misalliance or a transference-countertransference bind develops, the analytic relation is placed in jeopardy. In such cases, if the crisis cannot be worked through and resolved, it may be necessary to interrupt or terminate the analysis.

It is in the interpreting, clarifying, and working through of the introjective components, especially as they come to their fullest expression in the transference neurosis, that significant shifts can be identified in the therapeutic alliance. These changes reflect alterations in the basic patterns of identification. As the underly-ing dependencies are resolved, subtle shifts occur in the patient's functioning within the analysis. There are increasing signs of the patient's autonomy, in the sense of a growing capacity to carry on the work of the analysis independently of the analyst. The patient may feel more comfortable about coming a few minutes late when circumstances reasonably call for it and may more freely and responsibly negotiate, or even decide on appropriate occasions, when to miss an appointment. The patient may begin to take on more responsibility in the analytic work and show initiative in clarifying and interpreting his own analytic productions and in relating their content to various realms of his experience, including his infantile experience. With these shifts, one may observe various imitative adoptions of the analyst's words, attitudes, mannerisms, and even ways of thinking about and processing analytic material. One can even think of this phase of the analytic experience as involving forms of trial identification in which the patient attempts to assimilate aspects of the analyst's personality that seem useful and adaptive to the patient (these aspects may even be idealized as such to some degree).

As these fragmentary identifications play themselves out, they directly influence the quality of the therapeutic alliance. The character of the alliance in the early phase, when the patient is establishing basic trust and increasing dependence, is quite different from that in a later phase, when the patient is establishing and consolidating a sense of autonomous functioning within the analysis. The analyst's approach to the alliance and the ways in which he fosters and supports it must shift accordingly. In the earlier phase the analyst supports the regressive aspects, tolerates the patient's often intense dependency, and tries to create the conditions of empathic understanding required for the patient to enter into the analytic process. As the regressive phase continues, the analyst maximizes the conditions for regression by tending to be passive and silent, allowing the regressive pulls to assert their influence and providing the fullest possible opportunity for the pathogenic introjective configurations to express themselves. The analyst's concern in this phase is merely to maintain the alliance, making sure that it is not regressively undermined and that no influences arise, whether of a countertransference variety or otherwise, that would put the alliance on a false footing and lead to a therapeutic misalliance (Langs, 1975a).

As the patient moves into a more autonomous phase, the quality of the alliance also shifts. The analyst becomes more concerned with creating conditions that foster the patient's nascent attempts at independent functioning and with avoiding those subtle defeats and devaluations that can frustrate and even kill the patient's highly vulnerable attempts at self-definition and growth. The analyst must be careful not to convey the attitude that the patient, after all, does not really understand his difficulties and that only the wisdom of the analyst can bring illumination and success in the analytic work. The model here, as we shall see in greater detail later, is that of the good parent, who does not defeat or devalue the child because the child is clumsy, awkward, or ineffectual in his attempts to do more complex things. Rather, the good parent values the child's attempts and encourages the effort, providing helpful assistance that enables the child to do better than he might otherwise have done.

Thus, the good analyst must learn to moderate and minimize his own interpretative function as the analysis progresses in the interest of supporting those tendencies in the patient which offer opportunity for potential growth and increasingly autonomous functioning. In the course of this process, the patient develops an increasing sense of confidence in his own ability to deal with inner states and feelings and a more secure sense of his own capacity to deal with real life problems. These are all steps in the direction of establishing a sense of personal identity, which integrates the various stages of identification that have marked the progression of the alliance.

Optimally patients leave an analysis with a sense of personal competence and capability, a sense of their own individuality and personal value, and a feeling of separateness and freedom from dependence on the analyst which allows them to take responsibility for the course of their own lives. They retain, we might hope, a bond of affection toward the analyst, but one uncontaminated by feelings of dependence. They now have an identity that is truly their own, independent of the analyst. Here again we can draw a parallel between the analyst and the good parent, who not only allows the child to separate and individuate, but who helpfully and constructively facilitates the child's further venture into adult autonomy and identity.

Throughout the analysis the relationship between the analyst and the analysand reflects the relative contributions of available introjects and identificatory capacities. The intent of the analytic process is increasingly to mitigate the introjective components and to allow for the expansion and amplification of identificatory processes. Needless to say, a major concern in assessing analyzability is an evaluation of the intensity, scope, and strength of the introjective aspects of the patient's inner psychic organization, as well as an assessment of the patient's achieved identificatory capacity. The importance and the complexity of these criteria of analyzability cannot be underestimated (Knapp et al., 1960; Sashin, Eldred, and van Amerongen, 1975; Zetzel, 1970; Zetzel and Meissner, 1973).

4

THERAPEUTIC ASPECTS OF INTERNALIZATION IN THE PSYCHOANALYTIC PROCESS

We shall now examine the psychoanalytic process itself, keeping the major focus of our study on the role of internalizations within this process. We shall begin by looking at the nature of the psychoanalytic encounter as a process and then move to a consideration of the specific phases of this process, from its beginning through its termination.

PSYCHOANALYSIS AS A PROCESS

Process versus Situation

In discussing the psychoanalytic situation, we were concerned particularly with the structural dimensions of the analysis and with the way in which internalizations contributed to and shaped that structure. We observed that this structure undergoes certain progressive changes through the course of analysis. We shall now shift our emphasis to the dynamic aspects of these same elements and the manner in which they interact to move the psychoanalytic process from one stage to the next. Inherent in the notion of process is the concept of changing action and interaction over time along with progressive modification of the variables involved in the process. In referring to internalizations in this context, we are referring to them not merely as structural entities—that is, as organizational schemata within the psychic integration of either the analyst or the analysand—and not only as constituents of the

139

structural organization and integration of the psychoanalytic relationship and its various components, but specifically as *processes* having a dynamic impact and inherent motivational expression, which play a powerful role in the analytic interaction.

From this perspective, internalizations serve as motivating forces with a derivation and origin, a dynamic pattern of interaction and expression, an underlying motivation, and a history that can be characterized within the time span of the psychoanalytic process itself, as well as within the patient's life span. In other words, we cannot lose sight of the basic analytic principle that the understanding of analytic processes requires an account of all the metapsychological points of view. Internalizations must not be viewed merely as structures (the products of internalization), but must be seen to have dynamic (motivational), genetic, and adaptive aspects as well.

The Components of the Psychoanalytic Process

The components of the psychoanalytic process can be conceived as subprocesses, which combine their various elements into the psychoanalytic process itself. We shall focus here only on the major components, recognizing that other aspects may also play an important role. The present categorizing has at least the advantage of general familiarity, and it encompasses the major dimensions of the analytic process.

To be specific, we shall consider the elements of regression, resistance, transference, and alliance as functional subprocesses, which reveal their dynamic action and interaction throughout the course of the analysis. These components intertwine in a variety of subtle and important ways, and they compound their expressions in multiply determined ways to give rise to the analytic process. They are seen here as sources of activity, progression, and dynamic interaction. In addition, our discussion will focus on particular forms of internalization as they are affected by and themselves affect these components of the analytic process.

REGRESSION

It has long been recognized that the analytic regression is central to the analytic process. A number of elements within the analytic situation serve to induce the analytic regression, particularly the use of the couch, the quiet and nondistracting environment, the analyst's passivity and silence, and most particularly the patient's free association.

Theoretically the analytic regression is envisioned as a controlled and regulated regression that moves through various levels of psychic organization and developmental experience, until the core conflicts of the neurosis are reached and can be opened for exploration, and ultimately for interpretation and resolution. At each step of this regression, the patient comes closer and closer to the underlying conflicts so that, as the analytic regression proceeds, the level of anxiety tends to increase. The gradual and controlled quality of this regression is intended to avoid severe regressive episodes, which might induce an overwhelming degree of anxiety. Such malignant regressions within the analysis can be extremely disruptive and may signal the necessity for more active structuralizing intervention on the part of the analyst. Indeed, they may at times call for the termination of analysis or a shift to psychotherapy (Gudeman, 1974). A malignant regression suggests that the patient's ego defenses have become fragmented or are so permeable to drive derivatives that a useful level of ego control and therapeutic distancing is no longer operative.

The capacity to tolerate regression is an important consideration in the evaluation of a patient's analyzability. One must be sure that the patient has sufficient ego resources and the capacity to tolerate anxiety so that in the face of the analytic regression the structural aspects of the patient's ego will remain intact. In other words, the analytic process requires that patients be able to tolerate that degree of anxiety which will allow them to approach the underlying conflicts and to deal with these effectively and therapeutically. If a patient does not have this resource and runs the risk of being overwhelmed by a traumatic anxiety, the therapeutic effectiveness of the analytic procedure is considerably diminished, if not completely lost.

The distinction is often drawn between functional and structural regression. Functional regression of the patient's psyche takes place without major structural reorganization. The regression may be from a higher level of ego functioning to a more primitive level; it may be from a higher level of libidinal organization to an earlier, possibly pregenital level; it may involve a shift in the quality of object relations or in the level and quality of defenses. Such regression is not global, but can be highly selective. Patients may regress in one area of ego functioning without showing any significant regression in other aspects. Or patients may show regression in certain areas or contexts of their experience or in specific object relationships without showing any significant regression in others. Modell (1968) distinguishes such functional regressions from the more severe structural regressions, in which the cohesiveness of the self-organization and the sense of identity are also affected.

Modell articulates this distinction in terms of topographic versus structural regression. Modell bases his discussion of regression on the central distinction between structural and functional aspects encapsulated in the formula: "The same structure may be used for different functions at different times" (p. 122). The topographic metaphor refers to Freud's conception of mental contents and operations in terms of their relationship to consciousness (i.e., mental contents are either unconscious, preconscious, or conscious), thus it refers to what are essentially functional alterations within the ego. Freud's enlarging clinical experience, however, indicated to him that the merely functional metaphor was no longer adequate for describing the complexities of psychic functioning. The topographic model was based on repression and the genesis of hysterical symptoms; it grew out of a therapeutic approach centered on bringing unconscious contents to conscious awareness by association and interpretation, thus undoing the unconscious conflict and alleviating the symptoms. However, analysis rapidly reached beyond such symptomatic and conflict-based concerns and began to deal with the more resistant and deeply embedded characteristics reflected in abiding configurations and patterns of organization within the ego itself. It was this general shift in emphasis and focus that made it necessary for Freud to reorganize his conceptualization of the mental apparatus and to move from the topographic (functional) model to the structural model. The structural metaphor articulated the less apparent and more perduring configurations in the organization of the ego.

Modell describes the functional organization of the ego as "Janus-faced," that is to say, the ego involves two functional systems. One of these is oriented toward the external world and is organized to obtain gratification from it. This corresponds to what Freud called the reality ego. But another part is oriented toward the world of subjective inner experience and obtains gratification from within that inner world. In this light, topographic or functional regression can be defined in terms of a shift of cathexis from the external world to the internal world.

It is this functional regression, without structural regression or alteration, that is intended by the analytic process. It is also this functional regression that one finds in neuroses, where there is no significant regression of ego structure and no substantial interference with or distortion of reality testing. Within the analytic process, the regression-inducing components of the analytic situation lead to a shift of the patient's attention from the external world, the world of outer reality, to the world of inner psychic reality. In this way, the analytic regression serves to reactivate childhood fantasies, memories, and images and brings about a recapitulation of the infantile neurosis.

These aspects of the analytic regression are commonly accepted and understood, but in terms of our focus on internalization processes it is important to emphasize that an additional, and indeed central, aspect of the analytic regression is the reactivation and revivification of infantile introjects. As the analytic regression proceeds, the activation of earlier introjects creates a modification in the patient's sense of self, which is organized around and derived from the core introjective elements. As the introjective elements become increasingly available to the patient's awareness, and as their power and intensity increase, these introjective configurations increasingly take on the quality of primary-process presences (Meissner, 1971; Schafer, 1968a). They act as quasi-autonomous foci of influence within the psychic organization, at some phenomenological distance from the intentionally grasped core of the ego.

This experiential distancing of the introjects is usually a later aspect of the therapeutic reworking of the introjects. Earlier telltale signs of the emerging influence of these infantile introjective configurations can be found in the gradual modification of the patient's sense of self together with the mobilization of pain-ful pathogenic affects — usually depression, but frequently enough, when the titer of pathogenic narcissism is high, also ele-ments of shame and guilt. This pathological sense of self then dominates the clinical situation and the patient's interaction within the analytic relationship. Another important index of the activation of these infantile introjects has to do with the suscepti-bility to aggressive, libidinal, and narcissistic drive influences, particularly those derived from early infantile levels. The last im-portant index of the activation of these introjects lies in the inten-sification of the patient's tendency to projection as a mode of de-fense. Often this use of projection can be detected in the patient's activities outside the analysis, where the influence of the introjects may be acted out in a variety of ways, but the most important and central place for the acting out of these derivatives through pro-jection is in the therapeutic relationship, specifically in the organization and intensification of the transference neurosis.

The analytic regression also has a developmental dimension. As the regression intensifies and successive layers of introjection are activated and worked through in the analytic process, earlier and earlier developmental strata, with their associated issues and conflicts, are reactivated. The introjective configuration tends to retrace this developmental course in reflecting successively deeper and earlier levels of developmental influence. Turning to Freud's model of fixation, which is intimately connected with the notion of regression in analysis, we may say that the patient suc-cessively moves to increasingly earlier levels of fixation so that one sees the gradual emergence of introjective elements stemming from the postoedipal, the oedipal, and even preoedipal levels.

A clinical example may help to clarify this process. My purpose is simply to illustrate that in addition to describing the clinical regression in terms of levels of drive organization, intensity and quality of anxiety, or patterns of resistance and defense, we can articulate it in terms of patterns and levels of introjective organization — and that seeing the regressive movement in these terms opens the way to additional perspectives on the analytic process and its workings. The example I have chosen is not unique, since something of the same process and the same evolu-tion of regressive phases can be seen in almost any neurosis.

A young married woman in her early thirties entered analysis because of her feelings of worthlessness, her sense of frustration about herself and her life circumstances, and particularly her distress over the infanticidal impulses that she felt toward her seven-year-old daughter. She recalled her intensely ambivalent feelings surrounding the birth of the child and how depressed, bitter, and resentful she felt at being saddled with an infant to take care of. She had wanted to kill the child and thus free herself from this intolerable burden.

As the analysis progressed, the theme of her worthlessness as a woman and her generally devalued position began to predominate. She was unhappy with her job as a part-time teacher and dissatisfied with her family life and with her home. She complained bitterly about her husband's inadequate salary and the burdens of maintaining her home and family in addition to having to work to supplement the family income and pay me what was a significantly reduced analytic fee. The general theme was that women have a bad time of it and that men have all the advantages, all the opportunities; they are not tied down with the burdens of family, home, and children, and are therefore free to express themselves and do significant things in the adult world. The patient's complaints and her feelings about herself and her lot in life expressed aspects of the underlying introjective configuration, but in these early stages of her analysis only the superficial, surface aspects of the introjects were manifested.

Under the pressure of increasing regression, I began to hear more and more about the patient's oldest brother and about her mother. The oldest brother, an accomplished concert pianist, had been a brilliant student and had attended one of the best Ivy League colleges, graduating with high honors. This boy had been the apple of mother's eye and apparently was the mother's great consolation and source of pride in what seemed otherwise a desert of disappointment and disillusionment. The mother herself was portrayed as a woman of extraordinary capacity—intelligent, well read, and practically omniscient in the fields of literature, current events, art, music, and drama. It was only after many months of working through this highly idealized and intensely overdrawn portrait of the mother that other, less flattering aspects became apparent. It turned out that the mother had dropped out of college at the end of her freshman year, and that in fact her life had been a series of disappointments and failures. The picture gradually emerged of the mother's chronic depression and progressively worsening chronic alcoholism.

In the patient's eyes, however, the mother remained a paragon of intellectual virtues and attainments, who was somehow beyond the patient's reach. The mother and the oldest brother shared a special bond, the privileged communication belonging to people of genius and great accomplishment. The patient, with her lack of special talents, was left out of this special bond of communication between the mother and the son. It was at this level of regression that the patient's intense penis envy emerged, as well as her wishes to take in and incorporate a penis, the source of power and wisdom, so that she could become like her idealized image of the phallic mother. This was also translated into transference terms. The patient saw me as the brilliant, all-knowing, and all-providing wizard, who was the possessor of the powerful penis-brain. The solution to her problem would come through her submission to me and through her compliance with my expectations in the performance of the analysis. If she did what was expected of her and fulfilled my expectations of her, I would give her the secret magical knowledge that would enable her to change herself into a more worthwhile and valuable human being. In other words, I would give her a penis-brain.

At this level of the analytic regression, both sides of the oedipal conflict were played out in transference terms. On the one hand, I was the powerful, all-knowing phallic mother who would provide the penis the patient so desperately desired, if she lived up to the level of performance I expected of her in the analysis. At the same time, I was the inept and somewhat bumbling substitute for her father, whom she regarded with contempt for his weakness and impotence, and especially for his incapacity to face down and control her mother. Yet for all his despicable impotence and lack of accomplishment, the patient had a fondness for her father, as he cared about her even if he was able to do little or nothing to help her.

More and more, the patient's fear of her mother as the powerful and demeaning criticizer came to the fore. In the analysis she was constantly afraid of my becoming critical, of my wanting to put her down, of my finally saying to her that the analysis had gone far enough, that she was not worth the trouble, and that she should get out of my office. For most of the analysis she could not shake the fear and the anxiety that I would suddenly one day turn on her and do her in. This was clearly related to criticisms from her mother that had made her feel worthless and totally incompetent. The fear was that whatever she confided to me, particularly of her inner sense of weakness and vulnerability, I would sooner or later use it against her to put her down and even further demean her. This vulnerable and worthless aspect of herself reflected the organization of the victim introject, whose determinants came primarily from the latency level with its strong unresolved oedipal elements. She was the incompetent, dumb one — the inadequate and worthless girl who could never accomplish or achieve what her brother had accomplished, who had no special talents or abilities, nothing to mark her out or distinguish her in any way. She was the weak female who had irretrievably lost out in the oedipal competition with the phallic mother.

It was only after much of this material had been worked through that we were able to reach another level in the evolution of the transference, in which the opposite pole of the patient's profound sense of vulnerability and helplessness became increasingly apparent. Only gradually was she able to reveal her feelings of superiority to people around her, her tendency to criticize and devalue people in her life, and particularly her desire to feel herself superior to me. She thought about withholding vital information and fooling me into thinking that she was healthy, so that she could finally leave my office and the analysis laughing behind my back. Slowly the components of her feelings of superiority and entitlement, that she was a special person to whom the world owed acknowledgment and acclaim, came into focus. Only then did her wish to see herself as the "exception," as the tragic figure sunk in a morass of disillusionment and disappointment whose life was a saga of frustrated desire and lost opportunities, become apparent, and only then did the narcissistic underpinnings of her masochistic and depressive posture reveal themselves. To suffer, to be unhappy, to be disappointed and set upon by the cruel forces of the world was the mark of her specialness. She was singled out to suffer in a way that ordinary human beings were not.

As this material became increasingly available, the depth of her narcissistic trauma and the intensity of the oral greed and envy that accompanied it revealed themselves. It became increasingly apparent how much she played out the family myth centered on the figure of her mother. These same narcissistic and pathological attitudes had marked her mother's life career. It became clear that it was through an acceptance of the mother's masochistic and depressive world-view and her attitudes of magical expectation, which were foredoomed to continual disappointment and disillusionment, that the patient maintained a special bond with her mother — even though her mother, so frequently lost and unavailable in a drunken stupor, knew little or nothing about this. It was this magical bond, steeped in the tragic stuff of pathological narcissism, that formed the basis of the organization of the patient's relatively archaic introjects. The pathogenic roots of the patient's difficulties lay in this primitive, narcissistic introject derived from the internalization of the maternal object. At its deepest roots, this patient's introjective configuration was built around early preoedipal elements embodying infantile oral dependence, aspects of archaic narcissistic omnipotence and grandiosity, envy, greed, and a deficit in the capacity for basic trust, which left this patient situated in a chronically, if muted, paranoid position.

There are no easy rules of thumb for predicting or anticipating the pattern of such regressive configurations. Each analysis tends to follow its own idiosyncratic course, but in general the earliest developmental issues and levels of introjective organization tend to require the deepest and most difficult regressive movements. For each patient it is important to determine the degree of regression that is optimally tolerable and manageable and that can be undergone without running the risk of inducing undue or irreversibly damaging structural alterations in the patient's ego. Structural regressions do in fact occur in the process of many analyses, but the critical question is to what depth they occur and to what extent they are reversible (Calder, 1958).

In some patients, the analytic situation induces a regression that is excessively precipitous and threatens the patient with overwhelming anxiety or with the intense pain of revivified infantile affects. This headlong rush of regression can often be tempered by the introduction of parameters—whether it be increased activity on the part of the analyst, support, intellectualization, or even sitting the patient up for a time. Usually the patient's capacity for tolerating such regressive stress can be measured by the degree to which the therapeutic alliance has been established and stabilized. But occasionally, the regressive rush cannot be muted or temporized, and the patient plunges into extremely painful and distressing pathogenic affects, with the result that the analytic work cannot be sustained.

This situation arose with another patient of mine, who sought analysis because of her long-standing chronic depression and her involvement in a succession of highly ambivalent and narcissistically traumatic involvements with men. This intelligent young woman had already established herself in a difficult and demanding professional career, but despite this she felt that her personal life was messed up.

As the analytic work progressed, the patient became increasingly aware of the intense ambivalence that permeated all her relationships, particularly those with men with whom she became emotionally involved. This same ambivalence played itself out in her relationship to me. Increasingly, she felt within her the pull to dependence on me and the analytic situation, and she found this increasingly threatening and intolerable.

Gradually the intensely pathogenic dimensions of her oedipal involvement began to make themselves clear. Her father had been a warm, sympathetic, kindly, and somewhat seductive figure for her. She had sensitively tender and loving feelings toward him, but also experienced intense guilt and sadness in relation to his death from a heart attack. Some months before his death, she had become sexually involved with a man, had become pregnant, and had had an abortion. The emotional turmoil and stress connected with these events, she felt, precipitated her father's heart attack and death. Consequently, her guilt in this regard was intense and extremely painful. Her sadness and grief were only gradually mobilized by the analytic work. As the work of mourning progressed and the patient's grief and sadness were to some degree worked through, her feelings of rage and anger toward her father for his softness and weakness and for his inability to stand up to the patient's mother and put her in her place became available.

The patient's relationship to her mother had been extremely conflictual and intensely ambivalent. The mother had not wanted a girl child, was continually critical of her daughter, and showed her little or no warmth or affection. The patient recounted seemingly endless episodes in which she had been rejected or demeaned by her mother and could respond only with impotent rage and self-hate. When her father died, the patient had felt thrown upon her mother for emotional support, and she got little or none. It was after the death of her father that she had plunged into a series of relationships with men, in which she would become intensely involved, emotionally and sexually, and then would turn on the man, devaluing, criticizing, and then hostilely rejecting him.

The theme of the patient's hostility to the mother and her hatred and fear of her gradually enlarged. There was a series of dreams in which the patient was smothered and otherwise attacked and hurt by the mother or mother-substitutes. We also began to get parallel hints of the opposite side of the patient's intense ambivalence toward her mother, namely, the deep and frustrated infantile longing for closeness, acceptance, and love from the mother. These frustrated longings were extremely painful for the patient, and gave rise to seemingly endless periods of heart-rending tears and laments.

These feelings were also increasingly mobilized in the transference, where the patient's longing to be dependent, loved, taken care of and protected, created a powerful regressive pressure within the analysis. But this regressive pull was extremely threatening to the patient, since it revivified all the rage and frustrated hatred that accompanied and reflected her infantile longing. At this point, the pain and sadness connected with her yearning became overwhelming and the patient decided to break off treatment. She decided that she could not tolerate these feelings, particularly the yearning to be close to and dependent on me, since it carried with it such a threat of frustration and disappointment. She believed that a resort to her own capacities for self-sufficiency and independence, along with a reinforcement of her obsessional defenses, was far preferable to undergoing and tolerating the pain that she had begun to experience and that she knew lay ahead of her in the analysis.

From our present perspective, we can guess that behind these dynamic issues, what the patient was experiencing and reacting to was the activation of an extremely painful, pathogenic introject which derived particularly from her mother and which was motivated by the frustrated, yet undiminished, yearning for acceptance and love from her mother. This introject was organized around the core of depressive affects that seemingly permeated her mother's life, and which had to do with the mother's devaluation and hatred of herself as a woman. No matter how hard my patient had worked, no matter what efforts she had poured into her professional career and into developing her intellectual capacities, she could not cover over or submerge the inner sense of worthlessness, helplessness, vulnerability, and self-hatred. It was the stirring reactivation of these inner components, bound into and sustained by the introjective organization, that terrified her and precipitated her flight.

Profound levels of regression are not inconsistent with the analytic process, but they may require important modifications of analytic technique (Dickes, 1967). These concerns have been voiced by Winnicott (1965), who speaks of the necessity of creating a "holding environment" to sustain the patient through such periods of significant regression, and by Balint (1968), who concerns himself at these levels of regression with what he calls the "basic fault." It should be remembered that developmentally the introjective configuration is constantly being remodeled and reworked by the progressive exchange and interplay of projections and introjections. The organization of the child's inner world is never static and does not consist of one pattern of introjective configurations, but rather a succession of dynamically interacting configurations. Consequently, in the context of the analytic regression, one can expect to see a certain degree of shifting and alteration in the introjective configuration. Nevertheless, there is a certain patterning in the patient's developmental experience which tends to cluster the organization of introjects from multiple levels of experience in terms of certain critical themes. We shall have more to say about this patterning of the introjects later on.

We must also remind ourselves that the analytic regression takes place along narcissistic dimensions as well. In his discussion of narcissistic personality disorders, Kohut (1971) has described the mobilization of the idealized parental imago and the grandiose self. These basic differentiations of primitive narcissism express themselves in characteristic forms of transference — the former manifesting itself in idealizing transferences and the latter in so-called mirror transferences. Under the stress of disturbance of the transference equilibrium and further regression, both of these narcissistic configurations can regress to more archaic forms of either idealization or grandiosity. Such degrees of regression can be tolerated in the analytic situation within the limits of the maintenance of a cohesive self. The sustaining of narcissistic cathexes in the maintenance of self-cohesion is entirely consistent with the functional regression of the analysis, and it is only under the pressure of more profound and self-fragmenting regressive pulls that structural regression may take place. Additional narcissistic regression leads to the emergence of primitive autoerotism and fragmentation and diffusion of the self, along with other regressive narcissistic disturbances.

An important dimension of our approach is the role of narcissism in the economy of introjects. As we have already indicated, the introjects are organized in terms of narcissistic vicissitudes and are embedded in and express the complexities of narcissistic components. As Kohut (1971) suggests, the decisive work of the analysis is an increased engagement of the central sector of the patient's psyche and its involvement in the transference so that there is an increasing activation of the patient's unconscious narcissism, which then becomes available for the systematic working through of the analytic process. It is only as a function of the analytic regression, however, that successively more archaic and more narcissistically organized and determined levels of the introjective economy become available.

The important issue here is the role of narcissism in the genesis of introjects. The critical factor is that the defensive implementation of introjection is based on underlying narcissistic needs as a way of, on one level, preserving narcissistic invulnerability and, on another level, preserving the ties to the all-important, self-sustaining object. Thus the dynamics, underlying the integration of the grandiose self, on the one hand, and the idealized parental imago, on the other, involve the elaboration and interplay of introjection and projection. From another point of view, the critical motivation for the organization and sustaining of the introjects has to do with the preservation of the patient's sense of self—however defensively motivated and maladaptively distorted—and the correlated pressures to maintain a sense of the integrity and cohesion of the self (Kohut, 1971; Meissner, 1978b). It will be more useful, I think, to enter into a detailed consideration of these issues in discussing the role of the transference in the analytic process.

RESISTANCE

The notion of resistance is one of the everyday staples of analytic life and one that is all too familiar to working analysts. The analytic regression and free association introduce a certain disequilibrium or imbalance into the patient's psychic life. Before undertaking analysis, the patient had achieved a delicate balance between the drive-derivative impulses, both libidinal and aggressive, and the defensive configurations designed to keep these impulses in check. Certain aspects of psychic functioning may have been effectively repressed in the interest of maintaining internal stability and cohesion, or in the interest of avoiding certain internal dangers—separation, castration, etc.

The undoing of the defensive organization and the corresponding imbalance in the intrapsychic alignment create anxiety and mobilize the patient's ego to a new line of defense. Inevitably the patient sees the analyst as the agent of this internal distress and thereby summons up his resources to defend against the analytic attack and to resist further progress in the analytic work. The analysis of the patient's resistances and defenses in a process of confrontation, interpretation, and working through leads to the further undoing of the defenses and the fostering of further regression. As we have already noted, the analytic process seeks to induce a controlled and manageable regression such that the corresponding anxiety from the inner disequilibrium is neither overwhelming nor traumatizing, but remains more or less on the level of signal anxiety.

Often the analytic process must work its way through many layers of resistance—the layers of the onion in Freud's classic allusion. With each penetration of the stratum of resistance and defense, another cycle of regression and resistance is set in motion. The giving way of resistances at one level leads to regression with a concomitant heightening of anxiety, which then signals the need for a tightening of resistances at the next psychic level. As the analytic process works through successive layers of resistance and regression, it comes closer to bringing to light the core conflicts that lie at the root of the patient's pathology. It is these core conflicts and the psychic elements related to them that will be most intensely and highly defended by the patient. Consequently, as the analytic regression proceeds, the level of resistance tends to deepen and to become more rigid and progressively more difficult to work through.

In our present approach, the level of the patient's core conflict is not simply conceptualized in terms of the opposition of drives or drive derivatives and the corresponding restraining defenses and countercathexes. Rather, we are concerned with the structuralized components that relate to the organization of drives, drive derivatives, and defenses in terms of the internalized objects or introjects. It is here that the structural theory of defense and defense organization is conjoined with a more explicitly object relations frame of reference (Dorpat, 1976).

The introjective organization centers on the internalized objects derived from those developmental levels that characterize the infantile conflicts and lie at the pathogenic root of the patient's neurosis. The drive influences and their derivatives, as well as the defensive organization, are integrated and organized in terms of these internalized objects, which have become integrated into the patient's inner world. Thus the introjects embody, reflect, and express the underlying developmental conflicts and issues. As the introjective configuration is increasingly activated through the analytic regression, the patient mobilizes defenses and resistances in the service of preserving that internal introjective organization. The motivation of these resistances is related to the underlying anxiety, but ultimately it is rooted in the motivation that lies behind and sustains the introjects themselves.

The point to be kept in focus here is that the defensive organization and its relation to drive derivatives are not simply matters of the economics or dynamics of instinctual impulses and the corresponding defenses. To see the organization of defenses and, in the analytic context, resistances only in these terms is to focus on a lower level of organization of psychic processes and to ignore the higher-order integration and patterning of these same processes in supraordinate structural terms. Defenses do not arise simply in response to the energic pressure of a drive stimulus. The choice of defense, its integration into a larger defensive organization, and its interaction with other aspects of psychic organization and functioning depend on the patterns of internalization derived from the experience of objects. From the dynamic perspective, this has important implications for the analytic work. The motivation for maintaining the defenses and resistances does not lie merely in the avoidance of specific instinctual threats, but often, more importantly, in the affective forces related to the specific object relation and the need to cling to the object or its derivatives. Consequently, it is not adequate (although it is often sufficient) to analyze the connection of defense and drive; a fuller understanding requires analysis in terms of the relevant internalizations (introjects) and the motives at play in the object relation from which these derive. This involves important dynamic, genetic, structural, and even adaptive issues that are otherwise left unattended.

The hierarchical organization of conflicts and defenses in relation to the introjective configuration can be seen quite strikingly in the chronically depressed young woman described earlier. At one level, the oedipal issues played a significant part. The sexual wishes toward her father were identifiable and contributed to the patient's rage toward her mother, as well as to her considerable fear of attack and retaliation from the mother. These elements were muted, however, by the quite devalued position of the father and the dominant and controlling position assumed by her mother. The penis envy became dramatically focused in relation to her idealized older brother, since it was the brother rather than the father who was the apple of mother's eye.

In this case, the conflicts stood out clearly and could be readily dealt with in terms of the patient's oral envy and narcissistic deprivation. In fact, these latter issues lie much closer to the roots of her pathology than do the more oedipal concerns. In terms of the organization of internalizations, the whole complex of influences and defensive reactions was shaped by the telling introjection of the maternal imago by the little girl. The pattern of the patient's needs, deprivations, wishes, defenses, and conflicts was set by the organization of her mother's personality in terms of the mother's own pathogenic introjective configuration. My patient reproduced that same configuration in a strikingly parallel and detailed fashion in her own perception of herself and in the organization of her defenses. Her introjective mirroring of the mother served profound infantile wishes for clinging dependence and loving acceptance from a narcissistically walled-off and self-involuted mother-figure, who was incapable of extending warmth, loving acceptance, and understanding to the patient. Moreover, the clinical analysis, interpretation, and working through of higher-level resistances did not effectively touch or transmute the narcissistically embedded, primitive wishes underlying the patient's clinging adherence to this pathogenic introject. It was only when the introjective elements were clearly delineated and the patient's motivations for clinging dependently to an idealized and magically inflated mother-figure clarified and analyzed that any significant change began to take place.

It is useful to distinguish levels of resistance in the analytic process. In the early phases of analysis, one meets a superficial level of defensive organization, where the focus is predominantly extrinsic, in that the resistance is directed primarily against the analytic pressures and the technical interventions of the analyst. In the early phases of the analysis, for example, the analyst's attempts to get the patient to free-associate will be met by a variety of defensive maneuvers, including rationalization, intellectualization, silence, lateness, and a whole host of defensive tactics.

But as the level of regression and the corresponding resistance deepen, the concerns behind the patient's resistance shift to a more internal frame of reference, where the resistance has more to do with the internal effects of the activation and the greater availability of the underlying introjective configuration. At this level, there is a decisive shift in the nature of the patient's anxiety and in the quality of the underlying issues that motivate the resistance. As the introjects become more forcefully activated and, as the analytic work progresses, more and more clearly delineated, the issues shift from a level of structural concerns and conflicts to a deeper set of concerns involving the object relations context out of which the introjects derive and providing the essential motivation for the preservation of the introjects in the inner world. This is particularly the case in dealing with introjective configurations that may underlie the structural organization and that have embedded in them conflicts over dependency and separation and loss that reflect early distortions or deviations in the experience of object relations. The resistances at these deep-lying levels of the introjective organization can be exceedingly difficult and highly resistant to therapeutic interventions. It has been my experience that at such levels, where the introjective configurations themselves are being dealt with, the defensive and resistance issues center on predominantly narcissistic concerns. The degree of the rigidity of the resistances and the defensive organization is directly proportional to the depth and level of narcissistic impairment and defect. In the severe forms of psychopathology, the narcissistic deficits lie at an extremely primitive or oral level and derive from the early mother-child interaction. In these cases, the issues revolve around the primitive object involvement — what Balint (1968) refers to as the "basic fault."

TRANSFERENCE

We have already discussed the structural aspects of the transference with particular reference to their contribution to the organization of the analytic situation. Our emphasis here, however, is on the transference specifically as process — as that constellation of factors which forms the core of the analytic process itself. Our essential thrust is that the dynamics of the transference reflect the underlying introjective configuration and in fact derive from the inherent dynamics of the introjects.

Two important points can immediately be made about the process dimensions of the transference. The first is that there is a discernible progression in the dynamic expression of the transference, which is correlated with and elicited by the analytic regression. As the transference develops in the course of the analysis, both an increasing activation of the dynamic influence of the underlying introjects and a progressive shift in the quality and dynamic basis of the transference itself occur.

We have already suggested that the shift in the organization of the transference is from a predominantly displacement model to a more specifically projective model. From one perspective, the transference involves a displacement from the level of infantile experience. Feelings, attitudes, and thoughts originally stimulated in relation to infantile objects are revivified in the relationship to the analyst, and the analyst as the present object is now responded to in the same terms as the original infantile one. The model essentially appeals to the displacement of affects and responses from one object representation to another. But this is a partial description which does not account for the full range of transference phenomena. Unquestionably, displacement does operate at some level of the organization of the transference. That is to say, the patient responds to the analyst as a sort of substitute father or mother or other significant transference figure. But this description applies more to the early phases in the organization and emergence of the transference. It is also valid as a description of the broad range of transference experiences that occur in almost any situation of significant human interaction.

The transference neurosis in the full maturation of its expression in the analysis is of a different order (Stone, 1961). The relationship with the original infantile objects was itself compounded by the interplay and intertwining of processes of introjection and projection, operating within the specific developmental matrix of that stage in the child's experience. In other words, the relationship to the infantile objects involved critical internalizations, and these have become a part of the patient's inner world and the structure of his own functioning personality. In the emergence of the full-blown transference neurosis, the patient is once again caught up in a process of projecting and introjecting; through the analytic regression the patient has retreated to a level at which the patterns of infantile projection and introjection are reactivated and play themselves out in the present therapeutic relationship (Bychowski, 1956).

Thus there is a re-creation of the original relationship between the self and its object within the patient's inner world, which is then externalized to involve the analyst. Subtle and unconscious pressures are created to draw the analyst into the inner psychic drama of the patient's introjects. The analyst is not only pulled into this infantile relationship and its inherent dramatization, but is also induced to take the role of the infantile object and thus to play out the part of the original object in the patient's infantile drama. We find a subtle interaction of symbolic manipulation, magic, and illusion in the development of the transference neurosis. As Modell (1968) notes in this connection:

> By symbolic manipulation, an illusion of control and mastery is created — an illusion that the original objects in the external world can be controlled by means of the symbolic representation in the internal world. In the transference neurosis, this internal reality is transferred upon the external reality, that is, upon the relationship with the analyst. It is not only that the analyst is perceived in accordance with older imagoes, he is also unconsciously manipulated to *act* in accordance with these imagoes so that the analytic process itself becomes a stage for the re-creation of the internal drama [p. 129].

This same interplay of projection and introjection in the evolution of the transference neurosis is identified by Malin and Grotstein (1966) in their discussion of projective identification:[1]

[1] This reference puts the interaction of projection and introjection within the transference in terms of "projective identification." In terms of our previous theoretical discussion, the concept of projective identification has no place since it is equivalent to the combination and interplay of projection and introjection. It is a bastard concept that serves only to obfuscate the metapsychological discrimination between introjective processes and identifications. For further discussion, see Meissner (1971, 1980b).

Transference phenomena are obviously very closely related to projective identification. Transference implies the projection of inner attitudes which came from earlier object relationships into the figure of the analyst during the analysis. A much broader concept of transference would state that all subsequent relationships are modified on the basis of the earliest object relationship of the individual which is now established in the inner psychic life. . . . If we accept a broad view of transference to include all object relations, internal and external, after the primary relationship with the breast-mother which is now internalized, then we are stating that all object relations and all transference phenomena are examples, at least in part, of projective identification. This implies that there must be a projection from within the psychic apparatus into the external object. We emphasize that this includes parts of self as well as internal object representations [p. 28].

Let me try to focus the preceding discussion in terms of a clinical example. A young professional man came to analysis because of a persistent and chronic depression of more or less bothersome proportions. He was also concerned about the pattern of his heterosexual involvements. The initial attachment was usually intense and rapid, but, as the relationship progressed, he became increasingly bored, dissatisfied, and finally critical and distancing, leading to his breaking off the relationship. He had had previous experience in psychotherapy, but felt dissatisfied because he had more or less evaded the therapist's attempts to deal with any core problems. He felt he had gotten the most out of the therapy when the therapist had expressed support and reinforcement for his more positive attributes and capacities. Since his underlying problems had persisted, however, he now felt he needed a more serious and extensive treatment.

In the beginning of the analysis, this patient's attitude was circumspect, deferential yet distant. He seemed to be testing the water, uncertain how to respond to me, and generally playing it close to the vest. However, he gradually warmed up to the analytic task over the ensuing months, and I felt he had developed a basically positive transference. His demeanor was one of trying to do the right thing, trying to please me by working at free-associating, and generally being a good boy.

His history revealed that his father had died of a heart attack quite unexpectedly when the patient was ten. In describing this event, the patient passed over it with apparent equanimity and matter-of-fact-ness. Following his father's death, however, a different story emerged, a saga of intensifying tension, conflict, mutual resentment, recrimination, and hostility between the patient and his mother. After his father's death, it seems that his mother had become quite depressed and resentful, constantly complaining bitterly about losing her husband, about being left to bring up her sons without him. She complained about having to work, about my patient's lack of cooperativeness and helpfulness, etc., etc.

My patient resented her endless demands, which seemed more than he could possibly bear. Anything she asked him was too much to expect from him. Her constant complaints and bitter recriminations frustrated and infuriated him. But it also became apparent that neither mother nor son could let things be. They were drawn to each other, and each contributed in their measure and turn to the unremitting struggle between them. Neither one could leave the waters unmuddied. When one threw down the gauntlet, the other seemed compelled to take it up, to continue the struggle, to fan the flames of anger and resentment.

With the analytic regression, the patient gradually became able to deal with his repressed and long-standing grief over the loss of his father. As the tears flowed, his repressed hostility and resentment toward his father became more available and he could express some of it and begin to work it through. His father had always been distant and unavailable. The patient could remember only one or two instances where his father had spent any time with him or even seemed inclined to play with him. His father had rarely been at home, and when he was, he seemed always to be hidden behind a newspaper. The patient recalled scenes of his playing on the floor at his father's feet as a little child, trying to get his father's attention and constantly feeling himself too little, too insignificant. The complaint was that he got little or nothing from his father, despite his attempts to please, to gain his father's attention and approval, to be a good boy.

It was not long before this repressed and frustrated homosexual yearning was translated into the transference. He began to complain that he got little or nothing from me, that he knew nothing about me, and that I seemed distant and unavailable. I became the Olympian father-figure, to whom he had no choice but to submit and comply, to try to please as best he could, and against whom his anger and resentment were impotent and meaningless. His resentment of this unapproachable Olympian deity became more conscious as the transference evolved. His resentment took the form of feeling cheated out of something, even as he felt cheated out of something in life. He had been cheated out of any closeness with his father, cheated out of any warmth and maternal affection from his mother. He felt generally resentful and bitter toward the whole world.

His life was filled with burdens — burdens in his work, burdens from his girlfriends, burdens in his analysis. Everywhere he turned, people made demands on him to perform, to produce, to respond to their needs, and to satisfy their expectations. On all these fronts, he felt increasingly burdened and depressed and harried. Getting out of bed in the morning was agony; it meant leaving the warmth and comfort of his blankets to face the cold demands and unrelenting expectations of a hostile and uncaring world. Even his sexual relationships oppressed him. At first he felt gratified, stimulated, and excited by involvement with a new girlfriend. The sex was intriguing and the challenge of getting to know her and becoming sexually intimate invigorated him. But as soon as the relationship began to deepen and she began to have expectations of him and to put demands on him, he became ambivalent, dissatisfied, and resentful. He felt burdened, constrained, put upon and taken advantage of.

As these feelings became elaborated within the analysis, the striking parallel between the patient's posture in this regard and that evinced by his mother came increasingly into focus. His life, his experience, and his behavior were all governed by and organized around a powerful introject, which derived in large part from his mother. On the one side, there were his feelings of inadequacy, insignificance, worthlessness, and the feelings of being bored and burdened, cheated and deprived. The opposite side, however, displayed his wishes for admiration and respect, his conviction that things should be given to him and that he should not have to work hard for them, that the world owed him something. His constant complaint was: "Haven't I suffered enough? Haven't I done enough already? Who do they think they are expecting anything more from me?" It was in these terms that the profound sense of narcissistic entitlement, which had been shared by both mother and son and which formed the basis for their continual struggle to achieve narcissistic gratification from each other, expressed itself.

These aspects of the maternal introject were complemented by a contribution from the father, who had received acknowledgment and respect without apparently having to work for it — at least at home and in the experience of his little son. The transference neurosis, then, took shape around these introjective elements. As we have already noted, the patient saw me in Olympian terms, demanding compliance and submission from him, particularly to the terms of the analysis. I was not called upon to give him anything or to provide him with any meaningful response or acknowledgment. It was this Olympian aspect of his own inner self, repressed and unacknowledged, yet fed into in complex and interacting ways by derivatives of the personalities of both his parental objects, that created the matrix out of which the transference neurosis emerged.

Following the lines of our previous discussion, the analytic regression introduces a cathectic shift from the external real order to the patient's inner world. As the regression intensifies, a corresponding progressive activation of the underlying introjects occurs. This is followed by a second phase in the evolution of the transference, in which the activated elements of the introjects serve as a basis for ensuing projections, which qualify the object relationship between the patient and the analyst. Thus, as the regression deepens, the level of the interaction of introjection and projection tends to become more infantile. The patient in effect re-creates the same kind of relationship he had with infantile objects with the present analytic object. As this complex organization emerges, the patient begins to experience the same yearnings for gratification, the same frustration, rage, and jealousy, that were once felt toward the original objects and which have become repressed in the course of time. Both paternal and maternal imagoes play themselves out in varying combinations (Le Guen, 1974), but their expression takes place through the activation of processes of projection and introjection. The quality and patterning of the integration of these respective imagoes within the transference neurosis derive not only from the pattern of their interaction in the patient's developmental experience in relating to parental objects, but also from the ongoing interaction with the analyst. This interaction involves, as we shall see, not only countertransference determinants but also specific qualities embedded in the real relationship between the analyst and the patient.

Essentially, then, this interplay of introjection and projection tends to re-create a certain aspect of the content of the patient's inner world in the outer world of his experience with objects. The inner world can be said to invade or interpenetrate the functions of the patient's reality ego. In effect, the emergence of the transference neurosis creates a transitional object relationship, which is compounded out of the interplay of introjection and projection in the analytic relationship (Meissner, 1978b). The regression is in fact close to being a "regression in the service of the ego," to use Kris's (1952) excellent phrase; it is also, in the analysis, put in the service of the analytic process and its therapeutic objectives.

It is in terms of this subtle interplay between projection and introjection that the transference neurosis is organized and emerges within the analytic situation. The transference neurosis re-creates, in some approximate sense, the elements of the oedipal involvement, which, as we have already suggested, may in varying degrees reflect oedipal and preoedipal constituents. The re-creation of these infantile elements is not identical, but is influenced by the pattern of interaction that emerges in the therapeutic relationship. In other words, although infantile elements are reactivated, they become focused and realized in a newly created interaction with the analyst, which provides not only the access to these elements, but also the matrix for their reworking and resolution.

In some broader sense, the interaction of projection and introjection takes on what can be called a paranoid flavor in that the analytic object becomes the receptacle for projective modifications. Le Guen (1975) has highlighted this "paranoid" dimension of the transference interaction: "In psychoanalytic treatment the analyst is the stranger *par excellence*: his being can never quite be grasped, he is the object of fantasy, he is never present where we expect him, the full sense of this presence is revealed through frustration and he appears to mean the losses and desires of the analysand. He is the distant inheritor of the non-mother and his function is inexorably paternal, because of his original configuration—and this despite the varied imago representations he assumes during treatment" (p. 372). Here we can say that the transference neurosis reactivates and reprocesses the same basic constituents of projection and introjection that played themselves out in the earlier oedipal drama, in which the dialectic of motherness and non-motherness is constructed into the triangular oedipal conflict. The role of the interaction of introjection and projection in the organization of the oedipal situation and their correlative role in the processing of underlying pregenital ambivalences have been discussed in detail elsewhere (Meissner, 1978b).

The transitional object relationship of the transference neurosis, elaborated out of interlocking projections and introjections, operates in the realm of transitional phenomena so aptly described by Winnicott (1965, 1971). This realm cannot be simply reduced to either subjective experience or objective reality. Rather, it is an area in which the subjective and the objective overlap to create a third realm of experience, the realm of illusion. Within this realm of the patient's experience, brought about by the analytic regression and expressing itself in terms of the distinctive qualities of illusory experience, the most powerful creative potentials of the patient are realized and unleashed in the service of the therapeutic goals (Olinick, 1975). Reading backwards in history, it must have been something like the creative potential of this area of illusory experience that Freud (1915b) had in mind when he referred to the transference as the most powerful instrument at our disposal for therapeutic change.

Within the analysis, the analytic object may be perceived as an object of projection, that is, as being endowed with qualities from the patient's inner world (the introjective configuration). The analyst is thus seen as an object within the range of illusory experience. But, in general, in clearly defined cases of neurosis, the patient retains the capacity of reality testing and the capacity to recognize, acknowledge, and accept the separate existence of the external object. The maintenance of this capacity to acknowledge and tolerate the separate existence of the object reflects the underlying structural integrity of the patient's sense of self in the face of regressive pulls toward merging and fusion. In such patients, we find the critical developmental achievement of a cohesive sense of self, which the analytic regression cannot undermine. Modell's (1968) comment focuses the crux of the matter here:

> The persistence of structural organizations safeguards the function of reality testing. Although there may be a blurring of the distinction between the inner and outer worlds so that the symbolic elements of the inner world invade the representation of the outer world, the structural integrity of the sense of self preserves the capacity to separate the object from the self. The object may be perceived in accordance with qualities of the inner world — that is, an element of illusion enters into perception — but the capacity to acknowledge the separateness of the external object is maintained [p. 133].

As aspects of the introjective organization are reactivated, these neurotic patients can enter into a transitional object relationship with the analyst without losing their sense of integrity and self-cohesion; they are able to preserve their capacity to acknowledge the separate existence of the object. The regression here is primarily functional (topographic) and only minimally structural. In other patients, however, where the developmental process has not resulted in a level of secure integration and a coherent sense of self, the analytic regression can lead to a level of functioning in which the patient is unable to maintain a coherent sense of self, and in which the diffusion of the patient's sense of identity and the fragmentation of the sense of self bring about an incapacity to recognize the separateness of the analyst as an independently existing extrinsic object. There can be a failure in the patient's capacity to test reality, so that the projective modification of the analyst is accepted as no longer merely illusory, but real. This is the pattern of the transference psychosis, which involves not only functional regression, but structural regression as well.

It must be kept in mind that the transference, and particularly the transference neurosis, involves multiple levels of developmental experience. The construction of the transitional object relationship thus takes place on different levels, levels that reflect the patient's developmental experience and express, often in very vivid ways, strata of the patient's psychic organization. In neurotic patients, the transference neurosis characteristically expresses the dynamics of oedipal involvements, but often it also expresses various aspects of preoedipal libidinal attachments. At different times in the progression of the analytic process, the transference dynamics reflect different configurations, and often they shift considerably from level to level of developmental derivatives.

One must also remember that the narcissistic derivatives of the introjective economy are reactivated by the analytic regression and inevitably play themselves out in the transference neurosis. The dynamics of the transference are not simply a matter of the organization of object libido, but are caught up in the vicissitudes of narcissistic development as well. As we shall see, the narcissistic elements in the transference relationship must be worked through on their own terms for the pathogenic introjective alignment to be significantly modified.

Kohut, in his admirable work on the dynamics of the self (1971), has described some characteristic forms of narcissistic transference observed in a fairly narrow segment of patients with what he terms "narcissistic personality disorders." His delineation of the mirror and the idealizing transferences reflects the underlying narcissistic dynamics of the grandiose self and the idealized parental imago. Here it is worth noting that the grandiose self and the idealized parental imago represent aspects of the introjective organization and the correlated projective components at a certain stage of narcissistic development.

It has been my own experience, in the treatment of analytic patients, that frequently enough a significant regression takes place within the transference neurosis, which elicits an underlying narcissistic configuration and brings some of the dynamic issues that Kohut discusses into play in the analytic process. Here I am not referring to patients with "narcissistic personality disorders." Elements of the narcissistic configurations that Kohut has described may appear in patients whose initial pathology does not present as especially narcissistic, and who seem classically neurotic, whether hysterical or obsessional or mixed. Apparently, in Kohut's narcissistic personality disorders, the narcissistic dynamics dominate the transference interaction. But in patients I am describing, the narcissistic issues emerge only as a result of the transference regression, and then only after considerable working through of other levels of transference meaning and involvement. In other words, the narcissistic configurations become a central issue in the analytic process only secondarily.

As we have seen, the emergence of the full-blown transference neurosis depends on the stimulation and organization of object displacements and, more particularly, projections, through the activation of the underlying introjects. In this regard, the transference neurosis is a specific manifestation of the analytic process as such; it is not seen, or is seen only rarely and exceptionally, in other contexts of human interaction. And it is the transference neurosis that provides the analytic setting with its unique qualities and its unique therapeutic potential.

The transference neurosis is the most vivid, the most direct and dramatic expression of the underlying introjective configuration around which the patient's sense of self is organized. As the progressive layers of introjective organization are mobilized by regression in the transference, they are successively worked through so that there is a gradual undoing, reshaping, and reorganization of the patient's introjective economy. This is accomplished by the delineation and clarification of the various aspects of the introjective configuration and the linking of these multiple aspects to dimensions of the patient's life experience, particularly to the context of the object relationship between the patient and significant — usually parental — objects.

We can discuss the analytic process in terms of the work of interpreting, and working through. But what I am emphasizing here is another level of therapeutic interaction, which is equally if not often more important than the level of verbal interchange. In the transference neurosis, a process is set in motion at an implicit, nonexpressed, and frequently unconscious level. The reworking of the patient's introjects takes place through the continual interaction and interplay of projection and introjection within the analytic relation. This process goes on in subtle ways that are often not explicitly focused in the analytic work, but which have a reality of their own nonetheless. It should be remembered, of course, that these processes do not operate only on the analysand's part. The analyst, too, enters into and experiences them in his own way. We need constantly to remind ourselves that if there is transference, there is also countertransference. The analyst's countertransference plays out the same dynamic elements that are mobilized within the patient.

In other words, the analyst relates to the patient by way of the interplay of introjection and projection in his own head. The quality and nature of the countertransference have to do with the quality and nature of the analyst's own introjective alignment. More particularly, by way of this interplay of projection and introjection, the analyst, too, enters into a realm of illusory experience, which is shared with the patient and which thereby creates the matrix within which the analyst and the patient play out the dynamics of the analytic process. As the analytic work progresses, the patient's introjective configuration is gradually modified, and a major contribution to this process of modification is made by the projective aspects derived from the analyst.

In this view of the analytic process, the technical elements of free association, interpretation, and working through become a necessary vehicle for more fundamental processes taking place in the interaction between the analyst and the patient. It is these other processes, often unattended and unconscious, that frequently carry the burden of the effective therapeutic modification. And it is within the illusory realm of interaction of projection and introjection—from both the patient and the analyst—that the possibilities for mobilizing the patient's creative energies are realized. This aspect of the analytic process corresponds to what Winnicott so aptly delineates in his analysis of play (1971).

The direction and form of the internal remodeling, which is the primary therapeutic purpose of the analytic process, depend on and derive from the quality of the analytic interaction within this illusory realm. The analytic regression opens up and makes available the patient's powerful creative potential, which allows for more effective and adaptive reorganization. As the processes of projection and introjection work themselves through in this matrix of creative potential, the significant internalization which occurs as the analytic work proceeds bears particularly on the person of the analyst. The analyst becomes the significant object in relation to whom the work of progressive remodeling takes place.

The analyst serves as the basis for what has been termed the "analytic introject." The analytic introject is in fact formed by the patient's psychic processes, but it is contributed to by significant projections on the part of the analyst, which play into the illusory therapeutic matrix. This raises the critical question: What precisely is projected in this interaction? Our suggestion here is that what is projected is derived from the analyst's own introjective organization. This position carries certain important implications, namely, that a critical variable in analytic work and in the successful therapeutic outcome—if not with all patients, at least with a significant proportion of patients—is the quality of the therapist's own internal organization and the dimensions inherent in his own sense of self.

In a sense, the critical factor suggested here transcends the technical apparatus which serves as the vehicle for analytic interaction. This position inevitably raises difficult questions for analytic education and training. By inference, analytic institutes could not be satisfied with mere technical competence, but would have to address themselves to significant dimensions of the therapist's own personality. Ideally, the didactic analysis, successfully completed and thoroughly conducted, would satisfy any need for reorganization and integration of the therapist's own personality—but, in the practical order, there often seems reason to wonder whether such effective reorganization is really achieved, or whether, with the complexities of the training situation and the inevitable extrinsic pressures placed on the didactic process, what is more often achieved is not a form of analytic compliance, generated both by the expectations of the training analyst and by the wishes and narcissistic defenses of the analytic candidate.

As we have discussed, the pathogenic elements of the patient's introjects are reworked and remodeled in terms of the analytic introject. The consequent realignment in the patient's inner world releases an energic potential and a creative capacity for more effective and constructive forms of internalization. The reworking of the patient's self- and ego organizations undermines more defensively motivated and drive-influenced introjective alignments, and it may now be possible to mobilize higher-order identificatory processes within the analytic relation. There is the potential for reworking the analytic introject in terms of constructive identifications, which reprocess structural aspects of the patient's ego and superego formations in the direction of increasing autonomy and adaptive capacity.

Some important clinical implications of this discussion of the transference neurosis should not be ignored. The analysis of the transference neurosis requires that the underlying introjects be clearly and consciously delineated and that their genesis and source be determined and adequately described. The motives involved in the original object relation must also be carefully and fully examined and analyzed. Not only must the unconscious motives regarding the original introjection be thoroughly explored and reconstructed, but the continuing unconscious motives that underlie the patient's contemporary adherence to that introjective configuration must be adequately and, as far as possible, completely probed and interpreted. Finally, the specific issues related to the reemergence of these introjective components in the context of the ongoing relation with the analyst need to be thoroughly worked through and resolved.

In this regard, it should be emphasized that analyzing the transference from the perspective of the relevant internalizations brings into focus the complexity of the motivational strata that are built into the transference. In the long run, it is not adequate for the analytic work to settle for the interpretation and working through of the elements in the transference that derive from and reflect relations with previous significant objects. This accomplishes only a part of the transference resolution — a part focused only on the object relations aspects of the patient's pathology and the related instinctual vicissitudes. Including the introjective components into the picture, it seems to me, adds a quite distinct and different set of motivations, which require separate exploration, analysis, and resolution. With regard to

the narcissistic components, for example, a limited, object relations approach might bring to light certain aspects of idealization, along with the object-related derivatives of the idealized
parental imago, but such an approach would tend to ignore or
pass over the sense of inner grandiosity and the derivatives of
the grandiose self (Kohut, 1971).

A second point of importance is that the working through of
the transference elements is not accomplished exclusively on the
level of verbalization and interpretation. This is perhaps a
relatively uncontroversial point that is understood by most
analysts, but it deserves particular emphasis here. All the
aspects of the transference neurosis suggested above must be
clearly and explicitly delineated, and this requires continual
refocusing and interpretation. But one must also be aware that
the reworking does not simply take place on this conscious and
articulate level. Much of the work takes place on less conscious,
less explicit levels of personal interaction. How the analyst
responds to the patient; how the analyst feels about the patient;
the tone of voice used — whether lecturing, pedagogical, com-
forting, challenging, demanding, haughty, demeaning, caustic,
supportive, sympathetic, bored, hopeful, or impatient (the list is
endless) — the manner in which the analyst goes about conduct-
ung the analysis (different at different phases of the analytic
process); the attitude of respect, attentiveness, concern, interest, and empathy generated and maintained throughout the
analysis — all play an important role. The working through and
reshaping of introjective configurations occur at all levels of the
analytic interaction — just as the forming of the original introjects reflected not merely verbal or even consciously expressed
emotional attitudes between the parent and the child, but rather
was the product of the complex and largely unconscious levels of
communication that took place between them.

Here we should refer to the countertransference, to the reactive and responsive projections by which the analyst meets the
patient's projections. Countertransference projections play an
important unconscious determining role in the overall pattern
of the analyst's response to the patient. A crucial and central element is the extent to which the analyst is empathically attuned
to the patient's inner world and feelings and can respond in

ways which implicitly acknowledge, recognize, and respect the patient's unique individuality and personhood. As we have suggested, these matters relate more to the analyst's own personality integration and functioning than to specific technical aspects of the treatment. The point is that the analyst cannot deal with these dimensions of the analytic interaction by mere technical correctness — in fact, technical correctness may itself easily become the vehicle of countertransference manifestations.

I would, nevertheless, argue that analytic interpretations — having their own inherent validity and impact on the process of psychic change — also serve in large measure as the medium through which these other aspects of the interaction take shape and are expressed. It must be remembered, however, that interpretations are not the sole vehicle of this expression. It is entirely possible that the technically correct analyst, whose interventions are appropriate, well timed, and accurate, and whose interpretations are exact and valid, may find his effectiveness mitigated and the analytic outcome less than optimal precisely because of subtle, unacknowledged, and largely nonverbal communications which tend to run counter to the drift of the conscious interpretative work and tend to reinforce and maintain the patient's basic introjective organization. As we well know, the best intentions and conscious attitudes of parents do not prevent unconscious projections from influencing the child's introjections.

A third important point of emphasis — actually a correlate of the first — is that the resolution of transference elements depends ultimately on the surrendering of the introjects and their implicit object attachments and the appropriate mourning of this loss. The perspective provided by the paranoid process suggests that projective elements (out of which the transference neurosis is compounded) derive from the underlying introjective components (Meissner, 1978b). The working through of these projections in the transference leads to a reactivation (perhaps a reintrojection) of introjective elements and a corresponding sense of loss of the projectively transformed object. There must be, therefore, a mourning of the loss of the object as such. However, the mourning process is not completed nor are the roots of the transference resolved until the attachment to the introject is given up and renounced and the loss of this substitutive and internalized object adequately mourned. It can easily be seen that our understanding of internalization adds a significantly different and critically important dimension to the process of transference resolution and the working through of transference residues.

As the analytic process plays itself out, constructive identifications take an increasingly prominent role, and there is a gradual shift from the predominance of transference neurosis elements toward greater amplification of the therapeutic alliance within the therapeutic relationship. Within the emergence and reworking of the transference neurosis, we found a regressive movement, in the direction of increasing the intensity and vividness of projective elements, often through successively more primitive developmental levels and issues. But correspondingly, within the resolution of the transference neurosis, we find a progressive movement, which involves the processing of the analytic introject and the gradual emergence of capacities for identifications. Now the therapeutic alliance becomes a major consideration. Although the therapeutic alliance has all along been a stabilizing force and a controlling element in the staging of the analytic process, at some point in the resolution of the transference neurosis, the therapeutic alliance itself becomes a focus of the analytic process and must be worked through on its own terms.

THERAPEUTIC ALLIANCE

The therapeutic alliance, far from being a static or unitary phenomenon, in fact has a history and a development that can be traced through the analytic progression. Our major concern, then, in the process approach to the therapeutic alliance is to delineate some of the dimensions of this progression. But first we must answer a basic question. If the therapeutic alliance has a developmental progression, it must therefore have a beginning or starting point. What, then, can we define as the point of initiation of the therapeutic alliance?

Another way of phrasing this is to ask: What are the minimal conditions that allow for the setting up and putting into play of the basic constituents of the analytic situation? We are not at this point inquiring about the structural requisites for the therapeutic alliance, factors whose contribution to the analytic situation we have already considered. Rather, we are concerned with the basic conditions necessary to get the analytic process under way. At a minimum, it would seem that the necessary conditions for the patient's initial contact in the therapeutic situation are hardly different from the terms that bring any patient to seek assistance and alleviation of pain from a helping person (Friedman, 1969). These are the conditions that obtain generally in the doctor-patient relationship throughout the whole range of medical practice.

Patients come because they are in distress, because they are in pain, or because they realize that they are suffering from a condition that places them at significant risk. They seek alleviation of their distress, relief from their pain, or correction of the maladaptive condition. There is a certain fundamental trust that they place in the helping figure in presuming that that figure can do something to help them obtain the relief they seek. The process of coming to a physician and submitting oneself to the physician's care implies a basic willingness to accept the competence and capacity of the physician to cure.

There is both a rational and an irrational side to this willingness (Greenson, 1967). The reasonable component has to do with the physician's training, knowledge, experience, and competence, as well as the objective necessity for medical intervention. The irrational component, however, embraces a number of factors, including symbolic elements, sometimes magical expectations, superstitious beliefs, preformed transference elements, wishes, narcissistic defenses, as well as the basic capacity for entrusting oneself to the care of another human being.

Following Mehlman's (1976) clarifying suggestions, a critical element in this context is that in a situation of presumed narcissistic vulnerability, the patient moves to include the relationship to the analyst in the armamentarium of narcissistically protective elements used to guard a fragile sense of self. That quality which enables the patient to reorganize the narcissistic defensive organization to include the analytic relationship has been described in terms of "basic trust" (Zetzel, 1970). Mehlman

(1976) describes the initial therapeutic rapport as a "narcissistic alliance" which is rooted in basic trust. In her original discussion of the therapeutic alliance, Zetzel links the elements of basic trust to the successful negotiation of the early maternal one-to-one object relationship, in much the same terms as Erikson (1963).

Here a basic discrimination must be made. The patient must carry into the treatment context a capacity for narcissistic alliance. If, however, archaic narcissistic elements dominate the personality, this capacity may be seriously impaired. Such patients may be so involved in the demands instituted by the grandiose self or the need to maintain narcissistic equilibrium by attachment to an idealized object (Kohut, 1971) that even the first step of the narcissistic alliance becomes problematic. In such cases, the grandiosity of the self cannot tolerate any dependence on the helping object, or the need for an idealized selfobject generates such magical and illusory expectations that an effective alliance is subverted and brought into the service of the patient's narcissistic needs (Meissner, 1977c). These patients lack the capacity to form a narcissistic alliance and are deficient in basic trust. One would conclude that analysis with such patients is either impossible or can be done only with limited goals. In some cases, however, psychotherapy may sufficiently modify the patient's narcissism to permit a narcissistic alliance to emerge.

Our position here is that this first trusting rapport or narcissistic alliance provides the basic root out of which the therapeutic alliance will develop. The nourishing of these rudiments of the therapeutic alliance depends in large part on the empathic and intuitive responsiveness of the analyst from the very beginning of contact with the patient. Zetzel's description of this process in terms of the working through of primitive one-to-one issues in relationships with primary objects is very much to the point, since the model of that early parental interaction is operative from the very beginning of the therapeutic interaction.

The patient's willingness to include the therapeutic relationship in his narcissistic defensive organization must be responded to by the therapist in a way that is sensitive to the areas of narcissistic vulnerability, minimizes anxiety, and shores up the patient's faltering narcissism. Commenting on this process, Mehlman (1976) observes:

> In order to begin any kind of reasonable rapport, we are forced to allow to exist whatever latent willingness to trust in our charisma there is or whatever non-rational positive motivations already exist. Indeed, the appeal to reason so often only aggravates the situation, and the patient's initial comfort or fright can be said to be dependent on a variety of inarticulate factors which the successful practitioner intuitively responds to. He does a series of things that can be summed up by saying that he determines what the locus of the immediate narcissistic crisis or problem is, addresses himself to it, intuitively or cognitively, and in the process avoids *adding* to the fright and actually *diminishes* it sufficiently to allow the patient to include him *irrationally* as part of the adaptive-defensive system already operating [pp. 15–16].

In the mutuality and reciprocal responsiveness between mother and child the sense of basic trust is laid down and established (Erikson, 1963). Similarly, it is the therapist's capacity to respond empathically and intuitively to the patient's sense of vulnerability and to the patient's individuality that contributes maximally to the establishment and evolution of the therapeutic alliance.

It is important to realize that even at this initial level the issues of alliance are quite different from those of transference. The distinction has been adequately drawn in Zetzel's (1970) original formulations, but it needs to be reemphasized in the present context since our consideration of narcissistic issues may give rise to some confusion. The narcissistic alliance we have been discussing is to be distinguished from forms of narcissistic transference. In describing the formation of the alliance in the narcissistic personality disorders, Kohut (1971) observes:

> The observing segment of the personality of the analysand which, in cooperation with the analyst, has actively shouldered the task of analyzing, is not, in essence, different in analyzable narcissistic disorders from that found in analyzable transference neuroses. In both types of cases an adequate area of realistic cooperation derived from positive experiences in childhood (in the object-cathected *and* narcissistic realm) is the precondition for the analysand's maintenance of the therapeutic split of the ego and for that fond-

ness for the analyst which assures the maintenance of a sufficient trust in the processes and goals of analysis during stressful periods.

The idealizing transference, on the other hand, and the mirror transference are the *objects* of the analysis; i.e., the observing and analyzing part of the ego of the analysand, in cooperation with the analyst, is confronting them, and, by gradually comprehending them in dynamic, economic, structural, and genetic dimensions, attempts to achieve a gradual mastery over them and to relinquish the demands that are correlated with them. The achievement of such mastery is the essential and specific therapeutic goal of the analysis of narcissistic disorders [p. 207].

Once the realignment of the patient's narcissistic defensive organization has taken place and the narcissistic alliance is allowed to emerge, it permits a basic trusting rapport and dependency on the analyst and sets the stage for the transference neurosis to develop. It is by reason of the narcissistic alliance, then, that the patient places himself in the analytic situation. Once there, the patient is subject to the regressive influences of the analytic situation and the analytic process is set in motion. The emergence of the transference neurosis is an expectable consequence of the analytic regression and the movement within the analytic process. That movement may, however, be impeded. Highly developed and rigidly preformed transferences may interfere with the establishment of the narcissistic alliance and may indicate the operation of massive, pathogenically organized narcissistic defense systems. (This is often the case in psychotic or severely borderline patients.) The narcissistic alliance may also be undercut by the effects of the analytic regression, which may precipitate a response of traumatic anxiety or fragmentation of the patient's self. The latter circumstance may force the patient into a position of more primitive narcissistic defense which undermines the rudiments of basic trust and does not allow for the possibility of sustaining a narcissistic alliance.

This imperiling of the narcissistic alliance emerged in a patient whose analysis I have discussed in detail elsewhere (Meissner, 1978b). This young man was in his early twenties and had been referred for analysis because of his complaints of impotence, his phobic anxieties, and his persistent depression. The initial evaluation and the arrangements for the analysis were made before summer break, but the patient did not begin the analysis itself until late in the fall.

The intervening weeks provided ample opportunity for mobilization of the patient's anxieties about entering analysis and for the emergence of powerful preformed transference elements related to his obsessively anxious, intrusive, and controlling mother as well as to his perfectionistic and sadistically demeaning brother. In his first hours on the couch, the patient responded with intense anxiety in which fears of being hurt, attacked, or, as he put it, "shot down," pervaded his reaction to the analytic situation. He felt helpless and vulnerable. I became a powerful monster who was certain to pounce on him and tear him to shreds. The only alternatives were, as he saw it, to submit himself in total obeisance and placating submission to the will of the analyst, or to take flight. For several hours he hovered on the brink of fleeing from the analysis, and it was only by dint of reassuring and clarifying intervention on my part that the impulse to flee was short-circuited and the patient was able to moderate his persecutory anxieties. His alliance nonetheless remained a tenuous one through a significant part of the analysis and rested primarily on a narcissistic foundation. It was only when the transference wish to submit himself to an idealized but powerfully destructive and sadistically threatening object was clarified, and when he began to realize that I was not going to respond to his expectations of sadistic attack, that he was able to move from an essentially paranoid position to the beginnings of a narcissistic alliance.

To link this discussion to aspects of internalization, it would seem that the capacities that contribute to the narcissistic alliance derive from critical internalizations which take place early in the developmental experience, in the interaction with parental objects, particularly the mother. The internalizations derived from that context are difficult to conceptualize and can be aggregated loosely under the rubric of "basic trust." But this rubric does not do justice to the reality by any means, any more than it does justice to the full understanding of the elements that initially contribute to the narcissistic alliance. Here we must include both those elements that relate to an optimal symbiotic union with the mothering figure and those that contribute to an optimal distancing and separation from the symbiotic union. If, at this early stage, the child is overwhelmed by the threat of separation, loss, and annihilation, and experiences the pressures of severe anxiety and ambivalence, the balance of internalizing processes may shift away from constructive, positive identifications toward defensive, drive-dependent forms of introjection.

The resolution of the early developmental crisis that weights the psychic factors on the side of basic trust is accompanied by a predominance of constructive and relatively nonambivalent and nondefensive identifications. In contrast, if the crisis resolution leans in the direction of basic mistrust, the internal processes are caught up in the vicissitudes of ambivalence and defensive pressures. Introjective processes are then mobilized so that the external relationship with a bad or less-than-good object becomes an internally possessed sense of evil or defectiveness. Thus, from the very start of the narcissistic alliance, the analytic process begins to tap the fundamental roots of the introjective system and begins to activate and mobilize them within the analytic situation.

An important point in dealing with the therapeutic alliance is that within the analysis the alliance has a history and a course of development. In large measure, the articulation of this aspect of the analytic process remains relatively virgin territory. The emergence and development of the alliance in the analytic process can be envisioned, in broad terms, as following a progressive epigenetic course. Erikson's (1959, 1963) thinking regarding development has provided us with an epigenetic schema and a set of categories and a vocabulary in terms of which we can discuss these issues.

One can, for example, look at the emergent qualities of the therapeutic alliance in terms of Erikson's epigenetic schema and define its relevant parameters around the issues of trust, autonomy, initiative, industry, identity, intimacy, etc. Erikson (1964) has also provided us with a schema of strengths or virtues, including hope, will, purpose, competence, fidelity, love, care, and wisdom. I have no way of knowing at this point if

Erikson's categories will be the most useful or the most revealing in deepening our understanding of the therapeutic alliance, but it is at least one available set of categories.

In keeping with the overall epigenetic frame of reference, it should be noted that the individual elements of the schema may also have their own describable ontogeny. Mehlman (1976), for instance, has described a form of secondary trust, different from basic trust, in which, after the establishment of basic trust, a certain state of openness is maintained with the parents. According to Mehlman: "Secondary trust has to do with the willingness to cede over to the parental object some of those adaptive and defensive ego functions that would otherwise represent a *closed* system of previously internalized archaic parental images irrespective of their quality" (pp. 23–24). Thus the element of trust can be seen to have its own relatively independent ontogeny which reflects specific vicissitudes in the child's developmental experience. And this is paralleled in the analytic process. If the narcissistic alliance requires the operation of basic trust as a fundamental element, then the subsequent elaboration of the therapeutic alliance also requires trust, but it requires a more specifically evolved form of trust to sustain its functioning. In other words, as the therapeutic alliance emerges out of the narcissistic alliance, the element of trust undergoes a corresponding development. It does not by that reason lose contact with its roots in basic trust; rather, the element of trust goes through a progressive differentiation which maintains the rudiments of basic trust but organizes them in a form of secondary elaboration which in turn becomes more developed in the manner of its functioning and structure. Mehlman believes that it is this form of secondary trust that is operative in a genuine therapeutic alliance. He writes:

The failure of secondary trust or *premature* closure and solidification deprives the individual of the possibility of subsequent modifications developmentally (for instance of the superego) and makes the development of a genuine therapeutic alliance by definition relatively more impossible, since the kind of relating we are talking about in a therapeutic alliance is a late development in a relatively mature system and no longer subject only to primitive object relationships. The insistence upon the primitive usage of the parental object in avoidance of this progress, altogether representing an avoidance of closure (accepting an oedipal reality, for instance), also makes the development of a genuine therapeutic alliance impossible.

The development of trust, then, has its ontogeny, just as does narcissism. Basic trust would seem to be a necessary antecedent to the earlier establishment of sufficient object relationship to enable these early ego introjects to take place at all. *Secondary* trust or its failure has to do with the subsequent traumata that necessitate the child's becoming his own parent far too early and is probably a great deal of what we struggle with in developing a therapeutic as opposed to a purely narcissistic alliance. One could rephrase this by saying that premature closure calls a halt to the process of development that brings narcissistic need and therapeutic need closer together. We would hope by the later stages of treatment that the two had begun to approximate each other [p. 24].[2]

If we shift the discussion to the problem of internalization, secondary trust implies a continual openness to and acceptance of direction and influence from the parental objects. It implies a relative lack of ambivalence, the persistence of basic trust, and a receptiveness to positive, supportive, and constructive relationships with the parental objects. The premature closure implicit in the failure of secondary trust, however, suggests not only defensive fixation and separation from the influence of the parental object, but also a premature and defensively motivated internalization, namely, the forming of a pathogenic introject, which is tinged with paranoid elements. Both the elaboration of secondary trust and its failure are accompanied by significant internalizations — in the one case, constructive imitations and identifications, and, in the other, relatively pathogenic and defensively motivated introjections (Meissner, 1974d).

As we have seen, the patient's capacity for basic trust, reflecting the primary quality of the earliest mother-child one-to-one relationship, lays the ground for the patient's reorganization of

[2] We can note here that Stone's (1961) discussion of trust is cast in transference terms, but that the distinction of basic versus secondary trust follows a similar progression. He relates basic trust to the primary transference, as a reflection of the primary maternal symbiotic union. Secondary trust is thus related to the mother of separation.

narcissistic defenses to an extent that allows him to place himself in a relationship of dependence on the analyst. While it involves a reorganization of the patient's narcissistic defensive organization, the narcissistic alliance does not change the basic pathogenic configuration. It merely sets the conditions within which the initial tolerance of the analytic situation is made possible. The patient is now able to submit to the eliciting conditions of the analytic process, which leads in the direction of the emergence of transference elements and the evolution of a transference neurosis.

A transition, however, must be made from this initial level of narcissistic defensive alliance to a genuine therapeutic alliance. As we have noted, the critical element is the transformation of basic trust into a more elaborated and secure sense of secondary trust. What makes this transition possible is the empathic responsiveness of the analyst, who senses the locus of the patient's narcissistic vulnerability and provides sufficient support and reassurance for the patient to enter more deeply into the relationship without the threat of further narcissistic injury. It is at this critical juncture that the characteristics and sensitive empathic response of the analyst play a key role (Greenson, 1960; Olinick, 1975; Poland, 1975; Schafer, 1959). If the analyst's demeanor in the analytic situation does not respond to the patient's sense of narcissistic need, the patient will react by a premature closure, thus cutting off any emerging sense of reliance on the analytic object.

It is only to the extent to which the patient can move to a position of sustained openness and receptivity with regard to the analytic object that the possibility obtains for the transition to a more genuine therapeutic alliance. For most analyzable patients, the level of secondary trust is sufficiently established to allow this transition to occur almost inadvertently. But in those patients in whom the premature closure of basic trust has constituted a developmental problem, the interaction with the analyst at this juncture consists of an initial reworking of the developmental defect in order to allow for further progression within the analysis. Here I would like to quote Mehlman's (1976) discussion:

It is this secondary trust which I believe must be revived or maintained if a therapeutic alliance is to be established. Needless to say, this state may well represent the end stage of many analyses, rather than the beginning and represent in those obsessional patients I mentioned the repair and amelioration of a *secondarily* disturbed object relationship which also prevents the establishment of close and loving *adult* relationships involving this very same sort of trust. The degree to which this openness is *not* established would also seem to determine how little beyond the situation of basic trust going on to transference development, transference flooding, and private efforts to control the patient will go. This failure would appear to be intimately involved in the inhibition of the development of the *therapeutic* relationship which . . . is not only the cause of but also the *remedy* for this kind of narcissistic emergency in therapy.

It is at this juncture that the sequence of transference flooding or crisis, mobilization of defensive need, narcissistically protective resistance, analysis of the resistance and *enhancement* of the therapeutic alliance may be seen. On the basis of the narcissistic alliance on which the transference is based, a struggle is joined and not broken off, and the sequence of therapist interposing himself between the patient and danger by joining the patient in his struggles with it becomes the intermediary from narcissistic defense to therapeutic alliance [p. 22].

The therapeutic alliance thus becomes the essential vehicle for further progress in the analysis. But the therapeutic alliance itself is not a static entity. It is not simply established and then maintained during the emergence and resolution of the transference neurosis. Rather, the therapeutic alliance itself undergoes dynamic change within the analytic process. Moreover, at each stage of the analytic process, the status of the therapeutic alliance in fact sets the limits within which the analytic regression takes place, as well as the extent to which the ego can tolerate the emergence of infantile derivatives and their attendant anxieties.

The emergence of the transference neurosis occurs step by step, and each step of the regressive revivification of transference elements is correlated with a deepening and a consolidating of the therapeutic alliance. Or, to put it another way, at each level the transference revivification serves to challenge the therapeutic alliance. There is a reciprocal relationship between the predominance and intensity of transference elements in the therapeutic realtionship and the operation of alliance factors. The more the relationship with the analyst is contaminated by transference factors, the more difficulty there is in maintaining a stable and effective therapeutic alliance. Consequently, during the stages of analytic regression, a constant effort must be made to stabilize and maintain the therapeutic alliance, since it may be eroded by the emergence of infantile derivatives in the transference neurosis (Dickes, 1967).

During this phase of analytic regression and emergence of the transference neurosis, a key element in the therapeutic alliance is that of trust. As the regression takes place, the patient's trusting relationship with the analyst, particularly in terms of the differentiation and consolidation of secondary trust, must be continually reinforced and sustained. As the transference elements deepen and reflect successively more regressed aspects of the patient's functioning and personality organization, the therapeutic alliance is increasingly threatened and undermined. This effect is primarily buffered by the capacity of the analyst to stay the patient's anxiety and protect the critical areas of narcissistic vulnerability.

During the regressive phase, then, the therapeutic alliance serves a sustaining and buffering function to more or less allow this process to take place. However, as the analytic process moves into a more progressive phase, in which the elements of the transference neurosis begin to be analyzed, interpreted, and worked through, the therapeutic alliance itself undergoes a series of reworkings of developmental crises forming an epigenetic progression. It is the working through and progressive resolution of the associated and underlying instinctual conflicts that provide the frame of reference within which these epigenetic crises can be successively resolved. Thus, as the analysis moves forward, the quality and organization of the therapeutic alliance also shift and undergo progressive change.

It should be noted that in referring to an epigenetic progression we are not postulating some apodictic and unvarying organic sequence. Rather, the process varies considerably from patient to patient in terms of the underlying developmental issues, the patterning of the analytic process itself, the empathic and responsive capacities of the analyst, and a host of other variables. Moreover, as with any epigenetic sequence, the process does not involve an exclusive shift from one critical focus to another—rather, all aspects of the developmental sequence are involved at each phase. In the sequence we are suggesting here, for example, issues of autonomy do not arise without simultaneously implicating issues of trust and initiative. There is nonetheless an inherent sequencing and a consistent internal logic to the phases observed in the analytic process, although this is not an ironclad order.

The specific issues related to the working through of the alliance may alternate back and forth, such that a given issue may predominate at one point, then the focus may shift to a different issue, returning to the first issue at still another point. Nor are these issues cast in all-or-nothing terms. One does not deal with absolute trust as opposed to no trust, or absolute autonomy as opposed to no autonomy. Rather, these issues arise in varying degrees and are worked through in varying proportions at different phases of a given analysis. Thus, while it is perfectly accurate to describe secondary trust as essential for inaugurating a genuine therapeutic alliance, issues of trust may also play an extremely important part in the terminal phases of a given analysis.

In other words, the critical focus in the present consideration is that the therapeutic alliance is by no means a unitary or static phenomenon, but is composed of a variety of operative qualities which undergo a developmental progression both as a result of and as an active component of the analytic process. Moreover, we are emphasizing here the developmental aspects of this progression, and the fact that these aspects are inherent in the analytic process and, therefore, require analytic attention and consideration. These are real issues within the analytic process, operating in parallel and often critically important ways with aspects of the transference neurosis. There is an important reciprocal interaction between the aspects of the therapeutic alliance and the elements of the transference neurosis, which takes place throughout the course of the analytic process and provides the critical working area of the therapeutic effects of the analytic process. We shall discuss this area later in terms of critical internalizations involved in it. At this point, however, we are concerned with the descriptive aspects of the progression in the therapeutic alliance itself.

So far we have discussed only the first epigenetic phase, which has to do with the elements of trust. To reiterate: essentially the function of secondary trust within the analytic process is to maintain a condition of openness to the analytic influence and a willingness to commit oneself to the analytic process. This trust involves a certain willing dependence on the analyst and on the analytic process, along with a sense of reliance and hopefulness that the process has meaning and will eventuate in a good therapeutic outcome. We have already indicated that this sense of dependence and reliance on the other is an important factor in the initiation of the analytic process and the involvement in the analytic relationship. But clearly, if the patient remains locked in this state of willing dependence and trusting reliance, the analytic process will stalemate and a therapeutic progression will be short-circuited. The not infrequently seen hysterical willingness to trust may serve as a significant source of resistance, as much of a block to forward motion as the obsessional's premature closure of trust and the corresponding failure of secondary trust. In other words, a leaning in either direction, either toward excessive trust or toward excessive mistrust, impedes the patient's capacity to enter the next phase of epigenetic development. What we are emphasizing here is that, as the analysis progresses, the element of trust must differentiate and become integrated with other emergent qualities of the therapeutic alliance. As in the epigenetic sequence in childhood, trust is not lost or eliminated in the move to the next developmental stage, but rather serves as a foundation for the emergent qualities involved in the resolution of later developmental crises.

In most analyzable patients the issues of trust are sufficiently resolved so that the therapeutic alliance can be effectively sustained and movement to subsequent phases is not seriously impeded. Nonetheless, in many patients, and this is clearly the case in narcissistic disorders and other forms of more severe character pathology, the reworking of the elements of trust is an important aspect of the therapeutic process. Many of these patients *are* analyzable, but only with difficulty and with careful attention to the alliance issues. Often the issues of trust remain a focus of analytic work throughout the course of the analysis. The resolution of the infantile determinants that impede the development of a genuine sense of trust presents some of the most difficult and problematic questions confronting psychoanalysis today.

To the extent that the patient is able to resolve and integrate the issues of trust, he is capable of moving on to a stage of emergent autonomy. Within the framework of a positive trusting relationship with the analyst, the patient begins to establish and test out areas of autonomous functioning within the analysis. The ontogeny of autonomy within the analytic process is a subject worthy of study itself, and little or no attention has been paid to it thus far. Perhaps the most pertinent work in this area is the contribution of object relations theorists dealing with the progression in the analytic work from dependence to independence (Winnicott, 1965). The analogy to the toddler's testing of autonomy is also relevant here.

The emergence of autonomy within the analysis implies that the patient is ready, able, and willing to enter into the work of the analysis and to take the responsibility for it. This is quite different from the earlier attitude of trusting reliance and dependence. The emergence of autonomy implies that the patient is an active agent and a vital force in the work of the analysis, and that he contributes in important and significant ways to the forward movement of the analytic process. It is in this context that the patient takes responsibility for meeting the appointment times, for paying his bills, for producing material and working effectively and productively within the analytic hours, for reporting dreams, and so on.

The process of establishing and maintaining autonomy is a delicate one and requires a careful tuning on the part of the analyst to the needs of the patient. The analyst must be careful to respect the patient's emerging autonomy and not to subvert it with implicit demands for analytic subservience or compliance. The line between signs of the patient's resistance, which need to be analyzed and interpreted and effectively diminished, and aspects of the patient's growing autonomy, which need to be supported and sustained, is often a difficult one to tread. Within a given analytic context, the patient's missing a therapy hour may express important resistances, but it may also indicate an emerging autonomy. The therapist must take a careful reading of the state of the patient's defenses, the status of the alliance, the level to which the analysis has advanced, and must situate the patient's behavior within the complex context of the overall analytic progression.

In addition, it is important to note that the emergence of genuine autonomy allows for the acceptance and acknowledgment of autonomy in others. Thus it is important for the fostering of the patient's autonomy that the therapist's own autonomy be genuine and well integrated. The critical question here is the extent to which the patient's modified dependence and emerging independence are a source of stress or difficulty for the analyst. It is altogether too easy to interfere with and truncate the patient's growing autonomy. This difficulty is inherent in the parent-child relationship. A parent's insistence on conformity and compliance, for example, can undermine and diminish the child's beginning efforts at autonomy. Similarly, in the analysis, an excessive quickness to interpret on the analyst's part can effectively take the play away from the patient and deprive the patient of an area of hesitantly emerging autonomous functioning.

Here, too, any deviation from genuine autonomy in the direction of excess or deficit will have its effects on the analytic process. If the patient immaturely asserts his independence of the analyst in an excessive way, the alliance is disrupted and one can presume that this retreat to hyperindependence is serving defensive needs. On the other hand, if the patient is overly compliant and fails to exercise his independent judgment at the appropriate phase of the analytic process, the alliance also suffers. The critical point here is that at a certain phase in the development of the therapeutic alliance an appropriate balance between the relative autonomies of the patient and the therapist must be obtained for the effective progression of the analytic work. A patient may come to the threshold of a more autonomous relationship to the analyst, and then may retreat to an earlier position of accepting trustfulness and nonconfronting dependence. Clearly such a retreat or such a holding to the earlier position is defensively motivated and forms a type of resistance within the alliance.

Given a persisting and differentiated sense of trust and a relatively stabilized sense of genuine autonomy, the patient is gradually more able to express his own initiative within the analytic process. Essentially initiative in this context involves a willingness to initiate within the analytic process and to undertake on his own recognizance, as it were, the interpretation and application of his own therapeutic material. Initiative in this sense also includes a willingness to undertake change in his attitudes, beliefs, values, and ways of behavior, both within and without the analysis. The critical question at this juncture is whether the patient can undertake this initiative without the risk of rejecting, deflating, or attacking the analyst. Here a vital element is the narcissistic resiliency of the analyst, who must tolerate and even encourage the patient's initiative within the limits of the analytic work.

For many of our patients this is a crisis point in their developmental experience, since so often the emergence of the child's individuality and self-assertion and the undertaking of critical initiatives in various areas of life experience have somehow come to mean a rejection, a defeat, an attack on the narcissistic vulnerability of the parents. The negotiation here is a sensitive one in that the patient's initiative must be integrated within the analysis in such a way as to extend the analytic work as a collaborative effort between the analyst and the patient. The patient's initiative must be exercised in a manner congruent with the position of the analyst and the ongoing requirements of the analytic process.

Closely related to the issues of autonomy and initiative is the question of industry. In Erikson's (1963) terms, the sense of industry has to do with the child's application and implementation of emergent skills toward the achievement of recognized and accepted goals. A deficit of industry, stemming from discouragement of the child's use of newly acquired skills, leads to an abiding sense of inferiority. One of the objectives of the analytic process in this regard is that the patient gain a sense of capacity and reliable skill in the application of analytic insights and in the internalization and utilization of the analytic frame of mind as a permanent possession. This is what is generally intended by references to the internalization of the analytic process as one of the therapeutic outcomes of analysis.

Finally, the more or less terminal point in the development of the therapeutic alliance is the emergence of a cohesive, integrated, mature, and adaptive sense of self. Erikson formulates this concept under the rubric of identity, and it can be loosely employed in the present context as well. In an abstract sense, one can say that the establishing of a stable and adaptive sense of identity is the ultimate step in the analytic process itself. But one can question the degree to which this objective is intrinsically related to a particular analysis. It may be that in many analyses one does not envision the emergence of a stable and mature identity so much as the resolution of fundamental aspects of the transference neurosis and the underlying infantile conflicts, as well as the opening up of the *potential* for the subsequent formation of a more effective and stable sense of identity. To the extent that the earlier issues resident in the therapeutic alliance have been effectively mobilized, the forces are set in motion for a gradual reworking of elements of the patient's self, which ultimately leads in the direction of the consolidation of a sense of identity.

That consolidation, however, may take place only over a considerable period of time, even after the termination of the analysis itself. In this light, we can conceive of the analytic process not as a specifically time-limited and phased operation, but rather as an open-ended process, which continues to act within the patient in a gradual modification and shaping of the patient's personality. The effective working through of the analytic process sets into motion certain critical mechanisms, which serve as an effective matrix within which the expanded issues of a stable sense of self and the related narcissistic crises embedded in the life cycle are progressively resolved and integrated.

I shall not detail the subsequent Eriksonian phases which stretch out into the broad range of the life cycle. Intimacy, generativity, and integrity are issues that in general reach beyond the limits of the specific therapeutic interaction between the patient and the analyst. Nonetheless, they are the abiding issues permeating the progressive integration and adaptive functioning of the patient. One can hope that the rudiments established by the analytic process will extend themselves into the resolution of future crises, so that the patient can maintain a sense of self-coherence and adapt effectively throughout the life cycle.

To shift our perspective, we should note that the succession of the developmental phases of the therapeutic alliance is a function of and depends on the resolution of the underlying instinctual conflicts and instinctually derived issues that have been revivified and reactivated in the transference neurosis. From the point of view of internalization processes and their role in this epigenetic course, the analytic regression activates selective aspects of the introjective economy, which encapsulates and organizes the different levels of developmental conflict and fixation.

In other words, each level of resolution of the infantile derivatives bound up in the transference neurosis involves a corresponding revivification and reworking of a particular developmental level of the introjective organization and economy. At each level, then, the introjective organization is to some degree regressively dissolved and the potential for working through the correlated developmental issues is reopened. In the course of development, it was the failure or deviation within the significant object relations of the child that shifted the balance of internalization processes away from constructive and positive identifications toward defensive, drive-derivative pathogenic introjects. The same internal process is revived in the analysis, but now in terms of the relationship that obtains between the patient and the analyst. In the reworking of developmental crises with the analytic object, the balance in the introjective organization is shifted away from the ambivalence and pathogenic defensiveness inherent in the original introjects toward a considerably less ambivalent and more positively toned introjective content.

At each step of the elaboration of the therapeutic alliance, then, critical defensive issues and introjective alignments are reworked to allow for the emergence of positive and constructive identificatory processes. These underlying identifications carry with them ego-building and increasingly secondary-process and autonomous capacities and functioning, which serve to reinforce and differentiate the therapeutic alliance. Step by step, as the therapeutic alliance develops, it is accompanied by the internalization of significant ego capacities and ego strengths and a progressive move in the direction of a stable, secondarily autonomous structuralization of the patient's internal world.

In the elaboration and integration of a cohesive, functional sense of self in the patient, we are not implying that the patient did not have a sense of self before entering analysis. However, aspects of it were to some degree conflicted, caught up in defensive struggles of one kind or another, or maladaptive or deficient in certain areas of the patient's life experience. In the most analyzable patients, the sense of cohesive self is already fundamentally established, and the analytic reworking of certain elements contributes to a reshaping and a reintegration, which preserve and build on that underlying cohesion. It is rare in well-conducted analyses for patients to regress to a point of fragmentation or disorganization of the sense of self, but in cases where a developmental arrest or defect has severely affected the level of self-organization, the restructuring of the self may take on a more central and significant role.

The development of the therapeutic alliance, in this frame of reference, cannot simply be regarded as an emergence of specified qualities in the patient's ego, or even for that matter as an integration of ego and superego. Rather, we are dealing with a complex organization reflecting the interplay between the structural components of the psychic apparatus, both ego and superego, and the integration of a cohesive and adaptive sense of self. The emergence of this sense of self and its correlated sense of identity cannot be divorced from the processing of narcissism.

One of the major instinctual components, which is deeply embedded in the introjective organization and gives the introjects their special quality in the organization of the patient's pathological sense of self, is the inherent narcissistic investment. In other words, the introjects can be envisioned as narcissistically invested psychic structures which form the core of the patient's pathological sense of self. It is in the dissolution of these pathogenic structures that the narcissism bound into them is unleashed and becomes available for a developmental reworking leading to narcissistic transformation.

In the progressive elaboration of the therapeutic alliance, the underlying instinctual components undergo various vicissitudes. Aggressive and libidinal components may be sublimated or neutralized, while narcissistic components are more likely to undergo transformation. These narcissistic transformations are an integral part of the processing of the therapeutic alliance, as well as of the formation of a cohesive sense of self. It is this reprocessing, this transformation of narcissistic elements that constitutes a central instinctual dimension of the shift from an introjective organization to patterns of constructive identification.

In addressing ourselves to this issue we are touching on an as yet unexplored frontier of psychoanalytic theory. The function of narcissism and the organization of these internalization processes are still not fully understood. However, the later transformations of narcissism, as later correlates of the development of the self and a sense of identity, have been described by Kohut (1966) in terms of man's creativity, his ability to be empathic, his capacity to contemplate his own impermanence or transience, his sense of humor, and his wisdom. As we have already suggested, the narcissistic elements of the transference organization frequently remain unresolved at the point of termination of the analytic relationship. There is now, however, the *potential* for the resolution of these elements and their integration. It is precisely through the subsequent reworking, resolution, and integration of these narcissistic elements that the narcissistic transformations take place which contribute to the highest level of human capacity (Kohut, 1966), and to the resolution of further developmental stages in the life cycle (Erikson, 1959).

PHASES OF THE PSYCHOANALYTIC PROCESS

We can now turn our attention more specifically to the phases of the analytic process. Insofar as it is an organic process with its own inherent development and progression, the psychoanalytic process can be conveniently divided into an initial opening phase, an evolving middle phase, and a final terminal phase. Yet it should be obvious that our classification here cannot be rigid or exclusive. An identifiable shift in emphasis and focus characterizes each phase, but no element of the analytic process is entirely isolated within one particular phase. Concerns or issues predominant in the early stages of an analysis may extend into other phases and may recrudesce in variant forms at different periods of the analysis. Similarly, issues that stand out in later stages of the process may emerge in inchoate and less determinate forms in the earlier stages. Nonetheless, it is possible to delineate a certain organic progression.

We need to remind ourselves at this point that our discussion does not aim to embrace the generalities of psychoanalytic methodology or technique. Rather, our intent is to pinpoint the role of critical internalizations and their progressive evolution within the psychoanalytic process. While it is obvious from our previous discussion that these internalizations cannot be divorced from the organic complexity of the psychoanalytic situation and process, our focus here is somewhat narrowed. Instead of surveying the wide panorama of the psychoanalytic process as a whole, we shall take a close look at the mobilization and interaction of internalizations within the analytic process, most specifically and relevantly, introjection and identification.

The Initial Phase

The opening phase of the analytic process concerns itself primarily with establishing the psychoanalytic situation. It is in this phase that the groundwork is laid for the further development of the analytic process and the progression of the analytic work. During this stage the seeds are planted for a number of elements of the analytic process, which will come to a fuller flowering and maturation in later stages. It is rare indeed for a patient to enter into the analytic situation easily or without difficulty, so that this opening phase often requires careful attention and sensitivity on the part of the analyst to discriminate those areas within which specific effort is required to establish and secure the analytic situation.

A primary concern in establishing the psychoanalytic situation is the formation and initial consolidation of the therapeutic alliance (Zetzel and Meissner, 1973). The early narcissistic alliance which allows the patient to submit to and tolerate the analytic involvement must give way to a more stable and less fragile form of therapeutic alliance. Obviously the .patient's capacity for object relatedness plays a significant part in this development. What is required is that the patient place himself in a position of dependent reliance and trusting involvement with the analyst (Friedman, 1969). For this to occur, there must be a certain capacity for basic trust and a certain willingness to open oneself to the risk of narcissistic injury. From the analyst's side, the facilitation of the patient's shift to a more therapeutic form of alliance demands an empathic responsiveness to the areas of sensitivity and narcissistic vulnerability in the patient (Kohut, 1977).

The shift to a more effective therapeutic alliance is particularly complex and difficult in those patients in whom the narcissistic pathology is more marked. This is especially true in cases of narcissistic character pathology and other forms of narcissistic impairment where the more archaic expressions of narcissistic pathogenicity are operative. In such cases, the shift to a more genuine therapeutic alliance may not be possible or may be so difficult as to preclude effective analytic work. The risk is that whatever alliance evolves will continue to emerge along narcissistic dimensions, so that the alliance that develops in the course of the analysis is determined more by narcissistic needs and vulnerabilities than by genuinely therapeutic and growth-facilitating concerns. What arises is a kind of narcissistic misalliance which may allow for the continuation of the analytic process, but which sets severe constraints on the potential for effective therapeutic work and for achieving a good analytic result. This may, in fact, have been the problem Freud and Brunswick faced in their attempts to treat the Wolf Man (Meissner, 1977c).

The analytic situation is a unique and somewhat strange experience for all patients, and one that is heavily weighted with expectations and hopes. A significant degree of anxiety may attach itself to this initial strangeness, as well as to the pull toward regression. More often than not the analyst must respond by providing a greater degree of structure to cushion the patient's anxiety and to stay the regressive pulls of the analysis in order for a certain degree of adjustment to take place. This may be particularly necessary with patients who have suffered early object deprivations. As Fleming (1972) has observed:

> Object deprivation in childhood tends to perpetuate an intense and immature ego-object-need which distorts the reality of later object relations in the service of trying to restore a sense of the presence of the object needed for development. The parent-loss patient requires special responses from the analyst in tune with the level of object need to aid in the functioning of an observing ego and to interrupt the transference defenses against grief and mourning. The analyst's empathically symbiotic responses provide a temporary substitute for the 'coördinates', necessary for 'refueling' throughout childhood and adolescence, a diatrophic alliance for continuing growth that was prematurely interrupted by early parental loss [p. 45].

The analyst can provide such structure by adopting a relatively greater degree of activity, either by delaying the patient's advance to the couch or by a more active if tempered pacing of interventions in the early stages of the analysis. The titration of such activity is a function in large measure of the patient's capacity for engagement in a therapeutic relationship with the analyst, which is in part determined by the patient's capacity for object relationship. The analyst's responsiveness in this context is dictated by a sensitivity to issues of separation and object loss, as well as by the need to establish and consolidate the analytic situation, a need that takes precedence over any concern with inducing the analytic regression. As we shall see, the latter concern assumes increasing prominence as the analytic process moves forward.

One of the major risks in this phase of the analysis is that the attempts to stabilize the therapeutic alliance may be excessively contaminated by transference elements. Frequently enough, the analyst has to deal with precipitant transference reactions, which may distort the analytic relationship and interfere with the establishment of the therapeutic alliance. These transference reactions can be distinguished from the later development of a transference neurosis. Usually these reactions are more in the form of generalizations from previous object-related experiences, particularly relationships with authority figures, professional personnel, or even parental figures. In some patients, however, this tendency to transference reaction is exaggerated and correlates with a more general tendency to projection in their interpersonal relations. Such patients often reveal relatively paranoid inclinations in which this tendency to projective defense is associated with a higher degree of narcissistic vulnerability and a predominance of narcissistic issues in the pathology.

The emergence of such projections in the analytic interaction is difficult to deal with and makes the establishing of the analytic situation a complex task. In extreme cases, such transference distortions can lead to a transference psychosis which may necessitate interruption of the analysis. Even projective distortions of minor degree, however, call for a specific response from the analyst to counter these tendencies and to shift the balance in the analytic interaction back toward the therapeutic alliance. In these cases, efforts must be taken to minimize the regressive pulls and to emphasize the more realistic elements in the analytic situation. Great care must be taken to consolidate the therapeutic alliance so that the increasing pressure toward regression will not mobilize the patient's anxiety to an excessive degree. It is the precipitous emergence of these anxieties, usually linked to underlying narcissistic vulnerability, that gives rise to the projective tendencies.

As we have already suggested, such transference distortions may occur with the mobilization of preformed transference elements. In the case of the young man previously described, his anticipations of involvement in the analysis activated transference elements which placed him in a paranoid position characterized by severe persecutory anxiety, fright, and a corresponding impulse to flee the analysis. To establish the psychoanalytic situation, the analyst had to assume a much more active and confronting posture. It was necessary to point out to the patient the nature of his distortions, that they must be coming from other areas of his experience than those involved in the present situation, and that if he let his fears get the better of him, he was in danger of destroying the analysis. In this particular patient the basic capacity of his ego to observe and assess reality enabled him to respond positively to this strong intervention. Although this did not change the basically paranoid quality of the patient's transference and of the subsequently elaborated transference neurosis, it did sufficiently break through the paranoid defense to allow the more adaptive portions of the patient's ego to engage in the therapeutic interaction and the analytic work.

It should be noted that such disruptions of the alliance are not restricted to the initial phase but may occur in later phases, particularly where the alliance has not been solidly established to begin with and where the contamination of the alliance by transference factors operates at a fairly high level of intensity. One highly threatened young woman defensively assumed an argumentative and competitive stance through most of her analysis. She was particularly resistant to any attempts on my part to clarify her resistance, to work through her defensiveness and the obvious concealed layer of intense anxiety, fear, and inner sense of overwhelming weakness and vulnerability that motivated her posture within the analysis. Even the most tactful observations or clarifications and the most gentle, relatively innocuous interpretations were taken as personal attacks, meant only to demean, devalue, and critically undercut and defeat her.

This attitude became increasingly intense and began to seriously threaten not only the work within the analysis, but the patient's continuing in the analytic situation. She finally came to a point where she angrily and bitterly accused me of making her lie on the couch as a demeaning and humiliating exercise in which she had to submit herself unwillingly to my probings and questionings. It was for her a defeat, a degrading exposure of those parts of herself about which she felt most ashamed and vulnerable. Her associations clearly related this to a gynecological examination, with her legs spread and strapped helplessly, her most private parts open to the cold, uncaring observation of the gynecologist.

At this point I asked the patient why she was lying on the couch anyway. The question startled and confused her. It had never occurred to her that lying on the couch was in any way a matter of choice or decision. She had automatically, unquestioningly put herself on the couch, thinking that that was what analytic patients were expected to do and what I expected of her. I suggested that lying on the couch might not be the most useful way for her to go about the analysis, and that she might think about whether or not she wanted to use the couch and whether it helped her; perhaps she wanted to do something different. When she returned for the next hour, she announced that she had decided to sit in the chair and to work facing me. We did this, and in the course of the ensuing months the patient's extremely defensive and argumentative stance disappeared completely, along with the intensely paranoid distortions that accompanied it. During the period of sitting up, we were able to establish a relatively solid alliance and many of her defensive attitudes and their underlying unconscious derivatives were exposed, analyzed, and productively worked through.

An important condition for the therapeutic alliance is that the initial narcissistic alliance not be precipitately distorted by the emergence of narcissistic transference elements. In typically neurotic patients this risk is minimal insofar as these patients are generally capable of engaging in a meaningful relationship with the analytic object without the issue of narcissistic vulnerability looming too large. In these patients, the narcissistic issues remain in the background, although they may gradually become operative under the pressures of the analytic regression. For other patients, however, in whom the narcissistic pathology plays a more predominant part, the tendency to shift to the level of narcissistic transference, more or less bypassing the issues of therapeutic alliance, can be a complicating factor. We shall have more to say about the emergence of the narcissistic transference later, but at this point it is crucial to reiterate that in such cases establishing a meaningful therapeutic alliance is a major issue in the initial stage of the analysis and may remain a critical dimension of the analytic work throughout the entire course of the analysis.

Correlated to the establishing of the therapeutic alliance in the initial phase is the overcoming of the patient's initial anxiety and resistance. For all patients entering psychoanalysis, certain basic anxieties are intensified because of the importance the patient attaches to the undertaking. It represents a serious and often burdensome investment of time, effort, and financial and emotional resources. In addition, patients often come to analysis after a series of therapeutic frustrations, and this places their self-esteem in further jeopardy as they undertake what must seem to them a radical, if not desperate, procedure.

The basic question is whether the patient can become engaged in a trusting, dependent, and therapeutically productive relationship with the analyst in the face of this elevated titer of narcissistic vulnerability. It is important, therefore, that the analyst be present in the interaction with the patient as a relatively constant, confident, reasonably optimistic, secure and professionally competent object. These qualities in the analyst set the stage for the shift from basic trust to forms of secondary trust and provide the patient with some degree of reassurance in the undertaking. Frequently, in the initial stages of negotiation of the analytic contract, patients try to check out and evaluate these aspects of their potential analyst.

Ample opportunity should be provided for patients to make such assessments, particularly in the face-to-face interviews before the beginning of the analysis. The determination of these issues not only sets the stage for the emergence of the therapeutic alliance, but also allows for and to some degree induces the initial dependence which the patient must be able to tolerate in order to enter into the analytic situation and to enjoy some degree of openness to analytic influence. Beyond these qualities in the analyst, however, is the important initial work of identifying and empathically working through the patient's early resistances and anxieties in order to foster the patient's engagement in the analytic process and in a meaningful therapeutic alliance.

We can see that the opening phase of the analytic process involves a complex interaction between the analyst and the analysand. However, the importance of establishing the psychoanalytic situation cannot be underestimated, since it provides the basic foundation on which the analytic work is built. But this initial fundamental work cannot be taken for granted in the further progression of the analysis; it must be continually reinforced, refocused, rearticulated, and developed throughout the analysis. In other words, the psychoanalytic situation is not definitively or conclusively established in the opening phase, but rather requires a constant effort toward consolidation and reinforcement. The opening phase only accomplishes the first, major effort in this direction.

The importance of the therapeutic alliance cannot be emphasized enough. It provides the buffering and sustaining dimension to the analytic process that allows other aspects of the therapeutic relationship to develop. The patient's tolerance for dependence within the therapeutic relationship contributes to the therapeutic alliance; at the same time it serves to elicit and facilitate the transference neurosis. To the extent that the therapeutic alliance has been consolidated, the subsequent emergence of the transference neurosis can be regarded as therapeutically productive.

For many patients it is the buffer of the alliance that permits them to tolerate the beginning transference neurosis. These, however, tend to be patients in whom the maintenance of structure has a primary importance and for whom the analytic regression may carry the risk of overwhelming anxiety or constitute a threat to an underlying narcissistic vulnerability. In other patients, the propensity to plunge into a transference relationship reflects an ease of transference mobilization that may derive from underlying character or structural defects. Here the risk is of precipitous engagement in the transference neurosis without the safeguard and point of analytic purchase provided by a relatively stable therapeutic alliance. This is particularly true for patients with more primitive forms of character pathology, especially borderline personalities, as well as for patients with various forms of narcissistic character pathology.

Such early narcissistic transference distortions place the therapeutic alliance in considerable jeopardy. The emergence of a therapeutic alliance requires the capacity to accept the separate reality of the analyst and the capacity to enlist oneself in a meaningful relationship and collaboration with the analyst in the work of effecting therapeutic goals and internal change. In the narcissistic transferences, however, the patient may place himself in a position of relatively grandiose isolation from the analyst—rejecting, devaluing, and demeaning the analyst's contributions, as though the analyst's interpretations or clarifications were meaningless or even worthless. The patient wards off any initiatives from the analyst as a threat to his rigidly protected, fragile narcissistic core. Such patients may to some degree establish a misalliance, in which they cooperate with the external requirements of the analysis, but within their internal frame of reference they withhold themselves from a commitment to the analytic process and maintain a posture of splendid isolation and contempt.

Some narcissistic patients, on the other hand, may tend to idealize the analyst. Here the narcissistic misalliance is based on magical expectations and the illusion of attachment to an idealized, all-powerful object. Modell (1975) has described this constellation most succinctly: "What substitutes for therapeutic alliance is a magical belief that to be in the presence of the idealized analyst will effect a change—[the patient] will acquire the idealized characteristics not by means of an active identification but by means of a magical process. As one patient described it, choosing the right analyst is like joining the proper club—one derives a sense of identity by means of a contiguity" (p. 280). The inherent risk with such patients, of course, is that the implicit narcissistic contract allows them to enter the analytic process with a hidden agenda of their own. These patients will comply in elaborate detail with the expectations of the analytic situation and the analyst, performing all the externals of the analytic work, even to the point of elaborate production of dreams and associations—in effect being "good" patients. But their belief is that this compliance will be responded to by the exercise of analytic omnipotence to bring about the changes they want.

This was clearly the case in the chronically depressed young mother I described earlier. She became a dutiful, compliant, and diligent patient within the analysis. Only in the closing stages of her analysis, when the narcissistic components became more available and more clearly defined, did it become obvious that her work in the analysis was motivated by a persistent belief that, if she performed well enough and responded to my demands and expectations, I would bestow upon her all the changes she desired to satisfy her narcissistic illusions and entitlements. By successfully completing the analysis, she would automatically become a more effective, dramatic, and dynamic person. She would prosper in her career and would be admired and respected by everyone she came in contact with.

As I have discussed elsewhere (Meissner, 1978b), this posture within the analysis is equivalent to the organization of a false self (Winnicott, 1965), and may constitute a more frequent outcome of analytic endeavors than has previously been thought. The difficulty in dealing with such narcissistic transferences may culminate in the patient's and even the analyst's settling for this false-self resolution. Modell (1975) has also drawn attention to the convergence of the false-self organization and narcissistic character pathologies.

It is worth noting that an analytic outcome based on a false-self conformity is at times a reasonable, if not preferable, analytic result. We can too easily run the risk of therapeutic omnipotence if we hold out for a puristic resolution which outlaws such conformity. For many patients, the nature of their pathology, rooted in relatively severe ego distortions or developmental defects or arrests, is such that the introjective realignment implicit in the false-self organization can provide significant therapeutic benefit. It substitutes an analytic introject for the pathogenic introjects. The analytic introject is considerably more benign, reasonable, moderate, and optimistic. It provides room in the intrapsychic sphere for less conflicted ego functioning and for the emergence of a significant increment of self-esteem. The fact that this resolution remains a false-self organization with its inherent weaknesses and susceptibilities does leave the potential for further difficulties. But for many patients this may be an optimal outcome. Certainly for others, it would not be. This determination is a critical one for the decision of when the analysis should be terminated.

To return to our discussion of the opening phase, the working through of the patient's initial resistances and anxieties sets the analytic process in motion. As the initial resistances fade, the patient begins to feel the regressive pulls of the analysis. Thus while the diminishing of anxiety and resistance facilitates the patient's engagement in free association, the concomitant regressive pulls tend to weaken repressive barriers so that new levels of resistance and anxiety are mobilized. This gradual activation of more and more primitive levels of resistance and anxiety is a familiar aspect of the analytic process and need not be commented on further at this point. It is this deepening, however, of resistances and related anxieties that marks the progression from the opening phase of the analysis to later stages.

To focus these issues in terms of our present concern, the primary impact of the work of the opening phase is the activation of latent introjects. The mobilization of these introjects correlates with the degree of regression and the diminution of resistance. With the establishing of the therapeutic alliance, the buffering context is set, within which the analytic regression and lessening of resistances can begin to take place. The activation of introjective configurations follows on this process. It may, however, require significant and prolonged phases of regression and modification of resistance before the full dimensions of the introjective economy become apparent.

The capacity for a therapeutic alliance depends on the patient's internal structure and therefore reflects the organization of internalizations. The capacity for basic trust, essential to the formation of an initial narcissistic alliance, reflects the influence of early identifications, particularly with the mother, but not exclusively so. At this early level of identificatory involvement with the significant objects of dependency, it is difficult to distinguish between identifications and early, relatively nonambivalent introjections. Nonetheless, we can infer that early experiences of good mothering and of interaction with an adequately responsive need-satisfying object lay the groundwork for relatively more positively toned and ego-building introjections and/or identifications. With these internal modifications comes a growing and gradually more consolidated capacity for basic trust, which allows further adaptive capacities to emerge in the parent-child interaction.

We can presume that to some degree the analytic interaction, particularly in the initial stages of the alliance, both expresses and relies on these fundamental psychic capacities and that it calls into play these internalized structures and their object-related aspects. By the same token, not infrequently these capacities are impaired because of the early contamination of object relations and the resulting acquisition of defensively organized and ambivalently motivated introjects. The analytic task then becomes one of working through the bases of these pathogenic introjects so that a more constructive and adaptive introjective alignment can replace the pathogenic one and thus provide the basis within the analysis itself for the emerging therapeutic alliance. As we have indicated, in more primitively organized personalities — the borderlines and narcissistic disorders — this effort may constitute a major focus of the entire analysis. In the more ordinary run of the analytic experience, however, this work belongs primarily to the initial phase of the analysis.

In a certain sense, the business of the opening phase is little more than the initiation of a process that extends itself through most of the analysis. The activation of introjects and the diminishing of resistance and defense lead to the mobilization of projections, which give rise to the more specific transference neurosis. It is this progression of emerging projections with the correlated formation of the transference neurosis that definitively marks the transition from the initial phase to the middle phase.

The Middle Phase

As noted above, the transition to the middle phase of the analytic process is specifically distinguished by the emergence of an identifiable transference neurosis, in contrast to earlier less organized and more fragmented transference elements or reactions. We can consider the developments of the middle phase in terms of two subphases: a regressive subphase and a subsequent progressive subphase. The clarification of these two subphases is particularly useful in discerning discriminable aspects of the analytic work, which takes place in the middle phase.

But, as always in such artificial delineations, we find that the elements and interactions that characterize the regressive subphase also permeate and extend into the progressive subphase, and vice versa. In other words, the phenomenology of the middle phase cannot be completely described in terms of exclusive categories. To be more precise, the middle phase works itself out in a sequential shifting back and forth and in an often complex intermingling of aspects of both subphases. Nonetheless, we can say that in most analyses there is a detectable shift in emphasis from the concerns of the regressive subphase in the direction of progressive modification as the elements of the transference neurosis are resolved and worked through.

THE REGRESSIVE SUBPHASE

In the regressive subphase the regressive processes set in motion in the initial phase extend themselves and eventuate in the emergence and elaboration of the transference neurosis. It is during the regressive subphase that the transference neurosis deepens and intensifies.

As we have seen, the tolerance for controlled regression that allows the transference neurosis to emerge requires a continual stabilizing and reinforcing of the therapeutic alliance. The basic issue concerns the shift from a narcissistic alliance, organized around the elements of basic trust, to the firmer footing of a therapeutic alliance, organized in terms of an increasing capacity for secondary trust. The strengthening of these elements of the alliance provides the context for the gradual diminution of resistances and the penetration of successive layers of regression.

The major emphasis in this subphase is on the modification of the patient's resistances to the analytic process and the corresponding induction of the analytic regression and facilitation of free association. Thus the major preoccupations are with defense analysis and with maintenance and consolidation of the therapeutic alliance. It should be recognized immediately that this particular subphase may be long drawn out, since it requires the sequential working through of the layers of an onion. As each defensive layer is resolved, further regression is precipitated, which in turn elicits its own appropriate resistances. The analysis frequently becomes caught up in a cycle of resistance, analysis of resistance, regression, further resistance, and so on.

From the viewpoint of our present concerns, this regressive cycle serves to activate more and more primitive aspects of the introjective organization. As we have already indicated, the organization of the patient's introjects is complex and reflects developmental vicissitudes from various levels of experience. The introjective organization embraces and envelops these different levels which are subject to varying degrees of repression. As the regressive pressure of the analytic process works its way along, successive layers of the introjective organization are derepressed and activated so that they begin to play an identifiable role in the analytic interaction. In other words, as the analytic regression takes effect, introjective components from various levels of developmental experience can be identified. At first these come from later levels of developmental organization—adolescence and latency. With the deepening of regression, earlier infantile determinants appear, from the oedipal and preoedipal levels. The activation of these levels of introjective organization elicits the corresponding projections which come to bear on the analytic relationship. It is the mobilization of these projective elements that serves as the basis for the organization and emergence of the transference neurosis.

It should be noted that the view of the transference neurosis propounded here differs somewhat from that traditionally articulated in analytic theory. In our view, the transference neurosis is not based simply on transference elements and reactions that represent generalizations from previous object relations experiences. The traditional view suggests that the transference neurosis can be understood merely in terms of the translation of previous experiences to new object relations contexts. In other words, if a child experienced one kind of relationship with a parental figure at a given level of development, that experience will tend to reproduce itself within the analytic context. While there is little doubt that such elements do play a role in the elaboration of the transference neurosis, this conceptualization seems to provide a pallid reflection of the intense and powerful experience we feel the transference neurosis to be. Moreover, such a limited formulation does not consider the potent forces of internalization. In our view, the critical elements in the transference neurosis have to do with specific projections. These serve as transference projections and derive from the regressive activation of introjects which reflect specific developmental influences.

Thus the transference neurosis has a unique dimension which tends to separate it radically from other contexts within which transference elements or reactions can be identified more generally. Although in other contexts the powerful and dynamically significant transference projections may play a role, it is the analytic situation that is characterized by the mobilization of these transference projections and the precipitation of the transference neurosis. This dimension of the analytic process tends to discriminate it from other forms of psychotherapy. There seems to be little doubt that most forms of psychotherapy involve, whether consciously or unconsciously, transference elements. Transference elements and reactions play themselves out in every treatment situation and provide the general matrix for the doctor-patient relationship. But the explicit and self-conscious focusing and working through of the transference neurosis is specifically characteristic of psychoanalysis, and in mitigated form, of some forms of intensive analytically oriented psychotherapy.

Certainly the transference neurosis, reflecting the powerful dynamic force of the underlying introjective organization, provides a unique tool for therapeutic intervention. As I have suggested elsewhere in relation to the paranoid process (Meissner, 1978b), there are any number of indices that provide the therapist or analyst with information about the patient's introjective organization. These elements can be identified in the patient's history, his behavior, his expressions of attitude about events in the world about him, and more particularly and relevantly in his direct and indirect expressions of attitudes toward and valuations of himself. But these indices remain at a degree of remove and lack the necessary immediacy and therapeutic force to allow them to carry any significant degree of therapeutic potential. The mobilization of such elements and their expression in the transference neurosis, however, provide an immediate, vivid, dynamically impressive and therapeutically powerful medium within which both the patient and the analyst can experience and grasp the significance of their import. Freud's (1915b) dictum that the transference neurosis is the most powerful therapeutic tool can be understood here specifically in terms of the activation and expression, and thus the inherent availability and therapeutic immediacy, of the introjective organization.

Keeping this in mind, we can see the regressive subphase as

characterized by the emergence in the analytic transaction of an area of "illusion," within which the dynamic reworking of the transference neurosis takes place. Olinick (1975) has denoted this aspect of the transference:

> I am trying here to clarify an adult phenomenon of passage between illusion and reality, of an 'intermediate area of *experiencing*', of 'transitionalism' as Winnicott has expounded it with reference to infancy (1953). In the infant's progress towards functioning within the reality principle, the separation-individuation from the mother involves several factors. I need mention here only the beginnings of mental activity and 'the growing sense of process', the latter entailing 'remembering, reliving, fantasying, dreaming; the integrating of past, present, and future' (Winnicott, 1953). These are analogous and cognate to the experiences of the analysand. In the regressive aspects of the middle phases of psychoanalysis, transitional objects and phenomena appear. Illusion, disillusionment and 'weaning' are experienced [p. 150].

This area of illusion, as we have suggested, is constituted by the interlocking processes of introjection and projection contributed by both the analyst and the analysand. There is a subtle, unconscious play between the analysand's own introjections and transference projections, just as there is a similar play within the analyst. But, in addition, between the analyst and the analysand, there is a continual, progressively modified intermingling and exchange of projections and introjections.

In his recent discussion of psychoanalysis as art, Loewald (1975) emphasizes this illusional and creative potential of the transference neurosis. He comments:

> In the movement toward reflection, the transference neurosis becomes apparent in its aspect as fantasy creation which has its own validity and function in the patient's life. While intensely experienced, the transference feelings are prevented from being acted upon, from materializing in deeds, so that the transference neurosis seems to remain in the realm of trial action. But insofar as the development, flowering and resolution of the transference neurosis requires the active presence of, and responsive thought interaction with the analyst, and is the result of the collaboration of patient and analyst, this fantasy creation is more than an intrapsychic process, it has a form of reality different from pure thought or dreaming or daydreaming or remembering. The trans-

ference neurosis is not only, as Freud called it, a transition between illness and life, it is a transitional state between inner fantasy and actuality. I am here, I believe, in the neighborhood of
Winnicott's "third area, that of play which expands into creative
living and into the whole cultural life of man" (1967) [pp.
297–298].[3]

The conspiracy of the analyst and the patient in the creation
of the transference illusion opens the way to diverse considerations. The transference neurosis can be envisioned in dramatic
terms (Loewald, 1975), or more specifically as "charac-
terization" (Meissner, 1973). The emphasis thus shifts from a
static and relatively economically determined model of the
transference formation to a more active, authentically genetic
and adaptive conceptualization. The emergence of the transference is seen as a dynamic process, which can be accounted
for not simply in terms of the reactivation of historically embedded introjects and imagoes, but in terms of the mobilization of
these genetic constituents in a present context of adaptive interaction between the patient and the analyst.

The quality and nature of transference distortions are
familiar to all practicing analysts so that there is little need to
describe that phenomenology at this juncture. I would,
however, like to make some additional observations about the
organization of the introjects as they express themselves in the
transference neurosis. Insofar as the introjects serve as the focus
and repository of underlying drive determinants, they reflect
the influence of libidinal, aggressive, and narcissistic components in the organization of the patient's inner world. The integration of these components can be identified (as has been
characteristic of the traditional analytic approach) in terms of
developmental levels — oral, anal, phallic, genital, oral-sadistic,
anal-sadistic, etc.

What needs to be emphasized here, however, is that the
regressive mobilization of the introjects brings about the cor-

---

[3] It should be noted that Loewald's formulation is cast in terms of "creative fantasies." Such fantasies are an operative part of the transference transaction, but, in
terms of our focus on internalizations, this fantasy aspect must be regarded as secondary to and derived from prior internalizations.

responding projections which structure the transference neurosis. This regressive component induces a split in the introjective configuration so that the corresponding projection tends to operate in terms of one or the other pole of the introjective split. In one such configuration, for example, the analyst may be seen as powerful, knowledgeable, and influential. The correlative aspect of this split places the patient in a position of relative helplessness, ignorance, and weakness.

Such regressive splitting reveals an important dimension of the organization of the introjects and the influence of the analytic regression. We have come to recognize that the inherent organization of introjects is bimodal, or bipolar. The usual polarities can be expressed in terms of inferiority versus superiority, victimization versus aggression, vulnerability versus power, or equivalent variants. Through the processes of splitting and projection within the transference neurosis, one aspect of these inherent polarities is typically projected, and it is around this aspect that the transference interaction is structured. The patient may opt for a position of inferiority, weakness, and vulnerability in relation to the analyst. The opposite polar attributes are then bestowed on the analyst, that is, superiority and the role of powerful victimizer. The patient thus re-creates within the transference neurosis a constellation of roles and relationships which not only reflects the developmental experience, but more often than not is played out in the patient's day-to-day experience.

This regressive play of projective and introjective elements within the transference neurosis is hardly surprising, but we must not lose sight of the inherent bipolarity of the introjective organization. If a given portion of the introjective configuration is regressively split off and projected, it must be remembered that the opposite dimension is retained as an integral part of the introjective organization. The power, influence, and omniscience that may be thrust upon the therapist are projective elements derived from the patient's own introjective configuration. These elements then remain latent or repressed in the patient's own self-awareness.

For neurotic reasons, one dimension of the bipolar organization is allowed to remain unrepressed and to play itself out on a conscious and explicit level. In this sense, the regressive split-ting and projective mobilization of only one aspect of the intro-jective configuration can be seen specifically as a defensive maneuver. The analytic work consequently must move in the direction of eliciting and clarifying both aspects of the bipolar introjective organization so that both aspects can stand side by side in conscious awareness. In the regressive subphase, however, the emphasis falls on the mobilization of one aspect through projective focusing within the transference neurosis and the subsequent elucidation of the corresponding aspect. It is only when this has been accomplished that effective working through and analysis of the introjective material become possi-ble.

It should be noted that invariably this introjective organiza-tion involves important elements of narcissism, even though these elements may remain at a relatively unexplicit and latent level for significant periods of the analytic work. In a fun-damental sense, the introjective organization is structured in such a way as to protect the patient's underlying narcissistic vulnerability. Narcissistic elements, however, arise in complex integration with other determinants and are expressed at a variety of developmental levels. In more classically neurotic pa-tients, varying levels of libidinal and aggressive determinants usually must be worked through before the narcissistic deter-minants of the introjective organization come clearly into focus and take on a significant role in the analysis. The narcissistic determinants are thus a major component in all analyses, not simply in those of more primitive states or of the "narcissistic personality disorders" (Kohut, 1971).

Nonetheless, in the more specifically narcissistic disorders, the vicissitudes of narcissism and its role in the introjective economy predominate. We can look at the forms of narcissistic transference that Kohut has described so well—the idealizing transference and the various mirror transferences—in terms of the narcissistic components of the introjective organization. The rudimentary differentiation of ideal object and grandiose self itself involves the operation of primitive projective and introjec-tive mechanisms. For instance, a projective idealization of the analyst frequently arises in the evolution of transference neurosis, and this is accompanied by a corresponding devaluation or diminution of the patient's sense of self. However, in terms of the bipolar organization of the introjects, we must remember that behind this more or less conscious configuration, there lurks a latent, repressed grandiosity which attributes a specialness and importance to the patient's own self along with a corresponding devaluation of the analyst-object. Thus the idealizing transference may mask a considerable amount of underlying envy and narcissistic rage.

Similarly, we can examine the interlocking roles of projection and introjection in the mirror transferences. Kohut (1971) describes several varieties of mirror transference involving increasing degrees of differentiation. The most primitive form is that of archaic merger in which "the analyst is experienced as an extension of the grandiose self and he is referred to only insofar as he has become the carrier of the grandiosity and the exhibitionism of the analysand's grandiose self and of the conflicts, tensions, and defenses which are elicited by these manifestations of the activated narcissistic structure" (p. 114). The primitive nature of this projective movement is apparent, and it seems to approach what we have described as "incorporation." In the second, less archaic form of mirror transference—the alter-ego or twinship transference—the object is narcissistically cathected in terms that allow it to be experienced as like the grandiose self or similar to it. The analyst is assumed to be like the patient and the analyst's psychological makeup, feelings, and attitudes are taken as similar to the patient's own. Finally, in the third, most differentiated form—the mirror transference in its narrowest sense—the analyst is maintained as a separate object, but at the same time the analyst is important to the analysand only to the degree that he participates in the patient's narcissistic needs for approval and confirmation.

These forms of mobilization and projection of the grandiose self reflect an underlying sense of deficit and narcissistic vulnerability. In all these cases, the narcissistic vicissitudes of the introjects can be seen in terms of defensive needs and instinctual pressures. The critical note here is that focusing on only one end of the bipolar organization of the introjects is inadequate, specifically in that it allows the underlying fixations to go unattended and provides a circuitous route by which the significant vulnerabilities escape analytic processing.[4]

As the transference neurosis develops, the patient's defenses move into the arena of the transference, giving rise to a transference resistance. The analysis of defenses and working through of resistances thus take place within the ambiance of the transference. Here, too, successive layers of resistance must be worked through within the transference. This is obviously a critical area of the analytic work, since it allows for the emergence of successively more primitive and more narcissistic elements of the patient's transference involvement. As the analytic process draws closer to the narcissistically determined levels of the introjective organization, the predominant issue that emerges is that of narcissistic vulnerability. It is this underlying vulnerability that mobilizes and motivates the patient's resistance to analytic intervention.

In healthier patients, the issues may be primarily those of self-esteem and the threat of loss of self-esteem, but in more severely disturbed patients, the issues become increasingly those of loss of love of a significant object, or even loss of the object. In the most severe cases, the issues are those of loss of self-cohesion and internal disorganization and fragmentation (Kohut, 1971). Such cases of primitive narcissistic disorganization lie within the realm of psychotic decompensation and are clearly beyond the limits of analytic effectiveness. The underlying narcissistic vulnerability, however, even at more differentiated levels, provides the most powerful motivation for adherence to the introjects, regardless of their consequences. For these patients the introjective organization is the stabilizing matrix within which the cohesiveness of the self is maintained. A discussion of the clinging to and persistence of these infantile introjective organizations and the undoing of the concomitant resistances leads us into the progressive subphase.

THE PROGRESSIVE SUBPHASE

The move from the regressive subphase to the progressive subphase hinges on a shift from the regressive mobilization of

[4] This is not the place to enter into the ongoing debate between Kernberg (1970a, 1974, 1975a) and Kohut (1968, 1971; Ornstein, 1974) in regard to the treatment of narcissistic disorders, but the above discussion is obviously pertinent.

introjective components and the correlated emergence of the transference neurosis to the analysis and resolution of the different levels of introjective organization. This shift in emphasis carries with it the beginnings of the resolution of the transference neurosis. As we have already observed, these two subphases are not exclusive, and they do not occur in a segregated manner. Part of the work of analysis and resolution takes place *pari passu* with the emergence and deepening of the transference neurosis.

At this juncture in the analysis, the well-known technical dimensions of the analytic process play themselves out in critical ways. The work of the analysis forms itself around the processes of free association, clarification, interpretation, at times even forms of confrontation, and finally the working through of elements of the transference neurosis. The progressive elaboration of the reactivated introjects and the resolution of transference components take on complex, relatively unpredictable patterns, which emerge only gradually during the course of the analysis and which vary idiosyncratically as a result not only of the unique dimensions of the patient's personality, but also of the particular interaction between the analyst and the patient.

An important dimension of the progressive subphase involves the therapeutic alliance. Whereas previously the therapeutic alliance served in a more or less buffering capacity, allowing the dynamic functional regression to take place, in the progressive subphase the therapeutic alliance begins to assume a more complex role. The analytic process must not only focus on the transference dynamics, but must increasingly concern itself with the emergent qualities of the therapeutic alliance. We shall look at this more closely later, but at this point it is important to note that the continuing attention to the consolidation of the therapeutic alliance and to the repair of any disruptions in it is a significant aspect of the progressive subphase.

The shift to the analysis and resolution of the transference neurosis and, by implication, the underlying introjective organization also leads to the facilitation and fostering of the *analytic introject*. We have already noted the inherent bipolar dimensions of the introjective organization. The analytic work in the regressive phase concerns itself primarily with the regressive mobilization of both sides of the polar split. In the progressive subphase, however, the emphasis moves in the direction of increasing clarification and elucidation of these polarities and a gradual articulation of their reciprocal reinforcement. A critical insight at this juncture is that the bipolar aspects are mutually related and interdependent and that they form interlocked perspectives of the underlying introjective organization. Patients must be able to understand and realize that in attempting to divorce themselves from one aspect of the bipolar economy, they run the risk of surreptitiously and implicitly embracing the other aspect. To phrase this slightly differently, they cannot simply renounce one polarity; they must also renounce the other. Conversely, it is metapsychologically impossible to adhere to one polarity without at the same time retaining the other.

It is particularly important in the working through of the attachments to these introjects that the internal structure of the introjective configuration be clarified, delineated, interpreted, and finally renounced. It is at this stage of the progressive subphase that the analytic work may seem to reach a plateau, as the patient faces the prospect of surrendering his attachment to the introjective organization with the greatest reluctance. This process is facilitated, of course, by the analyst's ability meaningfully and effectively to interpret the content of the introjects, specifically in relation to the originating objects. It becomes increasingly clear that the introjects represent the residues of infantile experience and also generate the fantasy products, which people the patient's inner world and which prevent the patient from dealing effectively and realistically with his current living situation.

To clarify this progression, let me describe the treatment course of a type of patient frequently seen in analytic practice. The patient, a young woman with a hysterical neurosis, proved to be very productive and was able to achieve a good analytic result. In the following account, I shall emphasize the progressive emergence of introjective material, particularly in the context of the transference neurosis, and the clarification of the patient's infantile dependency and its strongly narcissistic overtones.

I first met the patient when she was 25 years old and not yet married. She came to the outpatient clinic with complaints of acute depression and anxiety symptoms related to a "memory" of her father's having impregnated her at an early age. This so-called memory was extremely disturbing to her and left her in a near panic state. I agreed to see the patient in once-weekly psychotherapy.

Almost from the beginning of the treatment, the therapeutic issues are brought into play. The analyst can begin to read the "printout" of the patient's introjects in the patient's reported feelings, patterns of behavior, and particularly in the patient's verbalized and nonverbalized (acted-out) attitudes toward himself. As Freud so knowingly observed, no patient can keep a secret. This young woman's initial presentation told me clearly enough that she was dealing with a depressive introject in terms of which she saw herself as devalued, worthless, and helplessly victimized. The material suggested that these issues were intimately connected with underlying conflicts around sexuality — particularly her own feminine sexuality.

Just before she actually began therapy, the patient precipitately married a young man who was rather immature and ineffectual. He had been addicted to heroin and was at the time on methadone maintenance. I saw the patient for about a year in psychotherapy, during which time we determined that beyond her superficial symptoms there were long-standing depressive issues, and that she had rashly saddled herself with an unsatisfactory marriage relationship. When I felt confident that the depressive issues could be worked with and that her resources were sufficient for undertaking analysis, I suggested this to her and, over the course of several months, we gradually moved in this direction. The patient got a job to enable her to pay for the analysis, and we eventually began the analysis. We should note here that the hasty union with an unsuitable object was an expression of this woman's devaluation of herself and a form of acting out of the introject. Marrying such a man only proved how worthless a female she was. In contrast, the later decisions — to enter psychotherapy and to undertake analysis — reflected the mobilization of her resources to deal with her problems more effectively. She had started a process by which the introjects and their hold over her, especially the view of herself as devalued, helpless, and victimized, would be undermined. The decision to do something about her feelings about herself and their effects on her life and behavior ran diametrically counter to the demands of the victim-introject.

During the course of the patient's psychotherapy, many of the issues that were later discussed in the analysis came up, but only in a superficial way. The therapy focused primarily on the patient's problems in dealing with day-to-day difficulties and on helping her to support a sense of self-esteem, thus moderating and dealing with her depressive symptoms. When she began the analysis, however, the increased intensity of her feelings was striking. Under the influence of the analytic regression, a host of early memories, feelings, and associations, of which we had heard nothing before, came into focus. The effect of the analytic regression was specifically to reactivate the introjective components, to vivify their expression, and to mobilize them so that they began to play a more immediate and vital role in the analytic interaction.

From the very first hour, the patient was concerned about her performance in the analysis, whether she would measure up to my expectations and would be able to please me as an analytic patient. This had been an issue during her therapy, but became considerably intensified on the couch. About four months into the analysis, she had a dream of a man in magician's robes, who drove up in a small car and asked her for coffee. She had wanted to put honey in the coffee and struggled to make up her mind whether to give him cookies or pie, wondering which would please him most and afraid to give him one or the other because he might be displeased and leave her. She saw me as a powerful, magical figure, whom it was terribly important to please, since otherwise I might abandon her and she would be helpless and lost. This material reflected the projective distortion of the analytic relationship. (In case there is any doubt about the identity of the magician, at the time I was driving a VW.) The projection of these magical expectations of power onto me derived from her own introjective organization, specifically from that repressed and unconscious aspect which could be characterized in terms of magical omnipotence. The projection served to reinforce the more available aspect of the introjects which cast her in the role of the weak, helpless female who could only survive by compliance and placating devices. It is important to remember that both aspects — the powerless and the powerful — reflect the influence of the introjective configuration.

The need to please me quickly brought into focus the need she felt to please and to be important to her father, whom she also saw as a powerful and even magical figure. She felt that she could have no value herself unless others approved of her, most particularly men. This reflected her feeling that she could not be special or important because she did not have a penis; she could only gain importance by being acknowledged by those who did have penises. She recalled her feelings of being displaced from her parents' affections by her little brother, who was born when she was about two and a half. She felt intensely competitive with him, particularly when he began to play baseball with her father. Similarly, she felt that the analysis would somehow make her special and important, if she could please me, be a good analytic patient, and gain my acknowledgment and approval. Here one can recognize the rudiments of a narcissistic alliance.

This material also makes clear the extent to which similar projections colored her early relations with significant objects. We should also note that the quality of such projections and the character of the introjects from which they derive are not divorced from important instinctual and defensive vicissitudes. The introjects serve to give shape and organization to these elements and provide the context and medium for their expression. Thus, in the present case, libidinal, narcissistic, and aggressive impulses and their respective defenses were complexly integrated in the patterns set by important internalizations within the context of specific object relations. These patterns were reactivated in the analytic situation.

The issue of penis envy became a primary focus early in the analysis. The patient remembered her intense interest in examining her little brother's penis, which was small and gave her a feeling of power, as though she could control it. There were also wishes to bite off his penis and to make him like a girl, equal to herself. The sibling rivalry was intense and related to the deeper

rage against her parents for not having provided her with a
penis. She tearfully recalled leaving a doll out in the rain so that
its head rotted and it had to be thrown out. She had wanted to
do the same to her brother, to get rid of him, to get him out of
the way so that she could be the only one, the most important
one. Related to this was a deep resentment of all men, a wish to
castrate and destroy them. These feelings, and particularly the
resentment of her brother, were displaced into her marriage
relationship, where she belittled her husband as weak and ineffectual and deeply resented the fact that he could get away with
being lazy and not working or taking responsibility because he
had a penis.

Associated with the penis envy was her intense wish to
possess and incorporate a penis. She felt that she was empty and
of no value herself, but that she would be all right if she could
possess a penis by taking one inside herself. This related to oral
wishes to incorporate her father's penis and gave rise to
memories of taking showers with father, in which she was both
fascinated and terrified by her father's penis. She revealed her
wish to orally incorporate her husband's penis as well as mine,
since the penis was the source of the power and strength she intensely wished to possess. Related to this, however, were suf-
focation dreams, in which she was being choked by something
in her mouth. She would awake in a panic.

Early in the analysis, her anxieties were connected with fears
of lying down on the couch and assuming a sexual position. In
this position she felt vulnerable and open to being hurt and
taken advantage of. Her seductive wishes toward me also made
her feel bad, as though these wishes were somehow evil and
reprehensible. She was afraid that someone would lie on her
and that she would suffocate to death. This related to her wishes
to take my penis into her mouth, thus combining her wish to
please me with her wish to incorporate and control my power.
She felt that by taking a man's penis into her mouth she could
control it, but that when she was penetrated vaginally she was
open to injury and could exercise no control over the penis.
Thus, to be a woman meant to be helpless, castrated,
vulnerable, and victimized.

Her memories here had to do with the size and strength of

her father's penis and her wishes to touch and be touched by his penis in the showers. Apparently her father had washed her in those showers. His right hand had been deformed by the loss of two fingers in a boyhood accident and thus had an elongated appearance, which the patient associated with the shape of a penis. It became clear that her "memory" of her father's penetrating her had more to do with his washing her in the shower and the related genital wishes than with any real event.

In the analysis, the penis envy was displayed in an intellectualized displacement in which my penis-power was seen in my capacity to understand. She saw this as a masculine activity and strove from time to time competitively to show that her "penis" was as good as mine by her capacity to do the analyzing herself. At the same time she felt that without a real penis she was entirely vulnerable and at my mercy. She could only express her aggressive feelings and her anger toward me if she had a penis. Without one, such feelings would only lead to my retaliation; I would turn her out and terminate the analysis. Thus it was of maximal importance for her continually to please me and to avoid any competitive, aggressive feelings. The penis as the symbol of a power was somehow dreadful and frightening. Being a man and having a penis was equivalent not only to having strength, competence, and knowledge, but also to being aggressively destructive. The unconscious equation seemed clear: female = victim introject, inferior, devalued; male = aggressor introject, superior, idealized.

While she herself wished to bite and incorporate the penis, she also saw the penis as itself a penetrating, biting, hurtful instrument. In intercourse she feared that the penis would pierce her abdomen and tear her insides to shreds. This sense of vulnerability and openness was related to her fear of pregnancy, which she fantasized in terms of her insides swelling, becoming larger and larger, and finally bursting open so that she would die. She saw pregnancy as a punishment, as the penalty for sinful sexual wishes, and the ultimate penalty for being a woman. The penis was a weapon and without one she could not fight back. She was left helpless and vulnerable, and could only survive by being pleasing and making herself agreeable to others. Here we can see that the projection of aggressive destructiveness bears witness to the underlying aggressor introject. The patient's own orally destructive and aggressive wishes, as well as her fear of them, provide direct evidence of the operation of the same aggressive components in her introjective organization. The more consciously available feelings of weakness and vulnerability (derived from the victim introject) are in part maintained defensively against the threatening destructiveness of the aggressor introject.

This patient's wishes to bite and incorporate the penis and thus make men equal to women ultimately went back to deeper regressive wishes to bite her mother's breast and to thus incorporate it so that she would not have to lose it. It was interesting that the patient was a nail-biter; in fact her fingers were quite raw and macerated from this. She related her nail-biting not only to the motif of punishment for masturbatory activities, but also to the wish to bite and incorporate her father's penis (which she related to the shape of his hand).

It comes as no surprise that the patient saw intercourse as rape, in which she was the vulnerable and helpless victim. She preferred to think of it in these terms because then she could feel that her anger at men was justified and that there was no need to please them. During the sexual act, she was frigid and had no feelings at all except fright, but later she could feel her anger and resentment, which protected her from feelings of dependency. If she were to allow herself to feel that dependency, she would feel all the more helpless and vulnerable in the face of abandonment. Here the oral contact with the penis helped to soothe these feelings of vulnerability and attack. Sucking on the penis was like sucking on the mother's breast; it helped her to feel more comfortable and protected.

Corresponding to the patient's idealization and admiration of her father, with his magic penis-wand, was an increasingly clear pattern of antagonism and hatred toward her mother. Even as a child, she saw her mother as depressed and self-sacrificing, a martyr to her condition as wife and mother, a slave who was tied down with family responsibilities, could never leave the house, and had no recourse but to resign herself to the unfortunate lot of being a woman. A woman was good only for making babies, nothing more. The patient saw her mother as weighted down, heavily burdened, always having to do the unpleasant menial tasks. In contrast, she saw her father as a happy, carefree man—able to come and go as he wished, enjoying life in a way that her mother could not.

The patient felt that her mother was never pleased with her, never liked or really loved her. This was because the patient herself was also female and thus could never be pleasing to her mother. The patient's deep resentment of her own femininity was expressed in her description of her own genitals as messy, foul—a dank, dark hole. Her view of her own genitals had a marked cloacal quality; she felt that anything that came out of her was only good enough to be thrown away. In contrast, a man's penis was strong, clean, and powerful.

It should be noted that these sexually divergent attitudes—feminine devalued, masculine overvalued—not only derived from the respective parental object relations, but also served as the basis of and expressed a configuration of introjects in the patient's own psychic organization. Lax (1977) has recently delineated the dynamic and genetic patterns that contribute to such internalizations. To her illuminating account of the development of female masochism, I would add the following points:

1. The organization and motivation of such internalizations follow the pattern we have described here for introjective configurations.

2. Both aspects of the introjective organization are simultaneously active, although only one configuration may be operative in a given context; the other tends to be repressed.

3. Both aspects of the introjective organization, characterized as masculine or feminine, are subject to projection, but usually it is the repressed member that is projected.

4. Although the respective configurations are characterized as masculine and feminine, this does not imply exclusive derivation, i.e., masculine from father, feminine from mother. Rather, the victim introject (devalued) may derive from the vulnerable aspects of both parents, the aggressor introject (valued) from the more potent aspects of both parents. The association with separate parental figures suggests a projective reexternalization of elements actually internalized from both.

The interlocking currents reflecting the underlying ambivalence involved in this patient's relationships with both parents took several forms. If she could not please her mother, she would try to please her father. This took the form of participating in her father's theatrical interests. He was an amateur song-and-dance man and would perform publicly on occasion. The patient learned to sing and dance and from time to time would perform with him. This was a very special activity which she shared with her father, and in which she saw him being applauded and admired by other people. It was not only something that enabled her to feel appreciated and special, but also something from which her mother was excluded. The patient associated this to her time with father in the shower, where she felt that she had her father to herself and resented her mother's intrusions. This triggered feelings of guilt about her sexual wishes for her father and her fears that her mother was watching her, knew what she was thinking and wishing, and was going to punish her for these wishes.

Connected with these feelings toward her mother was the memory of her constipation. It turned out that, about the time of her brother's birth, the patient was being toilet-trained. Her constipation was the occasion for frequent enemas, which were administered by her mother. In these experiences she felt violated and helpless and furious at her mother for taking away her feces. She had been cheated and deprived. Her mother had taken away something that was hers, that she had no right to take. The patient was left feeling empty and useless. In the analysis the patient associated feces with penises, saying that they were the only thing she had that was like a penis. She related this to having a baby, something precious and important which would be inside her and which was hers. But her feeling was that anything inside her could be taken away and that she would be helpless to prevent it.

Her mother had everything — her father, her brother, and even (so the patient felt) the power to give or take away penises. Behind this was the persistent fantasy that very early in her life the patient herself had had a penis, but that her mother had taken it away as a punishment for the patient's own wishes to take her brother's penis away from him. The anal struggles and retention of feces engaged the mother in a punitive attack, so that the patient could feel that she had been cheated and deprived

by her mother. These battles also served to intensify the resentment over the lack of a penis. The patient could not understand at
this primitive level why it was that even though she was the first
she did not get the penis, but instead it was given to her brother.

The retention of feces was associated with the patient's holding
onto her bad feelings, the feelings of anger, resentment, hurt, and
deprivation. She commented that holding onto her feces made
her mother notice her and pay attention to her, even though the
attention took the form of the enemas. Holding onto these feces-
feelings served a similar function in relation to me—gaining attention, interest, concern, making her feel special and important.
Holding on also prolonged the work of the analysis and postponed
the inevitable abandonment and rejection by me. The patient
remarked that holding onto such bad feelings made her somehow
feel that she was a real person, someone who would be noticed
and who was important, and that she would only be noticed if she
was unhappy and angry. She saw these feelings as equivalent to
the hurt, vulnerable, weak part of herself, that is, the feminine
part of herself. She contrasted to this the intellectual, logical part
of herself, which she saw as masculine and as having the power to
control. Allowing herself to have such feelings or to express them
was equivalent to a loss of control. She compared it to giving up
her feces—yielding to the power of another person by being pleasing and gaining approval, yet losing something that was important to her. This had immediate application to the analysis.

The motif of holding on was important since it helped defend
against her fears of loss. But holding onto her feces was also a way
of holding onto her mother. Similarly, it was important to hold
onto not only her view of mother as an object, but also the internalized introject-substitute for mother—the introject that formed
the nucleus of her view of herself as a woman.

Behind these apprehensions lay a deep separation anxiety.
This was mobilized at times of interruptions in the analysis, such
as vacations. Only gradually did the patient become aware of her
anger at me on these occasions and become able to express this
anger. She was angry because I was inaccessible and she was
powerless to control me and to keep me available to her. She felt
that, if she were really important to me, I would not leave or
abandon her. At one level, she related this to her father's in-

accessibility and her inability to possess him and his penis. But at a deeper level, the separation had to do with her fears of losing her mother. When her brother was born, her mother went to the hospital, thereby leaving her. At the time the patient felt that she had lost her mother, lost her own importance in her mother's eyes. When her mother returned, the patient was no longer the only one, no longer the most important one to her mother. She had been displaced by another, penis-bearing infant.

In the years of her childhood and even later, the patient was constantly preoccupied with the fear that her parents would get rid of her if she did not please them. In her fantasy, she had been deprived of both her mother and her "penis," and if she did not watch her step, her parents would get rid of her altogether. This was related to the feces, which were at one point somehow precious and important, and yet could be discharged into the toilet and flushed away to be lost forever. The patient described a dream in which little people were being flushed down the sink by a powerful witch. The little people were like feces, and the powerful witch was her mother. The patient feared that her mother would get rid of her like that, flush her away as if she were of no more importance than feces—or she might be thrown away, like the rag doll left in the rain. These associations reflected the patient's underlying assumption, derived from her narcissism, that if she was not important, that is to say, not only the most important but the only important one, then she was worthless and would be gotten rid of. Connected with these fears of abandonment, however, was a powerful wish for closeness and dependence on her mother. This was related to her fantasy of her mother as a phallic mother, which found expression in a dream of her having a homosexual affair with a woman who had a large penis.

These issues were displayed in the transference and had to be gradually worked through. At first the issues of the father transference predominated and expressed themselves in terms of her need to be pleasing in order to gain my acknowledgment and acceptance as a vehicle for making her somehow special and important. The need to please, however, was paralleled by the issues of submitting to the power of my penis-brain and the wishes to compete. The patient fought against her sexual and loving feelings toward me insofar as they made her feel vulnerable and weak. To feel loving or dependent toward me would put her in my power, and I could then attack her or get rid of her at my whim.

She also struggled with her hostile and destructive feelings toward me, particularly her anger at my inaccessibility and the constant frustration she felt in the analytic situation where her sexual wishes could not be fulfilled. In addition, she both envied and was enraged by my possessing so much knowledge, the power-penis which she could not take away from me and which she could not possess herself. On a deeper level, her anger at me and her fear of my power made her response to me all the more difficult, since the strong elements of the maternal transference also made me the good, understanding mother, who had the time to listen and to make her feel special and important. It was the loss of her mother's attention to her as the only child and her rage at her mother for this that had made her turn to her father in the first place. Her underlying vulnerability made the issue of control all the more intense, and this issue arose in all her relationships. The analysis was to some degree a power struggle, with the anal issues of control and submission very much in focus.

Another conflict surfaced with the feelings generated by her increasing dependence on me. The issue was one of whether she could trust me without having to place herself in such a vulnerable and devalued position. The same struggle manifested itself in her sexual relationships with her husband. She remained sexually unresponsive and in fact expressed this unresponsiveness in terms of turning off her genital feelings because they represented the weak, vulnerable, feminine part of herself which was open to violation and attack. She envisioned orgasm as a loss of control in which she could be completely taken advantage of. To counter this, she made herself the snake charmer, controlling the writhing, dangerous snake-penis.

As the elements of her father transference were worked through, the elements of the maternal transference became all the more prominent and intense. It became apparent that the refuge of the maternal transference, particularly the positive maternal transference, served as a defense against the intense sexual wishes involved in the father transference. But it also seemed to bring into focus deeper issues having to do with dependency and separation.

As I have already indicated, it is not enough to view the transference elements simply as displacements from previous object relations. Unquestionably the material can be seen in these terms, i.e., as object-related displacements of object representations, but this view of the transference serves little more than the interpretative objective of illuminating one aspect of transference dynamics and genesis. That is not to say that this kind of interpretation is insignificant; it is one of the major therapeutic props of analytic effectiveness. My point is that it follows on a limited analytic perspective (that generated within the confines of an instinct cum ego psychology), and thus ignores the impact of internalizations.

It was not enough for my patient, for example, to see that her wishes to please and placate me, so that I would not get rid of her, re-created feelings and attitudes she had had in relation to her parents as a child. This realization undoubtedly helps in the gaining of interpretive insight and has its own proportional therapeutic effect. More important, however, was the patient's coming to see that her view of me as having to be pleased was based on a projection from that part of herself which was demanding and perfectionistic, and from her own desire to be special, powerful, and influential. In gaining access to this other dimension of her introjective organization, a whole complex of wishes, motives, and important determinants was unveiled that otherwise would have remained unattended. It could be argued that these elements were also expressed in her relationship with her younger brother, but what is most important is that they be seen as currently active and that they be recognized as inherent aspects of the patient's own personality organization—then as now.

As the analysis progressed an important area of concern was the patient's unfortunate marriage. Her husband continued to behave in a rather irresponsible and immature fashion, and this infuriated the patient and stirred up many feelings that related to her childhood feelings toward her younger brother. It became increasingly apparent that the marriage relationship could not survive, and the patient had to deal with the problems of renouncing this relationship. She felt that she had married her husband out of a conviction that no one else would accept her and that he was the best she could do. She also felt that she could become important by saving a man who was weak and ineffectual. She could exercise her power by controlling him and making him into what she wanted him to be; this was the only way that she could get love.

Her husband in fact fulfilled many of her expectations of men, particularly in terms of her relationship to her brother. He was weak and lazy, but in her eyes he could get away with it because he had a penis. Further, if she left her husband and terminated the relationship, that would make me the most important man in her life. I would become the focal point for all the wishes and conflicts inherent in her relationship to her husband and, at a deeper level, to her father.

This renunciation became a major focus of the analytic work. First, the patient had to work through her oedipal wishes and attachments to her father. Gradually she came to see him in less and less idealized terms and in increasingly more realistic terms. Particularly striking was the patient's evolving perception of her parents. As they grew older, their positions became reversed. Her father seemed less happy and free and more burdened by the cares of advancing age. In contrast, the mother was viewed as increasingly liberated and productive after the children had left home, showing more of what the patient would have liked to have seen in her when she was younger. The mother had gone back to school to train as a teacher and was very caught up in and enthusiastic about her work. The patient had an increasing sense of communicating and sharing something with her mother. This stronger sense of positive identification came to replace the more hostile and resentful feelings connected with the image of the bad mother.

In terms of the marriage relationship, the patient began to see that her wishes to save and transform her husband were, in essence, attempts to make a silk purse out of a sow's ear. She was doomed to failure and disappointment. But it was difficult for her to acknowledge that she had made a mistake and that she would have to give up something that she had made important to herself.

The issue of renunciation also came to the fore in the analysis of the transference. During the course of the analysis, the patient's trust in and dependence on me grew. She felt that her relationship to me was one of the most important in her life. A major consideration in my undertaking analysis with her and one of the predominant features of her analysis, even in the face of the vicissitudes we have been discussing, was the strong therapeutic alliance that she had formed with me in the year of therapy before the beginning of the analysis. It, in fact, sustained her through the threat and the anxiety, the fear and the rage, experienced in working through the transference issues. As we approached the end of the analysis, the renunciation of the therapeutic dependence became a prime concern. The issue was whether the patient would see the termination of the analysis as something important being taken away from her, as with the enemas administered by her mother, or whether she could for the first time go through the process of building an important and positive relationship and then surrendering and renouncing it, together with her infantile dependency wishes, in the interest of further growth.

At this point in the analytic process it was necessary to work through the patient's wishes to remain dependent, to remain the special little girl who found her importance and her protection and appreciation in her relationship to powerful parents. The analysis had come to grips with the patient's underlying narcissism and her need to cling to her narcissistic fantasies. She had always felt worthless and empty in herself and had turned to the realm of fantasy as a way of making herself feel important and special. She was *the* significant, *the* central person in a fantasy world filled with fears and anxieties that allowed her to play the heroine in a tragic sense. She was unwilling to leave this world of fantasy behind her and to immerse herself in the world of reality where she was no longer special, but had to earn her rewards, compete with others, face possible failure and rejection, and submit to inevitable disappointments and frustrations.

The issue here obviously involved more than the patient's wishes to remain dependent on me. An additional concern centered on the patient's powerful attachment to and investment in her introjects. The two issues were related, but from the latter perspective one saw in much clearer focus her investment in being the helpless, dependent, vulnerable female, as well as her powerful "masculine" striving—the wish to be strong, competent, intelligent, controlling. Linked with these wishes were the intense narcissistic concerns over specialness, importance, being admired and approved, desired. Clinging to the configuration of introjects and the sense of self organized around them unquestionably served defensive needs, but it also preserved her inner fantasy—a kind of "golden fantasy" (Smith, 1977) which embodied treasured narcissistic elements. The patient's introjects themselves embraced narcissistic elements akin to the archaic residues Kohut (1971) has described in relation to the grandiose self. As we have already discussed, the grandiose self is one important narcissistically determined introjective configuration. For this patient, the renunciation of her introjects required the working through and resolution of the underlying narcissistic issues. It was necessary to work through the layers of idealization with its corresponding self-devaluation in order to approach in a therapeutically meaningful way the underlying grandiosity.

Gradually, these issues were worked through. At one point the patient decided spontaneously to increase the amount of her fee. She saw it as a reasonable adjustment. It was something over which she had control and power of decision rather than a submission to my power and influence. Her act was also in part a renouncement of her need to feel special and needy. As the analysis progressed, and particularly in the closing phases, the feeling of inner emptiness that had so marked her sense of self in the beginning of the analysis began to fade. Less and less did she find it necessary to recognize herself only in a reflection from those around her. Instead, she began increasingly to have a sense of her own self as a permanent possession, as something that was stable inside her, that could not be taken away by any outside force. She became less dependent on outside approval and no longer had the constant feeling of being on the brink of abandonment. She found herself more and more able to sustain a sense of self-coherence and stability during periods of my absence. Later on, in the course of her job, she had to spend periods of several days away from the analysis on business trips and found herself able to undertake these without anxiety and with a sense of fulfillment. Gradually she shifted from picturing herself as nothing but an empty hole, to feeling that there was something positive, valuable, and substantial within herself.

Along with this, there was a marked change in her self-esteem and in her initiative in undertaking responsible projects in her work. She was also finally able to give up her husband and to separate from him for a period of several months. Toward the end of the analysis, she began seriously to examine the question of divorce. The working through of the narcissistic issues and the gradual facing of the issues of renunciation progressively turned her neurotic fears and anxieties into a more appropriate sadness, connected with her surrendering both her idealized oedipal father and her husband. She was able to face the disappointment in both these relationships and to mourn them appropriately. She was also able, in the closing stages of the analysis, to express her sadness and the pain that she felt in terminating the analytic relationship, which had been one of the most significant and helpful in her life experience. But she took away from it a sense of trust in herself and a sense of her own inherent value and capacity to be a productive and happy human being. She was no longer the castrated and vulnerable—as well as special, important, and entitled—woman-child.

As this case followed its course, the emphasis shifted from oedipal concerns to more primitive narcissistic concerns, connected with the patient's loss of a sense of specialness and closeness to her mother, and the need to regain and retain that sense of specialness and importance. In this context, the two poles of the introjective organization were increasingly clarified and could then be interpreted. One side of this introjective configuration, which provided the depressive core of her neurosis, was characterized by weakness, vulnerability, powerlessness, and dependence on the good will and pleasure of those who had power and importance (penis equivalents). This was the helpless and emotional part of herself that she identified with her femininity. And it was this aspect of the introjective configuration that related to the depressed, self-demeaning, and self-effacing image of her mother. The opposite side of the introjective organization, however, drew a quite different picture. She was portrayed as special, important, magically influential and controlling, the central figure of the fantasy-riddled drama that she envisioned around her—an Alice in Wonderland. Although in her fantasy world she was often terrified and constantly victimized by the powerful forces that surrounded her, she was at the same time the heroine of the story, the most important character, more important than anyone else. To enter this fantasy world, she merely stepped through the looking glass, leaving behind the mundane world of reality with its ordinary satisfactions and everyday problems. Only when these polarities could be clarified and interpreted was it possible for this young woman to confront her narcissism and the infantile attachments with which it was inextricably entangled.

Here the analytic process runs up against the inherent rigidity of and the strong adherence to the introjective organization which characterize so many patients and which are embedded in the narcissistic dynamics. Patients often work their way through seemingly interminable and inexhaustible defensive maneuvers in order to retain some aspect of one or the other polarity. It is only in working through these resistances and gradually elucidating the nature of the introjects and their inherent unity that these patients ultimately come to confront the fundamental anxiety and the related issues of dependence that motivate their defensive postures.

Several points concerning the metapsychology of introjects can help sustain the analytic effort in this phase of the analysis and may serve as the basis for the development of critical insight. The first important point is that the organization of the introjects, their inherent bipolarity, is elaborated on the basis of defensive needs and in response to drive pressures, rather than on the basis of more reasonable, realistic (secondary-process) apprehensions. In the course of the analytic work, the patient evolves a set of self-images or self-appraisals which reflect the dimensions of the introjective organization. As these self-appraisals become more explicit and conscious, they can be regarded as imaginative byproducts which derive from the organization of the introjects and which express the introjective content. These self-imaginings represent what Loewald (1975) has called "fantasy creations." They are formed in the complex matrix which evolves out of the interplay of subjective components (introjective derivatives), objective factors, projective elements (from the analyst as well as the patient), and whatever else contributes to the illusory transferential matrix.

These mental products can be regarded as forms of self-representation, but self-representations that are nonetheless contaminated by imaginative byproducts derived from the introjective dynamics. They are in a sense forms of fantasy, although here specifically fantasies about the patient's own self. In fact the reality of the patient's self remains unknown, particularly to the patient, insofar as it is enmeshed in and masked by the pathogenic introjects. As the introjective organization is gradually elucidated and analyzed, the delineation of the fantasy dimensions derived from the introjects and the real dimensions (as yet unknown and undetermined) receives increasing emphasis.

To give a spatial sense to this conceptualization, it is as though the inherent tendency to splitting and projection which characterizes the organization of the introjects had split the introjective components on both sides of the ground of reality. The components of the introject deal in fantasied extremes of strength or weakness, superiority or inferiority, power or vulnerability. Both poles are extreme deviations from the reality and neither reflects the true state of affairs. Consequently, the analysand must reach a point where he is able to abandon both of these alternatives, and it is only when both alternatives are renounced that he can orient himself more adaptively in terms of reality and reality determinants.

A second important point has to do with the specific derivation of the introjects. It must be remembered that developmentally the introjects represent internalized objects derived from significant object relation contexts, usually and characteristically in relation to parental objects. Illumination of these derivative relationships provides the basis for critical insight, and in this way the infantile determinants, perduring in the introjective economy and extending themselves to the patient's current neurotic and maladaptive functioning, come to be clearly delineated. The emerging insight into these patterns of derivation makes it apparent that the underlying motivations, which preserve the pathogenic introjective organization, are no longer operative in the patient's present reality context.

Here again the developmental perspective tends to underline the differentiation between fantasy components and reality. At this level, the predominant issues are those of narcissistic vulnerability and infantile dependence. These issues must be worked through and resolved before the patient can come to a position of decisive renunciation and surrender of the residual infantile attachments. The regressive undoing and gradual renunciation of the dependent, infantile attachments, as well as the introjective organization they sustain, serve to release the patient's inherent developmental potential for intrapsychic reorganization along more realistic and adaptive channels. The effective renunciation of infantile attachments thereby opens up the potential for critical internalizations to take place within the analytic relationship.

The transition from pathogenic introjects to the more realistic and adaptive analytic introject is facilitated and accompanied by important learning processes. The mobilization of these processes within the analysis sets the stage for the gradual modification of the introjective organization and thus induces more realistic, secondary-process forms of identificatory process. The mobilization and integration of these modified forms of internalization take on increasing significance in the later portion of the progressive phase, leading to a reworking and reintegration in the terminal phase of the analysis.

The process of internalization of the analytic introject has been described by Dorpat (1974) in terms of progressive transformations, from the replication of patient-analyst transactions in the analytic introject to the gradual development of ego and superego functions by way of consequent identifications with the analytic object. Dorpat's somewhat narcissistic patients repeated analytic observational or interpretive transactions outside the analytic hours in the manner of a deferred fantasy imitation. He comments:

The analytic method and the analytic setting provide the environmental conditions for the formation of the analyst introject, and the patient-analyst transactions provide some of the content for analyst introject fantasies. Another set of conditions for the internalization process includes the patient's developmental capacities and motives for representing transactions with the analyst, and for using such imaginary transactions for the construction of ego and superego functions.... In the second transformation selective identifications with the object representations of the analyst were used for the formation of autonomous ego and superego functions.... the formation of selective identifications in these patients occurred at the same time as the analyst introject fantasies disappeared from consciousness. The analyst introject fantasies were a pre-stage for selective ego and superego identifications formed later out of the elements partially internalized in fantasy. There was a progressive structuralization and automatization of the functions formerly mediated self-consciously and imitatively in fantasy. Newly learned psychic actions were gradually experienced as an active process regulated and initiated by the self-as-agent [p. 187].

One of the useful ways of envisioning the neurotic's difficulty is that, because of internal fixations and defensive impediments, the patient fails to assimilate the fruits of experience and to learn from it. In other words, the rigid defensive organization of the pathogenic introjective economy prevents the normal integration of experience with its induction and facilitation of positive and constructive identifications (Meissner, 1974c). The undoing of these introjective impediments unleashes the patient's learning capacity which is then able to express itself in terms of meaningful patterns of social learning, including the imitative patterns which stimulate and reflect the emergence of the analytic introject.

The work of the analytic process is to set such learning potentials in motion. Once operative, they establish the conditions within which meaningful and constructive identifications can take place — particularly identifications with the analytic object. As I have observed previously:

The ultimate integration of imitative and introjective elements takes place through identification. As we have seen, the conditions promoting identification differ from those promoting introjections, and the integration of both these identificatory processes with imitative processes are likewise different. The operation of both introjection and identification is part of the normal course of personality growth. . . . Certain introjects serve to elicit and foster identifications, while others tend to impede them (Meissner, 1972). We can guess that relatively positive introjects have an inductive influence on further identification. Introjects that involve a relatively high degree of ambivalence due to unneutralized aggression tend to impede identification. We can suggest, therefore, that the conditions that allow for and encourage positive and meaningful object relations both promote imitative behavior and foster relatively nonambivalent developmental introjections, both of which can be integrated in developmental interests and serve to elicit meaningful ego identifications [1974d, p. 534].

The process operates in the developmental context no less than the analytic context — analogously, to be sure, and respecting the obvious contextual differences. In this light, the effects of the analytic process must be seen in terms of regressively dissolving developmental fixations which are built into the pathogenic organization of the introjects and which impede normal developmental attainments, particularly aspects of the developmental learning experience. The impact of interpretations in facilitating and advancing this learning process is considerable. The analytic process therefore involves much more than the restrictive undoing of pathogenic introjects.

We should not lose sight of the function of the introjects in the psychic economy. Not only must they be seen in reference to defensive needs of various sorts, but they should be seen particularly in terms of the underlying narcissistic issues. Theoretically, the organization of the introjects provides the core elements around which the inner sense of self is elaborated. For many patients who come to the critical point of renouncing the pathogenic introjects, a threat is posed to both the integrity and preservation of their sense of self — however desperate, conflicted, vulnerable, dependent, victimized, entitled, or omnipotent that pathological self may be. Such a sense of self is, after all, the best that the patient has been able to do through the vicissitudes of a lifetime.

The analysis must, in consequence, not only bring about the

interpretive resources for delineating and renouncing these introjects and their inherent attachments, but must help to mobilize those forces which will enable the patient to internalize the analytic introject as a replacement for pathogenic residuals. The patient, in turn, must work through the narcissistic perils of loss of love, loss of the needed relationship which has served to sustain self-integrity, or even, at its most pathogenic, loss of self-cohesion. For many classical neurotics, whose pathology involves predominantly structural conflict, this renunciation, followed by a turning to the analytic introject, is difficult enough. For the more severe personality disorders, in which narcissistic issues pervade the pathology, it is all the more difficult — and in some cases the possibility is much in doubt.

In this sense, then, the critical contribution of the analytic process takes the form of fostering and facilitating the analytic introject. The renunciation of pathogenic introjects sets the stage and provides the impetus for a more meaningful, less ambivalent and conflict-ridden internalization derived from the analytic object relationship. The analyst, in turn, continually makes himself available as an object for internalization. It is the dynamic aspects of the positive transference involvement that provide the matrix for this internalization. Only when the infantile attachments underlying the pathogenic introjects have been relatively effectively resolved can the inherent potential of the therapeutic relationship begin to assert itself.

The effectiveness of the analytic introject depends in part on the inherent qualities of the analytic object and in part on the status of the therapeutic alliance. The analyst strives within the analytic interaction to appear calm and trustworthy, both sympathetic and empathic, a nonjudgmental and consistent participant in the analytic process, the collaborative observer of the patient's behavior and productions. This demeanor of unruffled scientific objectivity has been variously described, beginning with the "mirror" concept advanced by Freud (1912), but subsequently reinterpreted in a variety of important ways, including the recent emphasis on the real qualities of the analyst as engaged in a real relationship with the analysand (Greenson, 1967).

The propensity for introjecting the analytic object is also facilitated by the supportive, positive dimensions of the therapeutic alliance. This alliance establishes itself primarily in terms of the trustworthiness of the analyst and the emerging capacity of the analysand to relate to the analyst through increasingly productive and meaningful forms of dependence. Involved in this is the consolidation of elements of secondary trust. The gradual resolution of pathogenic impediments and building of the therapeutic alliance have a self-reinforcing dimension which, as it develops, lays the ground for further, more meaningful and more effective forms of therapeutic internalization. As Boyer and Giovacchini (1967) comment in reference to the analyst's interpretations:

> As the analytic imago is introjected and as interpretive activity becomes internalized, the patient's range of secondary process functioning is expanded. The analyst superimposes his secondary process upon the patient's primary process, leading to greater ego structure. In a positive feed-back sequence, this enables the patient to introject more helpful aspects of the analytic relationship, which, in turn, leads to further structuralization and then to greater ability for internalization, etc. This increase in secondary process activity gradually extends to the patient's everyday life and no longer requires analytic reinforcement [pp. 233–234].

While the interpretation itself operates on a more or less cognitive level to produce meaningful insight and consequently facilitate therapeutic change and growth within the patient, other factors having to do with the alliance provide the context within which the interpretation can be meaningfully and productively communicated. The critical question in this regard concerns those factors which are most pertinent to the mobilization of growth potential and to the facilitation of a more coherent, consolidated, and adaptive sense of self in the patient. Addressing himself to this dimension of the analytic experience, Khan (1972) has made the following observation:

> The etiology of the dislocation of self, as Winnicott pointed out, starts always from maladaptive environmental care. We encounter the self of a patient clinically only in *moments* of true regression to dependence and holding. Quite often, such moments of self-experience actualize outside the analytic or therapeutic situation and our task then is how to enable the patient to provide ego coverage for them. Interpretation, as such, cannot engender

self-experience in the patient, although, once these experiences actualize, interpretations enable the patient's ego to find and elaborate symbolic equations through which these experiences can become a property of the inner psychic reality of the patient — conscious and unconscious. . . .

The two distinct styles of my relating to the patient I can differentiate as: (1) Listening to what the patient verbally communicates, in the patently classical situation as it has evolved, and deciphering its *meaning* in terms of structural conflicts (ego, id and superego) and through its transferential interpersonal expression in the here-and-now of the analytic situation. (2) Through a psychic, affective, and environmental *holding* of the person of the patient in the clinical situation, I facilitate certain experiences that I cannot anticipate or program, any more than the patient can. When these actualize, they are surprising, both for the patient and for me, and release quite unexpected new processes in the patient [pp. 98–99].

Undoubtedly this holding aspect of the analytic interaction plays a more prominent role in more primitive forms of personality organization. This "holding" may provide a kind of minimal condition without which the analytic transaction cannot take place at all. Berry (1975) observes:

In many cases, especially those in which paranoid factors are dominant, and in all cases where one reaches this kernel, the factors of presence, of good will and of listening, play a role which I see as the minimal condition necessary for the acceptance of an interpretation. Without this condition and this preliminary work ('holding'), the interpretation risks being received like milk, like a gift, an attack or a persecution, its contents not being comprehended. Without this 'minimal condition' the interpretation cannot be mutative [p. 366].

From the perspective of the present study, these appraisals of analytic "holding" can be extrapolated to all analyses. As I have already suggested, the analytic situation, particularly the emergence and development of the transference, carries within it an essentially paranoid dynamic that is built into the structure of the transference and can be responded to in meaningful therapeutic terms only by the careful establishing, maintaining, and unfolding of the therapeutic alliance. Particularly important in this regard is the transition from the earliest phases of narcissistic alliance to a position of secondary trust which ensures the patient of the analyst's continuing good will, presence, and support in the face of the patient's wishes to separate.

The critical question in all of this is whether the analyst can respond in such a way as neither to drive the patient back into a state of self-encapsulation, withdrawal, or isolation (equivalent to a paranoid entrenchment), nor, on the other hand, to force the patient into a position of false-self compliance or conformity. It should be noted here that the term "holding" describes the operation of those alliance factors on the part of the analyst which respond to the most primitive and maternally dependent vulnerabilities in the patient. Just as the mother's holding is attenuated, modified, and transformed in relation to the developmental changes in the child, so the analyst's holding undergoes a progressive modification in which the analyst maintains a sensitive responsiveness and attunement to the evolving vulnerabilities and sensitivities of the patient. In reference to later aspects of analytic responsiveness which have to do with the analyst's contribution to the progression of the therapeutic alliance, the term "holding" loses some of its appropriateness, although it continues to express the aspect of mutual involvement and reciprocal responsiveness that is optimally maintained throughout the developmental continuum. The holding needed for the infant is quite different and involves specific qualities quite divergent from the holding provided by a parent for, let us say, the adolescent.

The muting of elements of conflict and pathogenic ambivalence in the therapeutic alliance opens the way for the exercise of more effective ego resources and thus allows the patient's capacities for adaptive learning and the development of insight increasingly to assert themselves. The gradual shaping of the analytic introject is determined more and more by the patient's adaptive ego resources, rather than by the defensive pressures which played such a role in the organization of pathogenic introjects. Consequently, the analytic introject tends to be less ambivalent, less inherently conflicted, less subject to drive pressures and derivatives, and finally less susceptible to regressive pulls. The stage is set for the emergence of the ego's inherent developmental capacities for the induction of more constructive ego identifications along the lines of the "identification with the introject" (Meissner, 1972; Sandler, 1960).

As the progressive subphase advances, there is a shift from the emphasis of the transference neurosis to a consideration of the therapeutic alliance. As the component elements of the transference neurosis, derived from the underlying pathogenic introjects, are gradually clarified, worked through, and renounced, the patient's capacity for forming a meaningful analytic introject and the correlated potential for constructive identifications come more to the fore. What I am suggesting here, in somewhat schematic fashion, is that the progressive working through of elements of the transference neurosis induces a shift within the analytic relationship, in which corresponding elements of the therapeutic alliance are mobilized and placed in significant relief. This opens the way for the reworking of alliance issues in a meaningful way. The developmental model is useful in considering this perspective, since it provides a schema within which these processes can be articulated.

My point is that there is a progressive evolution within the therapeutic alliance, which is correlated with the relative resolution of levels of transference involvement. Thus, for example, the gradual opening and resolution of issues of infantile dependence in transference terms shift the equilibrium in the analytic relationship to an emphasis on issues of basic trust. Similarly, the work on issues of control and power may bring into focus the dimensions of the patient's emergent autonomy within the analytic relationship. In this sense, the analysis opens the way for the further reworking of developmental experiences in terms of the emergence and processing of the analytic introject. The extent to which such a reworking is at all possible remains a moot question. It may always be limited, and in some forms of character pathology and more primitive forms of personality organization, the prospects may be quite limited indeed.

What I am stressing here, however, is that too little attention has been paid to the analysis of the therapeutic alliance as such (Hani, 1973). I would suggest that it is in terms of the development of the therapeutic alliance that the matrix is provided for more constructive and transmuting identifications (as opposed to introjections) to begin to take place. As I have already indicated, Erikson's (1963) program of developmental tasks arises in varying degrees within the therapeutic alliance. It seems to me that the hurdles of trust, autonomy, initiative, industry, and identity readily find a place in this frame of reference.

At all stages of the analytic work, the qualities of the relationship to the analyst play a predominant role. At all points the empathic responsiveness and the facilitative stance of the analyst are critical. The analyst is placed in the difficult position of continuing the work of the analysis and resolution of transference elements while, at the same time, making way for and supporting the emergence of alliance components. It is important that these alliance elements be brought within the perspective of the analytic work so that the analytic internalizations do not take place in an implicit or haphazard fashion.

The patient's beginning attempts to establish some degree of autonomy within the analytic relationship, for example, must be respected in fact as well as in action. They are also appropriately and importantly the object of analytic scrutiny and reflection. The analysand should have the opportunity not only to experience an emerging autonomy in relation to the analyst, but also to explore the vicissitudes of autonomy in his own development and life experience. In this way, the analysand's growth to autonomy can be facilitated, consolidated, and made a more specifically reflective, self-conscious developmental possession. Such analytic scrutiny also provides the opportunity for insight into the patient's own inner needs and propensities, which serve to undermine the sense of autonomy, both in past experience and in the contemporary frame of reference.

However, and I wish to stress this point, the development of insight into these dimensions of the patient's ego functioning and self-organization has a limited value which must be supplemented and sustained—and in fact can only take on a significant dimension—in terms of the patient's ongoing experience of evolving autonomy within the analytic relationship. It is this aspect of the patient's experience that serves as the matrix for internalization, rather than the simple development of insight.

A last concern in regard to the progressive phase—last but certainly not least—has to do with the question of counter-transference. The term "countertransference" refers to a broad spectrum of processes involving the analyst's contribution to the analytic process. Clearly countertransference plays into the workings of internalization within the analytic process. My comments here focus on the formation of the analytic introject. In a previous discussion of the nature of introjection (Meissner, 1974b), I have argued that the child's introjections during the course of development are influenced not only by internal deter-minants but also by extrinsic factors, specifically the projections derived from significant figures around the child. The family emotional matrix, within which the child grows up, is characterized by the interplay of introjections and projections between the parents and the child, as well as those stemming from other family members who may be involved in this emo-tionally responsive interaction. In pathogenic family situations one often sees the pathologically affected child acting out elements of parental projections (Meissner, 1964, 1970b, 1978a).

In analogous fashion, the organization of the analytic intro-ject reflects the basic interaction of projections and introjections deriving from both the patient and the analyst (Little, 1951; Orr, 1954). The analyst's projective contribution depends to some degree on the analyst's own introjective organization. This countertransference projective interference may impede or distort the important work of resolution and progressive organization of the patient's introjects. As Searles (1965) has commented:

> To the degree that the patient needs to keep his personality incor-porated within what he conceives (largely through projection) to be the personality of the analyst, or to the degree that he needs to utilize the personality of the analyst (again, as the patient perceives that personality, distorted by many projections of his own repressed self-images) as a nucleus for his own functioning self, to that degree the patient's efforts towards individuation are unsuccessful. And insofar as the therapist himself needs to keep the patient's personality incorporated within his own, or to keep his own personality incorporated within that of the patient, he is

hampering the patient's efforts to achieve the goal of an independently functioning self [p. 62].

It is not merely that the analyst's introjective organization can
give rise to projections and thus impede the analytic work. One
can go further to insist that the patient's pathogenic dynamics
will seize on any projective element in the analytic object and
even strive to elicit such elements from the analyst. In immers-
ing himself in the therapeutic relationship, the analyst is sub-
jected to extraordinary pressures pulling him into a pattern of
responding that will confirm and reinforce the patient's inner
pathogenic needs — and thus give support to the patient's own
inner introjective economy.

Here we can say that the patient's projections promote and
induce a response in the inner world of the analyst. They
evoke a corresponding introjection on the part of the analyst,
which in turn may serve as the basis of further projections.
This form of introjective induction within the analyst has
been described in terms of "counteridentifications" (Fliess,
1953; Grinberg, 1962). And it is this interplay of projections and introjections between the analyst and the patient
that constitutes the illusory matrix of the transference with its
inherent creative potential. This matrix is also the place
within which the projective and introjective mechanisms
operate to support the empathic communication so essential to the effectiveness of therapy. As Schafer (1959) has
noted:

   . . . a subtle and relatively conflict-free interplay of introjective
   and projective mechanisms occurs, enhancing the object of contemplation as well as the subject's experience; thus the relationship between the two. Preconscious or conscious experimental
   fantasies concerning the object and the relationship express this
   interplay of mechanisms. . . . Empathy involves experiencing in
   some fashion the feelings of another person. This experience can
   only be approximate or roughly congruent, since the other self is
   not directly or fully knowable. The shared experience is based to a
   great extent on remembered, corresponding affective states of
   one's own. Observing a patient's life at any one point, we ten-
   tatively project onto him the feelings we once felt under similar
   circumstances, and then test this projection by further observa-

tion. . . . Affect may therefore be said to play a double role in the
comprehension of empathy. There is a re-creation of affect, that
is, becoming able to feel approximately as the other person does
through revival of past inner experience of a similar nature supplemented by projection and reality testing; also there is translation of one's own reactive affects into stimulus patterns in the
other person. . . . This double role of affect is a cardinal aspect of
the frequently referred to introjective component of empathic
comprehending; it amounts to carrying on a relationship with
another person internally, and with a relatively high degree of
cathexis. The free availability of affect signals in this process
presupposes superego tolerance, associated relaxation of ego
defense and control, and hypercathexis of one's own body ego [pp.
346–348].

As long as the analyst is able to utilize these currents of introjection and projection, his capability for empathic responsiveness
becomes a major therapeutic tool. But this requires that the
analyst be sufficiently in touch with these aspects of his experience and that his own internal identification be sufficiently
consolidated and integrated to allow this dimension of regressive
experience to take place in the service of the analytic process,
without bridging over into internal self-modifications on the one
hand, or into countertransference expressions on the other.

Moeller (1977) has recently emphasized the role of empathy in
elucidating the self-representational aspects of the patient's
transference. The persistent thrust of the present monograph has
been aimed at bringing the self-representations into effective play
as determining components of transference reactions. We must
continually remind ourselves that the transference develops out
of the interplay of projection and introjection, so that there are
objective aspects — representations of what the parents were
like — and subjective elements — representations of the patient's
own infantile self as determined in early interactions with the
parents. Projections in the transference can draw the analyst into
the parental role, where the dynamics allow the patient to assume
his familiar infantile role. When the analyst responds with projections and introjections of his own, the countertransference
is put into play. The result is that the transference and the
countertransference create a collusive and illusional matrix

within which the dynamics of the neurosis are replayed — or perhaps, better, re-created — with all the inherent potential for renovation and metamorphosis as well as regression and repetition.

It is particularly in this regard, perhaps more significantly and stringently than in any other, that the analytic insistence on neutrality assumes its most telling role. The tendency for such introjective and projective components to play themselves out at an unconscious level simply emphasizes the risk and difficulties inherent in the analytic process. Furthermore, this aspect of the transference interaction makes it apparent that analysts cannot just rely on elements of technique or analytic behavior to carry them through countertransference vicissitudes. Ultimately, they must rely on the organization of their own introjective configurations and the extent to which that has been effectively analyzed and resolved.

The Terminal Phase

The terminal phase is in many ways the least understood and, from the present point of view, perhaps the most critical. It is in this phase that the groundwork for the formation of positive, constructive identifications, which was laid down in the middle phase, is secured. The terminal phase carries forward the dynamic vectors set in motion during the progressive subphase.

It is altogether characteristic of the terminal phase that the issues that have been worked through in previous stages of the analysis are again regressively reactivated and must again be worked through. The issues of termination, however, lend a particular emphasis and quality to this reworking that distinguish it from the work in previous stages of the analysis. This later reworking is stimulated by and centers on the issues of termination and separation from the analyst. And it is in the face of this threat of loss and separation that the already-analyzed pathogenic components of the introjects are regressively reactivated.

The new reworking, however, does not take place on anything like the same terms, since it builds on previous insights and the patient's effectively realized attainments from the earlier work. At this point, the patient is no longer enmeshed in the constraints of the introjective network, but has to some degree won release. Although the threat of loss and separation reactivates regressive pulls which seem to draw the patient back, even transiently, to his former position, now the regressive pulls, whatever their strength and attraction, seem foreign and alien. Nonetheless, the process of renouncing the residues of the pathogenic introjects and the enduring infantile attachments remains a significant focus of the terminal phase of the analysis. Once again, as in the initial working through of these pathogenic elements, the undoing of the introjective components facilitates the emergence of constructive and transmuting identifications.

Particularly important in this phase is the emergence and analysis of separation anxiety. In many ways it has been the supportive and sustaining involvement with the analyst that has made it possible for the analysand to surrender the infantile attachments and dependencies. But, in the course of this work, the patient has developed an attachment to the analyst and a form of analytic dependency. Now, in the terminal phase, the patient is confronted with the necessity of renouncing the analytic relationship as well. This initiates a mourning process which must be dealt with on its own terms.

As Zetzel (1970) has pointed out, the working through of depression is a function of at least two aspects which place a significant demand on the patient. The first is the capacity to tolerate depression in more passive terms, and the second is the capacity to mobilize resources to deal actively with and alter the circumstances that give rise to the depression. In this light, the analytic work must not only concern itself with the toleration and working through of the depressive components, but must also support the patient's striving for autonomy and independence. Within the therapeutic alliance, the analyst must stand on the side of the potential for growth that is unleashed through the analytic work and the resolution of infantile fixations and attachments. The gradual resolution of the analytic dependence is accompanied by nascent expressions of autonomy. The working through of the issues of separation anxiety facilitates the resolution of the analytic dependence and serves to strengthen and stabilize those inherent ego capacities which gradually expand and are shaped by the emergence of significant identifications.

An integral part of the analytic process in the terminal phase is the continuing analysis of the therapeutic alliance. This involves the further resolution of transference neurosis residues, taking into consideration both the positive and negative aspects. The point is a critical one, since by overlooking positive transference elements or backing away from unanalyzed negative transference elements in view of the looming termination and the difficulties in separation one often leaves unresolved transference elements which may in time undermine the effectiveness of the analytic outcome. Obviously this is a matter of degree, and it is more than likely that in any analysis — no matter how successful — *all* the elements of the transference neurosis and its infantile determinants are never completely resolved. The analyst owes it to the patient, however, to be as thorough and as unrelenting in this regard as seems reasonable and judicious. Both positive and negative transference residues reflect the persistence of underlying introjective organizations which may serve as a nidus of further difficulty after the analysis has been brought to a close.

One important perspective in this context is the differentiation between the transference neurosis and the therapeutic alliance. This distinction provides the final testing ground for the patient to delineate elements of the introjective organization and to recognize their neurotic nature. The clarification and reinforcement of elements of the therapeutic alliance serve to stabilize and buttress the patient's inherent capacity to cope, to adapt, and ultimately to grow beyond the confines of the analysis. In this regard, a realistic appraisal must be made of the participation of both the patient and the analyst in this helping relationship.

The clarification and examination of the therapeutic alliance also contribute to the further delineation of the realms of fantasy and reality. Whereas this discrimination was an important component of the progressive subphase, it is now recast specifically in terms of the patient's grasp of and response to the therapeutic alliance. In these terms, the patient gradually comes to see and to begin to sense himself as a relatively autonomous individual with the capacity to function maturely and effectively in a realistic way in many, different life contexts. Correspondingly, the analytic introject is shaped in relatively nonconflictual and nonambivalent terms, thus setting the stage for transmutating and constructive identifications.

The point here is that the analytic work of terminal separation and individuation takes place explicitly and purposefully in terms of the therapeutic alliance. An important assessment concerns the patient's role in the analysis and the difficult, often painful effort at self-understanding and self-alteration that has contributed to the analytic outcome. This consideration must take into account the residues of infantile idealization and dependency that may have facilitated the analytic work in earlier phases, but now become an impediment and require the deliberate focus of analytic processing. As we have suggested, the analytic work in the preceding phases, particularly the progressive subphase, has moved in the direction of supporting, increasing the scope of, and facilitating the patient's sense of autonomy, responsibility, initiative, and industry within the analysis. The gradual and progressive amplification of these qualities is embedded in the process by which the pathogenic introjects are dissolved and diminished, and eventually replaced by the analytic introject. We can see this effect in the patient's increasing engagement in the analytic work, growing willingness to take responsibility for the analytic work, and widening ability to engage in the analytic process nondefensively or with diminished resistance. More and more the patient shows the capacity to free-associate, to initiate lines of exploration, and to share in the analytic perspective of both experiencing and trying to understand. Often the patient will dream more frequently and more productively. In addition, the patient begins to explore and extend the implications of interpretations or insights independently of the analyst. There are a host of such indices that experienced analysts have no difficulty recognizing. They might be regarded in a sense as reflecting the development of an analytic "work-ego" within the patient.

The building up of these capacities within the patient lays the foundation for the definitive tasks of the termination. The working through of residual transference elements and the associated dependence propels significant identificatory processes that help to consolidate and confirm the patient's emerging sense of a self with an existence and identity properly its own, exclusive of the relation with and dependence on the analyst. Increasingly, both within and outside the analysis, the patient finds ways and contexts to test out these new-found capacities. My "Alice in Wonderland" patient discovered a variety of ways to establish herself as an independent, self-respecting, capable and intelligent young woman, in contrast to the dependent nothing she had previously felt herself to be. To run down the list—she gradually took a more independent and demanding stance in her marriage, presenting her husband with the alternative of either shaping up or shipping out; she was no longer willing to put up with his behavior. She also became more assertive and competitive in her work, not merely acceding to the wishes or opinions of her male co-workers, but seeing herself increasingly as a valuable and competent contributor. In her sexual relationships, she became less clinging and demanding, viewing her involvement more in give-and-take terms. The sexual encounter was no longer a helpless submission to her partner's wishes in which she was reduced to the least common (feminine) denominator, but a situation of mutual giving-and-receiving whereby her attempts to please and satisfy were met by the man's attempts to please her and satisfy her.

Needless to say, parallel changes took place within the analysis. Her relation to me became less one in which she had to be constantly accepting and pleasing so that she would not run the risk of being criticized, devalued, or rejected, and more one in which she could exercise some selectivity in accepting or rejecting my interpretations, could gradually modify them in terms of her own understanding, and could increasingly become a collaborator with me in the analytic work. Gradually she began to exercise some assertion and control within the analytic sessions—feeling comfortable in coming a few minutes late when other matters got in the way, or even deciding to take the initiative of missing an appointment for a business trip that was not mandatory, but would enhance her standing in the company.

These movements in the direction of increasing autonomy and self-esteem were matched by her diminishing need to see me as the powerful agent of her salvation and a growing capacity to see herself as the responsible agent of her own life's course. Increasingly she directed her attention away from her inner neurotic preoccupations and self-doubts to considerations of what she wanted to do with her life. She speculated on the goals she might reasonably set for herself in relation to career ambitions, further schooling, and plans for marriage and family life. She tried to picture herself in realistic and hopeful terms. But, most important, she did not merely fantasize or dream about these matters; she thought about how to lay the groundwork and organize her life so as to make her goals a reality.

While from one point of view it seems reasonable to say that these changes in the patient's outlook were creative expressions of her own inherent potential, I would not wish to overlook the role of identification in bringing them about. The attitudes that the patient acquired were patterned after attitudes and observations that she had heard countless times from me during the course of the analysis. These attitudes toward herself and her life were introduced by me through observations, questioning of her generally self-derogatory view of herself, and clarifications of her fantasy distortions and their disparity from reality. As a general statement, one could say that the material of the identifications had been brought into the analytic work as interpretations. They were to some initial degree accepted as such, often acknowledged not as true or valid insights, but as points around which the need to conform and please found expression. Gradually they found more internal expression in the patient's own spontaneous views. They were little by little implemented in areas of the patient's experience, interestingly enough at first outside the analysis in the ways I have described, but then increasingly and tellingly within the analysis itself.

My contention is that these changes in the patient were the result of significant internalizations, and, in the latter stages of the analysis, most particularly of identifications based on the image of the analyst—the analytic introject—developed through the course of her analytic experience. I am by no means suggesting that the result of the analysis is a mimicking of the analyst—I would count such mimicry as mockery! The emergence of identifications is in some phase of its development marked by various imitative expressions. In my patient this could be seen in her frequent, more or less conscious attempts to take the attitudes or thoughts that I had expressed to her and apply them to various troublesome situations in her outside life, as she began to recognize her neurotic propensities and the ways in which she acted them out in her everyday experience. What experience with such patients suggests, however, is that in time these somewhat extrinsic imitative devices are further modified and give way to authentic identifications in which the attributes of the analytic model become an internal possession of the patient. At this level, it is no longer a question of imitation. Rather, patients acquire their own set of attributes, attitudes, feelings, and capacities, which are created within themselves as their own internal possessions, part of themselves and the way they function and act, but which nevertheless bear the stamp of the model.

A similar process could be identified in another young woman of considerable personal and intellectual gifts. She, too, saw herself as worthless, as having been deprived of a penis. She could have validity and meaning only by attaching herself to an important and powerful man, and basking in his reflected glory. In the terminal phase of her analysis, the issues of dependence and her attachment to me (and to the pathogenic introjects) became the central focus of our analytic work. As the changes of the terminal phase were taking hold, her capacity to take responsible action in her life grew apace. She was able to mobilize her considerable compulsive resources to finish her doctoral thesis and complete the requirements for her degree. She then undertook a long and frequently disappointing search for a job in a field where jobs were scarce and hard to find. Here, however, she refused to take anything that came along, but waited for a job that suited her needs and came near to fulfilling some of her expectations.

These steps were taken as we continued to work through the related analytic issues. Her degree was another hoop to jump through, another conquest to try to prove to herself that she was indeed worth something. Her dissertation was repeatedly devalued — not good enough, really someone else's ideas, not

read critically enough by her professors, etc. Missed job opportunities were repeatedly turned into defects, proofs that she was
not up to snuff, not good enough to be hired and paid, that her
defects were at last recognized for what they were. The people
who interviewed her could see that she was all fluff and no
substance, a nice little girl with nothing to put on the line.

Little by little, changes became apparent. She began to view
the disappointments less as defeats than as unfortunate circumstances that had nothing to say about her qualifications or
abilities. She was able to keep looking and became more appropriately selective in her choices, applying for jobs where her
skills and training might be better appreciated than not. Finally, she was offered a good job quite well suited to her own needs
and dispositions. Changes came more slowly in her relations
with her family and her husband. Gradually she was able to
take a stand against her parents' wishes for her to live closer to
home and to be more dependent on them. It meant countering
her own wishes to be regressively dependent on and protected
by them, and taking the risk of being responsible for her own
life. It meant opposing her mother's demands and taking her
own stance, regardless of the consequences for her relation with
her mother. With her husband, she had in the past tended to
become embroiled in his moodiness or fits of temper. In good
hysterical fashion, she could not disengage herself from the
emotional upheaval and was left angry and depressed by these
mutually destructive interchanges. Gradually she was able to
see herself as an essentially independent person, who need not
get caught up in or be unduly affected by her husband's emotional outbursts. This development came hand-in-glove with
her capacity to disengage herself from her parents' pathology
and to see that she had a life independent from theirs.

Within the analysis, the changes were slow in coming. The
issue was drawn in terms of her unwillingness to surrender the
analysis or her attachment to the analyst. Her complaint was:
"Why should I have to give up something that I want and has
been good for me?" The same question, of course, had to be addressed in relation to her attachment to her parents, who had
always been kind, loving, and giving to her, but who had ex-
tracted a price of continuing dependence and neediness. The

patient was increasingly able to acknowledge that she did not need them to protect and take care of her in her adult life as they had done when she was a child. She could acknowledge that she no longer needed me. She was no longer depressed, she was functioning better than ever before in her life, and she was once and for all able to take charge of her life. Yet the infantile side of her continued to cling. As she herself put it in the closing stages of analysis, "Damn it — I know I don't need you, but I want you!"

In this case there was little doubt that significant identificatory work would have to go on after the analysis was terminated. But the initial stages had begun and were well established. A part of the patient fought the inevitable almost to the end. A termination date was set — at her initiative. But once the date was set, second thoughts and doubts crowded the scene. She could not take the vital step toward renouncing me and the analysis and her dependence without significant misgivings and conflict. She struggled to undo, postpone, retract, suspend the termination — to no avail. She complained bitterly that if I cared a whit about her, I would not allow her to leave the analysis and push her out to be on her own. The question was whether I could tolerate her wish to be independent, to not have to depend on me, to be her own person — as her parents had not. But the decision had really been made. She was ready to take the step toward defining herself as a mature adult, though not without tears of regret and a deep sense of loss.

The identificatory process is not brought to a close at the termination of the analysis, but rather becomes internalized as an abiding propensity within the patient. To one degree or another, the capacity for meaningful, constructive identification is set in operation in the terminal phase and may begin to work in varying degrees on the analyst as an object of identification. I am not referring here to conforming introjections, which may serve as the basis for the organization of a false self (a danger that must be taken into consideration in the evaluation of any analysis). Instead, I am referring here specifically to identifications in terms of which ego capacities and resources are built up and a differentiated and maturely functional sense of self is realized.

It is in terms of these identifications, realized in part through the analytic process, that the potential is unleashed for additional identificatory modifications, which lay the ground for narcissistic transformations (Kohut, 1966, 1971). Levin (1969) has pointed out that "the mutual development of the ego and of the self gives rise to life-long endopsychic conflicts which (although related to) are different from, and not exhausted by, what we recognize as infantile conflicts. We might call these ordinary ego-self or narcissistic conflicts of adult living and we would hope to find their reflection in Erikson's age-specific stages" (p. 50). We can suggest here that the formation, internalization, and integration of the analytic introject—whether these processes are merely set in motion or to some degree achieved and consolidated during the analytic process itself—serve as the matrix within which further positive and constructive internalizations can take place. The modification of narcissistic elements embedded in introjective formations by the subsequent process of identification provides a mechanism for the transformations of narcissism, for the emergence of the mature qualities of humor, creativity, empathy, and wisdom described by Kohut (1966). The continuing identificatory process also provides for the progressive realization and internalization of those attitudes and capacities that Schafer (1970) has enshrined in terms of the "psychoanalytic vision of reality."

Another frame of reference for conceptualizing these transformations lies in the more familiar structural theory. The classical structural theory formulates at least a part of the introjective perspective in terms of the organization of the superego. The superego is conceived in some part and to some degree as an introjective structuralized configuration within the psychic economy. The introjective component was clearly stated in Freud's early formulations (1923) and has been sustained in subsequent presentations (Furer, 1972; Hartmann and Loewenstein, 1962; Sandler, 1960). The question remains open, however, even within the confines of the structural theory, whether or not the introjective perspective. pertains more to pathological superego formations than to adaptive and normally functioning superego integrations.

From the present point of view, while introjective components remain central to the organization and functioning of superego, these introjective components may be modified and consolidated by significant identifications. These new identificatory components would carry with them greater resistance to regressive pulls, diminished susceptibility to drive derivatives, greater autonomy and adaptive capacity, as well as an inherent secondary-process mode of operation. These qualities reflect the shift from an introjective organization to an integration based on identificatory processes. By implication, the modification of superego structures and correlated functions would reflect increasing degrees of superego-ego integration.

It is in these terms, then, that the modification of the pathological narcissism inherent in the structure of the introjects takes place. The theory of such structural modification remains relatively undeveloped but deserves serious reflection and investigation. It is my own persuasion at this juncture that these areas of superego-ego integration and consolidation are concerned primarily and uniquely with the formation and integration of value systems. The preliminary work of Hartmann (1960), Jacobson (1964), Erikson (1964), and others (Post, 1972) points decisively in this direction.

EPILOGUE

In this monograph I have undertaken a revision of the psychoanalytic theory on internalization and attempted to apply it, as an operative theory, to the psychoanalytic process. In assessing the results of this attempt, it has become apparent to me that what has been written here leaves more unsaid than said. The statement is really more programmatic than definitive. There is hardly a page of this monograph or a subject on which it touches that is not open to further elaboration, investigation, and clarification, both in theoretical terms and in terms of our understanding and implementing these processes in the psychoanalytic situation.

Nonetheless, viewing the psychoanalytic process through the lens of internalization opens up significant and difficult areas of rethinking and research, which potentially offer a considerable enrichment of our comprehension of the process of therapy, as well as of the basic functioning of the human psyche. A fundamental postulate of this monograph is that of the significance of developmental vicissitudes in understanding aspects of the analytic process. Focusing elements of the analytic process in terms of introjection, projection, and identification brings together these developmental issues in a particularly pertinent and immediate fashion. A considerable amount of clinical and theoretical work, however, will be required to articulate the points of connection between, for example, our advancing understanding of the separation-individuation process (Mahler, Pine, and Bergman, 1975) and its reverberation in the psychoanalytic process. The separation-individuation process can be described in terms of the inner dynamics of introjection and projection (Meissner, 1978b), and these dynamics are reactivated within the psychoanalytic process. Our knowledge of internalization processes and our appreciation of how they feed into the psychoanalytic process need to be both amplified and specified in the service of refining and deepening our understanding of the effects of therapy and the process of psychic cure.

Another very important dimension of the psychoanalytic process, which strikes me as relatively inchoate in its conceptualization, is the relationship between internalization processes and the learning transaction implemented in the psychoanalytic process. Psychoanalytic theorists and practitioners have so far carried on their work in relative isolation from the ferment of experimental and theoretical work on learning processes, which includes studies not only of animals but also of humans. And this omission applies no less to reinforcement and contiguity theories of learning, which have dominated experimental work, than to social and developmental learning models, as well as to the work of cognitive psychologists like Piaget. As we have suggested, important learning variables enter into the psychoanalytic process, both in the regressive phase, which allows for the activation and clarification of functional and structural formations in both the cognitive and affective realms, and in the progressive phase, in which primitive and archaic structural configurations, both cognitive and affective, can be meaningfully modified in the direction of more adaptive and functional resolutions (Greenspan, 1975; Peterfreund, 1971).

More central, however, to the concern of psychoanalysis itself, the approach through internalizations offers us the opportunity to reconceptualize clinical aspects of the analytic process, particularly in terms of a deepening understanding of the transference neurosis, the countertransference, and the therapeutic alliance. In all of these clinical areas, our thinking has stagnated, even though analysts are quite aware of the vast lode of conceptual enrichment that seems to elude our grasp.

Particularly intriguing here are the emerging and often provocative insights generated by the object relations approach. The way already lies open for a reconsideration of the transference neurosis and the countertransference from the perspective of internalization. By comparison, the potential contribution of this approach to our understanding of the therapeutic alliance remains a relatively untapped and virgin territory. We are only beginning to see more differentiated, more specifically honed concepts which will allow us to explore the elements that enter into and sustain the therapeutic alliance.

As I look back over these few pages, I cannot escape the impression that there is so much more to be done, so much more to be understood, and so much more to be said than could even be fantasized here. I hope that the formulations offered here will stimulate others to deepen and advance our knowledge of these important areas.

REFERENCES

Aarons, Z. A. (1975), The Analyst's Relocation: Its Effect on the Transference—
   Parameter or Catalyst. *International Journal of Psycho-Analysis*, 56:303–319.
Adler, G. (1970), Valuing and Devaluing in the Psychotherapeutic Process. *Archives
   of General Psychiatry*, 22:454–461.
Axelrad, S., & Maury, L. M. (1951), Identification as a Mechanism of Adaptation.
   In: *Psychoanalysis and Culture: Essays in Honor of Géza Róheim*, ed. G. B. Wilbur
   & W. Muensterberger. New York: International Universities Press, pp.
   168–184.
Balint, M. (1968), *The Basic Fault: Therapeutic Aspects of Regression*. London:
   Tavistock.
Beres, D. (1966), Superego and Depression. In: *Psychoanalysis—A General Psychology*,
   ed. R. M. Loewenstein et al. New York: International Universities Press,
   pp. 479–498.
Berg, M. D. (1977), The Externalizing Transference. *International Journal of Psycho-
   Analysis*, 58:235–244.
Berry, N. (1975), From Fantasy to Reality in the Transference: A Reply to the Dis-
   cussion by Pedro Luzes. *International Journal of Psycho-Analysis*, 56:365–366.
Birk, L., & Brinkley-Birk, A. W. (1974), Psychoanalysis and Behavior Therapy.
   American Journal of Psychiatry, 131:499–510.
Blos, P. (1962), *On Adolescence: A Psychoanalytic Interpretation*. New York: Free Press.
_____ (1967), The Second Individuation Process of Adolescence. *The Psychoan-
   alytic Study of the Child*, 22:162–186. New York: International Universities
   Press.

262

Blum, H. P. (1974), The Borderline Childhood of the Wolf Man. *Journal of the American Psychoanalytic Association,* 22:721-742.

Boszormenyi-Nagy, I., & Framo, J. L., Eds. (1965), *Intensive Family Therapy: Theoretical and Practical Aspects.* New York: Harper & Row.

Boyer, L. B., & Giovacchini, P. L. (1967), *Psychoanalytic Treatment of Schizophrenic and Characterological Disorders.* New York: Science House.

Breuer, J., & Freud, S. (1893), On the Psychical Mechanism of Hysterical Phenomena: Preliminary Communication. *Standard Edition,* 2:1-17. London: Hogarth Press, 1955.

Brodey, W. M. (1965), On the Dynamics of Narcissism. I. Externalization and Early Ego Development. *The Psychoanalytic Study of the Child,* 20:165-193. New York: International Universities Press.

Brody, M. W., & Mahoney, V. P. (1964), Introjection, Identification, and Incorporation. *International Journal of Psycho-Analysis,* 45:57-63.

Bychowski, G. (1956), The Release of Internal Images. *International Journal of Psycho-Analysis,* 37:331-338.

Calder, K. T., rep. (1958), Panel Report: Technical Aspects of Regression in Psychoanalysis. *Journal of the American Psychoanalytic Association,* 6:552-559.

de Saussure, R. (1939), Identification and Substitution. *International Journal of Psycho-Analysis,* 20:465-470.

Deutsch, H. (1942). Some Forms of Emotional Disturbance and Their Relationship to Schizophrenia. *Psychoanalytic Quarterly,* 11:301-321.

Dickes, R. (1967), Severe Regressive Disruptions of the Therapeutic Alliance. *Journal of the American Psychoanalytic Association,* 15:508-533.

Dorpat, T. L. (1974), Internalization of the Patient-Analyst Relationship in Patients with Narcissistic Disorders. *International Journal of Psycho-Analysis,* 55:183-188.

_____ (1976), Structural Conflict and Object-Relations Conflict. *Journal of the American Psychoanalytic Association,* 24:855-874.

Eissler, K. R. (1953), The Effect of the Structure of the Ego on Psychoanalytic Technique. *Journal of the American Psychoanalytic Association,* 1:104-143.

_____ (1958), Remarks on Some Variations in Psychoanalytic Technique. *International Journal of Psycho-Analysis,* 39:222-229.

Erikson, E. H. (1959), *Identity and the Life Cycle* [*Psychological Issues,* Monogr. 1]. New York: International Universities Press

_____ (1963), *Childhood and Society.* New York: Norton.

_____ (1964), *Insight and Responsibility.* New York: Norton.

Fenichel, O. (1926), Identification. In: *The Collected Papers of Otto Fenichel,* First Series. New York: Norton, 1953, pp. 97-112.

_____ (1953), *The Collected Papers of Otto Fenichel,* First Series. New York: Norton.

Fleming, J. (1972), Early Object Deprivation and Transference Phenomena: The Working Alliance. *Psychoanalytic Quarterly,* 41:23-49.

Fliess, R. (1953), Countertransference and Counteridentification. *Journal of the American Psychoanalytic Association,* 1:268-284.

Freud, A. (1936), *The Ego and the Mechanisms of Defense. The Writings of Anna Freud,* 2. New York: International Universities Press, 1966.

_____ (1954), The Widening Scope of Indications for Psychoanalysis: Discussion. *Journal of the American Psychoanalytic Association,* 2:607-620.

_____ (1965), *Normality and Pathology in Childhood. The Writings of Anna Freud,* 6. New York: International Universities Press.

Freud, S. (1900), The Interpretation of Dreams. *Standard Edition,* 4 & 5. London: Hogarth Press, 1953.

_____ (1905), Three Essays on the Theory of Sexuality. *Standard Edition,*

7:123-243. London: Hogarth Press, 1953.

———— (1909), Analysis of a Phobia in a Five-Year-Old Boy. *Standard Edition*, 10:1-149. London: Hogarth Press, 1955.

———— (1912), Recommendations to Physicians Practising Psycho-Analysis. *Standard Edition*, 12:109-120. London: Hogarth Press, 1958.

———— (1915a), Instincts and Their Vicissitudes. *Standard Edition*, 14:109-140. London: Hogarth Press, 1957.

———— (1915b), Observations on Transference-Love. *Standard Edition*, 12:157-171. London: Hogarth Press, 1958.

———— (1917), Mourning and Melancholia. *Standard Edition*, 14:237-258. London: Hogarth Press, 1957.

———— (1923), The Ego and the Id. *Standard Edition*, 19:1-66. London: Hogarth Press, 1961.

———— (1924), The Dissolution of the Oedipus Complex. *Standard Edition*, 19:171-179. London: Hogarth Press, 1961.

———— (1940), An Outline of Psycho-Analysis. *Standard Edition*, 23:137-207. London: Hogarth Press, 1964.

Friedman, L. (1969), The Therapeutic Alliance. *International Journal of Psycho-Analysis*, 50:139-153.

Frosch, J. (1967), Severe Regressive States during Analysis. *Journal of the American Psychoanalytic Association*, 15:491-507.

Fuchs, S. H. (1937), On Introjection. *International Journal of Psycho-Analysis*, 18:269-293.

Furer, M. (1972), The History of the Superego Concept in Psychoanalysis: A Review of the Literature. In: *Moral Values and the Superego Concept in Psychoanalysis*, ed. S. C. Post. New York: International Universities Press, pp. 11-62.

Gaddini, E. (1969), On Imitation. *International Journal of Psycho-Analysis*, 50:475-484.

Gardiner, M., Ed. (1971), *The Wolf-Man by the Wolf-Man*. New York: Basic Books.

Gedo, J., & Goldberg, A. (1973), *Models of the Mind: A Psychoanalytic Theory*. Chicago: University of Chicago Press.

Giovacchini, P. L. (1975), Self-Projections in the Narcissistic Transference. *International Journal of Psychoanalytic Psychotherapy*, 4:142-166.

Greenson, R. R. (1954), The Struggle Against Identification. *Journal of the American Psychoanalytic Association*, 2:200-217.

———— (1960), Empathy and Its Vicissitudes. *International Journal of Psycho-Analysis*, 41:418-424.

———— (1967), *The Technique and Practice of Psychoanalysis*, Vol. 1. New York: International Universities Press.

———— & Wexler, M. (1969), The Non-transference Relationship in the Psychoanalytic Situation. *International Journal of Psycho-Analysis*, 50:27-39.

Greenspan, S. I. (1972), Joining Aspects of Psychodynamic and Operant Learning Theories. *International Journal of Psychoanalytic Psychotherapy*, 1(4):26-49.

———— (1975), *A Consideration of Some Learning Variables in the Context of Psychoanalytic Theory* [*Psychological Issues*, Monogr. 33]. New York: International Universities Press.

Grinberg, L. (1962), On a Specific Aspect of Countertransference due to the Patient's Projective Identification. *International Journal of Psycho-Analysis*, 43:436-440.

Grossman, W. I. (1967), Reflections on the Relationships of Introspection and Psycho-Analysis. *International Journal of Psycho-Analysis*, 48:16-31.

Gudeman, J. E. (1974), Uncontrolled Regression in Therapy and Analysis. *Interna-*

tional Journal of Psychoanalytic Psychotherapy, 3:325–338.

Gunderson, J. G., & Singer, M. T. (1975), Defining Borderline Patients: An Overview. *American Journal of Psychiatry*, 132:1–10.

Guntrip, H. (1969), *Schizoid Phenomena, Object Relations and the Self*. New York: International Universities Press.

Hani, A. G. (1973), The Rediscovery of the Therapeutic Alliance. *International Journal of Psychoanalytic Psychotherapy*, 2:449–477.

Hartmann, H. (1939), *Ego Psychology and the Problem of Adaptation*. New York: International Universities Press, 1958.

_____ (1950), Comments on the Psychoanalytic Theory of the Ego. In: *Essays on Ego Psychology*. New York: International Universities Press, 1964, pp. 113–141.

_____ (1960), *Psychoanalysis and Moral Values*. New York: International Universities Press.

_____ (1964), *Essays on Ego Psychology*. New York: International Universities Press.

_____ & Loewenstein, R. M. (1962), Notes on the Superego. *The Psychoanalytic Study of the Child*, 17:42–81. New York: International Universities Press.

Hendrick, I. (1951), Early Development of the Ego: Identification in Infancy. *Psychoanalytic Quarterly*, 20:44–61.

Jacobson, E. (1954), Contribution to the Metapsychology of Psychotic Identifications. *Journal of the American Psychoanalytic Association*, 2:239–262.

_____ (1964), *The Self and the Object World*. New York: International Universities Press.

Kagan, J. (1958), The Concept of Identification. *Psychological Review*, 65:296–305.

Kernberg, O. F. (1966), Structural Derivatives of Object Relationships. *International Journal of Psycho-Analysis*, 47:236–253.

_____ (1967), Borderline Personality Organization. *Journal of the American Psychoanalytic Association*, 15:641–685.

_____ (1970a), Factors in the Psychoanalytic Treatment of Narcissistic Personalities. *Journal of the American Psychoanalytic Association*, 18:51–85.

_____ (1970b), A Psychoanalytic Classification of Character Pathology. *Journal of the American Psychoanalytic Association*, 18:800–822.

_____ (1971), Prognostic Considerations Regarding Borderline Personality Organization. *Journal of the American Psychoanalytic Association*, 19:595–635.

_____ (1974), Further Contributions to the Treatment of Narcissistic Personalities. *International Journal of Psycho-Analysis*, 55:215–240.

_____ (1975a), Further Contributions to the Treatment of Narcissistic Personalities: A Reply to the Discussion by Paul H. Ornstein. *International Journal of Psycho-Analysis*, 56:245–247.

_____ (1975b), Transference and Countertransference in the Treatment of Borderline Patients. *Strecker Monograph Series*, No. XII, Institute of Pennsylvania Hospital.

_____ (1976), Technical Considerations in the Treatment of Borderline Personality Organization. *Journal of the American Psychoanalytic Association*, 24:795–829.

Khan, M. M. R. (1972), The Finding and Becoming of Self. *International Journal of Psychoanalytic Psychotherapy*, 1(1):97–111.

Klein, M. (1932), *The Psychoanalysis of Children*. New York: Grove Press, 1960.

_____ (1948), *Contributions to Psycho-Analysis: 1921–1945*. London: Hogarth Press.

Knapp, P. H.; Levin, S.; McCarter, R. H.; Wermer, H.; & Zetzel, E. (1960),

Suitability for Psychoanalysis: A Review of One Hundred Supervised Analytic Cases. *Psychoanalytic Quarterly*, 29:459-477.

Knight, R. P. (1940), Introjection, Projection, and Identification. *Psychoanalytic Quarterly*, 9:334-341.

Kohut, H. (1959), Introspection, Empathy, and Psychoanalysis. *Journal of the American Psychoanalytic Association*, 7:459-483.

———— (1966), Forms and Transformations of Narcissism. *Journal of the American Psychoanalytic Association*, 14:243-272.

———— (1968), The Psychoanalytic Treatment of Narcissistic Personality Disorders. *The Psychoanalytic Study of the Child*, 23:86-113. New York: International Universities Press.

———— (1971), *The Analysis of the Self.* New York: International Universities Press.

———— (1977), *The Restoration of the Self.* New York: International Universities Press.

Kris, E. (1952), *Psychoanalytic Explorations in Art.* New York: International Universities Press.

Langs, R. (1975a), Therapeutic Misalliances. *International Journal of Psychoanalytic Psychotherapy*, 4:77-105.

———— (1975b), The Therapeutic Relationship and Deviations in Technique. *International Journal of Psychoanalytic Psychotherapy*, 4:106-141.

Lax, R. F. (1977), The Role of Internalization in the Development of Certain Aspects of Female Masochism: Ego Psychological Considerations. *International Journal of Psycho-Analysis*, 58:289-300.

Le Guen, C. (1974), The Formation of the Transference: Or the Louis Complex in the Armchair. *International Journal of Psycho-Analysis*, 55:505-512.

———— (1975), The Formation of the Transference: A Reply to the Discussion by A. Béjarano. *International Journal of Psycho-Analysis*, 56:371-372.

Levin, D. C. (1969), The Self: A Contribution to Its Place in Theory and Technique. *International Journal of Psycho-Analysis*, 50:41-51.

Lidz, T.; Fleck, S.; & Cornelison, A. R. (1965), *Schizophrenia and the Family.* New York: International Universities Press.

Little, M. (1951), Counter-transference and the Patient's Response to It. *International Journal of Psycho-Analysis*, 32:33-40.

Loewald, H. (1962), Internalization, Separation, Mourning, and the Superego. *Psychoanalytic Quarterly*, 31:483-504.

———— (1975), Psychoanalysis as an Art and the Fantasy Character of the Psychoanalytic Situation. *Journal of the American Psychoanalytic Association*, 23:277-299.

Mahler, M. S. (1968), *On Human Symbiosis and the Vicissitudes of Individuation.* New York: International Universities Press.

———— ;Pine, F.; & Bergman, A. (1975), *The Psychological Birth of the Human Infant.* New York: Basic Books.

Malin, A., & Grotstein, J. S. (1966), Projective Identification in the Therapeutic Process. *International Journal of Psycho-Analysis*, 47:26-31.

Mehlman, R. D. (1976), Transference Mobilization, Transference Resolution, and the Narcissistic Alliance. Presented to the Boston Psychoanalytic Society and Institute, Feb. 25.

Meissner, W. W. (1964), Thinking about the Family—Psychiatric Aspects. *Family Process*, 3:1-40.

———— (1970a), Notes on Identification. I. Origins in Freud. *Psychoanalytic Quarterly*, 39:563-589.

_____ (1970b), Sibling Relations in the Schizophrenic Family. *Family Process*, 9:1–25.

_____ (1971), Notes on Identification. II. Clarification of Related Concepts. *Psychoanalytic Quarterly*, 40:277–302.

_____ (1972), Notes on Identification. III. The Concept of Identification. *Psychoanalytic Quarterly*, 41:224–260.

_____ (1973), Some Notes on the Psychology of the Literary Character: A Psychoanalytic Perspective. *Seminars in Psychiatry*, 5:261–274.

_____ (1974a), Correlative Aspects of Introjective and Projective Mechanisms. *American Journal of Psychiatry*, 131:176–180.

_____ (1974b), Differentiation and Integration of Learning and Identification in the Developmental Process. *The Annual of Psychoanalysis*, 2:181–196. New York: International Universities Press.

_____ (1974c), Identification and Learning. *Journal of the American Psychoanalytic Association*, 21:788–816.

_____ (1974d), The Role of Imitative Social Learning in Identificatory Processes. *Journal of the American Psychoanalytic Association*, 22:512–536.

_____ (1975), Psychoanalysis as a Theory of Therapy. *International Journal of Psychoanalytic Psychotherapy*, 4:181–218.

_____ (1976), A Note on Internalization as Process. *Psychoanalytic Quarterly*, 45:374–393.

_____ (1977a), Cognitive Aspects of the Paranoid Process—Prospectus. In: *Psychiatry and the Humanities. Vol. 2: Thought, Consciousness, and Reality*, ed. J. H. Smith. New Haven: Yale University Press, pp. 159–216.

_____ (1977b), Psychoanalytic Notes on Suicide. *International Journal of Psychoanalytic Psychotherapy*, 6:415–447.

_____ (1977c), The Wolf-Man and the Paranoid Process. *The Annual of Psychoanalysis*, 5:23–74. New York: International Universities Press.

_____ (1978a), The Conceptualization of Marriage and Family Dynamics from a Psychoanalytic Perspective. In: *Marriage and the Treatment of Marital Disorders: Psychoanalytic, Behavior and Systems Theory Perspectives*, ed. T. J. Paolino & B. S. McCrady. New York: Brunner/Mazel, pp. 25–88.

_____ (1978b), *The Paranoid Process*. New York: Aronson.

_____ (1979a), Internalization and Object Relations. *Journal of the American Psychoanalytic Association*, 27:345–360.

_____ (1979b), Methodological Critique of the Action Language in Psychoanalysis. *Journal of the American Psychoanalytic Association*, 27:79–105.

_____ (1980a), A Note on the Differentiation of Borderline Conditions. *International Journal of Psychoanalytic Psychotherapy* (in press).

_____ (1980b), A Note on Projective Identification. *Journal of the American Psychoanalytic Association*, 28:43–67.

Miller, A.; Pollock, G. H.; Bernstein, H. E.; & Robbins, F. P. (1968), An Approach to the Concept of Identification. *Bulletin of the Menninger Clinic*, 32:239–252.

Modell, A. (1968), *Object Love and Reality*. New York: International Universities Press.

_____ (1975), A Narcissistic Defense Against Affects and the Illusion of Self-Sufficiency. *International Journal of Psycho-Analysis*, 56:275–282.

Moeller, M. L. (1977), Self and Object in Countertransference. *International Journal of Psycho-Analysis*, 58:365–374.

Moore, B. E., & Fine, B. D., Eds. (1967), *A Glossary of Psychoanalytic Terms and Con-*

cepts. New York: American Psychoanalytic Association.

Mowrer, O. H. (1950), *Learning Theory and Personality Dynamics*. New York: Ronald.

Nunberg, H. (1948), *Practice and Theory of Psychoanalysis*. New York: Nervous & Mental Disease Monographs.

────── (1951), Transference and Reality. *International Journal of Psycho-Analysis*, 32:1–9.

Olinick, S. J. (1975), On Empathic Perception and the Problems of Reporting Psychoanalytic Processes. *International Journal of Psycho-Analysis*, 56:147–154.

Ornstein, P. H. (1974), A Discussion of the Paper by Otto F. Kernberg on 'Further Contributions to the Treatment of Narcissistic Personalities.' *International Journal of Psycho-Analysis*, 55:241–247.

Orr, D. W. (1954), Transference and Countertransference: A Historical Survey. *Journal of the American Psychoanalytic Association*, 2:621–670.

Parsons, T., & Shils, E. A., Eds. (1962), *Toward a General Theory of Action*. New York: Harper & Row.

Peterfreund, E. (1971), *Information, Systems, and Psychoanalysis*. [*Psychological Issues*, Monogr. 25/26]. New York: International Universities Press.

Poland, W. S. (1975), Tact as a Psychoanalytic Function. *International Journal of Psycho-Analysis*, 56:155–162.

Post, S. C., Ed. (1972), *Moral Values and the Superego Concept in Psychoanalysis*. New York: International Universities Press.

Pressman, M. D. (1969), The Cognitive Function of the Ego in Psychoanalysis. I. The Search for Insight. *International Journal of Psycho-Analysis*, 50:187–196.

Rapaport, D. (1967), A Theoretical Analysis of the Superego Concept. In: *The Collected Papers of David Rapaport*, ed. M. M. Gill. New York: Basic Books, pp. 685–709.

Ritvo, S., & Solnit, A. J. (1960), The Relationship of Early Ego Identifications to Superego Formation. *International Journal of Psycho-Analysis*, 41:295–300.

Sandler, J. (1960), On the Concept of the Superego. *The Psychoanalytic Study of the Child*, 15:128–162. New York: International Universities Press.

────── ; Holder, A.; & Meers, D. (1963), The Ego Ideal and the Ideal Self. *The Psychoanalytic Study of the Child*, 18:139–158. New York: International Universities Press.

────── & Rosenblatt, B. (1962), The Concept of the Representational World. *The Psychoanalytic Study of the Child*, 17:128–145. New York: International Universities Press.

Sanford, N. (1955), The Dynamics of Identification. *Psychological Review*, 62:106–118.

Sashin, J. I.; Eldred, S. H.; & van Amerongen, S. T. (1975), A Search for Predictive Factors in Institute Supervised Cases: A Retropective Study of 183 Cases from 1959–1966 at the Boston Psychoanalytic Society and Institute. *International Journal of Psycho-Analysis*, 56:343–359.

Schafer, R. (1959), Generative Empathy in the Treatment Situation. *Psychoanalytic Quarterly*, 28:342–373.

────── (1968a), *Aspects of Internalization*. New York: International Universities Press.

────── (1968b), On the Theoretical and Technical Conceptualization of Activity and Passivity. *Psychoanalytic Quarterly*, 37:173–198.

────── (1970), The Psychoanalytic Vision of Reality. *International Journal of Psycho-Analysis*, 51:279–297.

_____ (1972), Internalization: Process or Fantasy? *The Psychoanalytic Study of the Child*, 27:411-436. New York: Quadrangle Books.

_____ (1976), *A New Language for Psychoanalysis*. New Haven: Yale University Press.

Searles, H. F. (1961a), The Evolution of the Mother Transference in Psychotherapy with the Schizophrenic Patient. In: *Collected Papers on Schizophrenia and Related Subjects*. New York: International Universities Press, 1965, pp. 349-380.

_____ (1961b), Phases of Patient-Therapist Interaction in the Psychotherapy of Chronic Schizophrenia. In: *Collected Papers on Schizophrenia and Related Subjects*. New York: International Universities Press, 1965, pp. 521-559.

_____ (1963), Transference Psychosis in the Psychotherapy of Schizophrenia. In: *Collected Papers on Schizophrenia and Related Subjects*. New York: International Universities Press, 1965, pp. 654-716.

_____ (1965), *Collected Papers on Schizophrenia and Related Subjects*. New York: International Universities Press.

Segal, H. (1964), *Introduction to the Work of Melanie Klein*. London: Heinemann.

Smith, S. (1977), The Golden Fantasy: A Regressive Reaction to Separation Anxiety. *International Journal of Psycho-Analysis*, 58:311-324.

Stone, L. (1961), *The Psychoanalytic Situation*. New York: International Universities Press.

Winnicott, D. W. (1953), Transitional Objects and Transitional Phenomena. In: *Playing and Reality*. New York: Basic Books, 1971, pp. 1-25.

_____ (1965), *The Maturational Processes and the Facilitating Environment*. New York: International Universities Press.

_____ (1967), The Location of Cultural Experience. In: *Playing and Reality*. New York: Basic Books, 1971, pp. 95-103.

_____ (1971), *Playing and Reality*. New York: Basic Books.

Zetzel, E. R. (1956), The Current Concept of Transference. In: *The Capacity for Emotional Growth*. New York: International Universities Press, 1970, pp. 168-181.

_____ (1966), The Doctor-Patient Relationship in Psychiatry. In: *The Capacity for Emotional Growth*. New York: International Universities Press, 1970, pp. 139-155.

_____ (1968), The So-Called Good Hysteric. In: *The Capacity for Emotional Growth*. New York: International Universities Press, 1970, pp. 229-245.

_____ (1970), *The Capacity for Emotional Growth*. New York: International Universities Press.

_____ (1971), A Developmental Approach to the Borderline Patient. *American Journal of Psychiatry*, 127:867-871.

_____ & Meissner, W. W. (1973), *Basic Concepts of Psychoanalytic Psychiatry*. New York: Basic Books.

INDEX

ABOUT THE AUTHOR

W. W. Meissner, S. J., M. D., is Associate Clinical Professor of Psychiatry at the Harvard Medical School, Boston, Massachusetts, and Instructor at the Boston Psychoanalytic Institute. He received his Ph.L. from St. Louis University, St. Louis, Missouri; his S.T.L. from Woodstock College in Maryland; and his M.D. from Harvard Medical School, where he graduated cum laude. Dr. Meissner is the author of more than 100 articles, which have appeared in various professional publications. He is the author of *The Paranoid Process* and the co-author, with Elizabeth R. Zetzel, of *Basic Concepts in Psychoanalytic Psychiatry*.

PSYCHOLOGICAL ISSUES

PSYCHOLOGICAL ISSUES

HERBERT J. SCHLESINGER, *Editor*

Editorial Board